Cut Your Client's Tax Bill: Individual Planning Tips and Strategies

By William Bischoff, CPA, MBA

T0338306

Notice to readers

Cut Your Client's Tax Bill: Individual Planning Tips and Strategies is intended solely for use in continuing professional education and not as a reference. It does not represent an official position of the American Institute of Certified Public Accountants, and it is distributed with the understanding that the author and publisher are not rendering legal, accounting, or other professional services in the publication. This course is intended to be an overview of the topics discussed within, and the author has made every attempt to verify the completeness and accuracy of the information herein. However, neither the author nor publisher can guarantee the applicability of the information found herein. If legal advice or other expert assistance is required, the services of a competent professional should be sought.

You can qualify to earn free CPE through our pilot testing program.
If interested, please visit https://aicpacompliance.polldaddy.com/s/pilot-testing-survey.

ISBN 978-1-119-72453-7 (Paper)
ISBN 978-1-119-72458-2 (ePDF)
ISBN 978-1-119-72459-9 (ePub)
ISBN 978-1-119-72457-5 (oBook)

Course Code: **732195**
CYCT GS-0419-0A
Revised: **August 2019**

V10018780_052820

Table of Contents

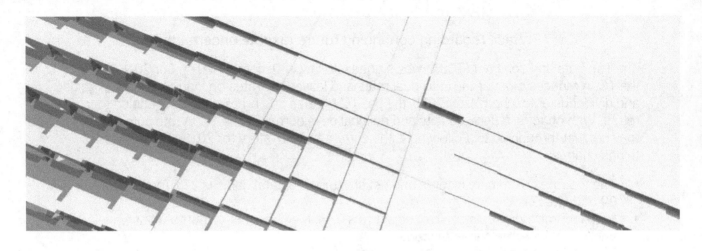

Chapter 1

Maximizing Tax Benefits for Sales of Capital Gain Assets and Real Property

Learning objectives

- Identify differences in the current federal income tax rate structure to help clients maximize tax benefits, taking into account tax rate changes included in the Tax Cuts and Jobs Act.

- Determine when selling capital assets, business assets, and real estate are to a client's advantage.

- Apply like-kind exchange rules under IRC Section 1031.

Introduction

This chapter covers what tax advisers need to know, from both the planning and compliance perspectives, to help clients maximize tax savings under the current federal income tax rate structure for capital gains and losses, and IRC Section 1231 gains and losses. We also cover some tax breaks that apply specifically to real estate transactions and the potential application of the 3.8% net investment income tax (NIIT).

Preface regarding continuing future tax rate uncertainty

The Tax Cuts and Jobs Act (TCJA) was signed into law in December 2017. For 2018–2025, the TCJA reduces most of the individual rates and leaves the rates on long-term capital gains and dividends untouched. After 2025, the pre-TCJA rates and brackets are scheduled to return. With ongoing federal deficits and political developments, the TCJA rate cuts may or may not last through 2025. Following is the current tax rate story for 2018–2025, unless things change:

- The top rate on ordinary income and net short-term capital gains is 37% (down from 39.6% in 2017).
- High-income individuals can be subject to a 0.9% Medicare tax on part of their wages and/or net self-employment income.
- The top rate on most net long-term capital gains is 20% for upper-income individuals (same as for 2017).
- Although the maximum rate is 20%, most individuals will not pay more than 15%, and individuals with modest incomes can pay 0%. These same preferential rates apply to qualified dividends.
- High-income individuals can be subject to the 3.8% Medicare surtax (the net investment income tax or NIIT) on all or part of their net investment income, which is defined to include capital gains and dividends.

Current capital gain and dividend tax rates

Rates on short-term capital gains

For 2018–2025, the TCJA retains seven tax rate brackets, but five of the rates are lower than before. In 2026, the rates and brackets that were in place for 2017 are scheduled to return. The ordinary income and short-term capital gain rate brackets for 2019 are as follows.

2019 Individual federal income tax brackets for ordinary income and short-term capital gains			
Filing status	Single	Joint	HOH*
10% tax bracket	$ 0–9,700	0–19,400	0–13,850
Beginning of 12% bracket	9,701	19,401	13,851
Beginning of 22% bracket	39,476	78,951	52,851
Beginning of 24% bracket	84,201	168,401	84,201
Beginning of 32% bracket	160,726	321,451	160,701
Beginning of 35% bracket	204,101	408,201	204,101
Beginning of 37% bracket	510,301	612,351	510,301
*Head of household			

Observation: Most individuals will come out ahead under the TCJA, but some who were in the 33% marginal tax bracket under the prior law may land in the 35% marginal bracket in 2019. That issue will mainly affect singles and heads of households with taxable income in the $200,000–$400,000 range. The lower rates on income less than $200,000 will offset some or all of the negative effect of being in the 35% marginal bracket.

Key point: Higher-income taxpayers may be subject to the 3.8% Medicare surtax on net investment income (IRC Section 1411), which can result in a higher-than-advertised federal tax rate on short-term capital gains. The IRS calls the 3.8% surtax the *net investment income tax* or NIIT. We will adopt that terminology.

2019 Individual federal income tax brackets for long-term capital gains and qualified dividends

Filing status	Single	Joint	HOH*
0% tax bracket	$ 0–39,375	0–78,750	0–52,750
Beginning of 15% bracket	39,376	78,751	52,751
Beginning of 20% bracket	434,551	488,851	461,701
*Head of household			

Key point: Higher-income taxpayers can also be affected by the 3.8% NIIT, which can result in a maximum 23.8% maximum federal tax rate on long-term gains and dividends (IRC Section 1411).

Key point: Qualified dividends do not count as investment income for purposes of the investment interest expense limitation—unless the taxpayer elects to have those dividends taxed at ordinary income rates [IRC Section 163(d)(4)(B)]. (The same rule has applied to long-term capital gains for many years and is explained later in this chapter.)

Higher rates on some gains and dividends

Unfortunately, the preferential 0%/15%/20% rates do not apply to all types of long-term capital gains and dividends. Specifically, as follows:

- The reduced rates have no impact on investments held inside a tax-deferred retirement account (traditional IRA, Keogh, Simplified Employee Pension, solo 401(k), and the like). So, the client will pay taxes at the regular rate (which can be as high as 37%) when gains accumulated in these accounts are withdrawn as cash distributions. (Gains accumulated in a Roth IRA are still federal-income-tax-free as long as the requirements for tax-free withdrawals are met.)
- Clients will still pay taxes at their higher regular rates on net short-term capital gains from investments held for one year or less. Therefore, if the client holds appreciated stock in a taxable account for exactly one year, he or she could lose up to 37% of the profit to the IRS. If he or she instead holds on for just one more day, the tax rate drops to no more than 20%. The moral: selling just one day too soon could mean paying a larger amount of one's profit to the taxing authorities.

Key point: For tax purposes, the client's holding period begins the day after he or she acquires securities and includes the day of sale. For example, if your client buys shares on November 1 of this year. The holding period begins on November 2. Therefore, November 2 of next year is the earliest possible date he or she can sell and still be eligible for the reduced rates on long-term capital gains. (See Rev. Ruls. 66-7 and 66-97.)

- IRC Section 1231 gains attributable to depreciation deductions claimed against real estate properties are called un-recaptured IRC Section 1250 gains. These gains, which would otherwise generally be eligible for the 20% maximum rate, are taxed at a maximum rate of 25% [IRC Section 1(h)(6)]. The good news: any IRC Section 1231 gain more than the amount of un-recaptured IRC Section 1250 gain from a real property sale is generally eligible for the 20% maximum rate on long-term capital gains. The same treatment applies to the deferred IRC Section 1231 gain component of installment note payments from an installment sale transaction.

Key point: Distributions from Real Estate Investment Trusts (REITs) and REIT mutual funds may include some un-recaptured IRC Section 1250 gains from real property sales. These gains, which are taxed at a maximum rate of 25%, should be separately reported to the investor and entered on the appropriate line of the investor's Schedule D.

- The 28% maximum rate on long-term capital gains from sales of collectibles and QSBC stock remains in force [IRC Section 1(h)(5) and (7)].

The reduced 0%/15%/20% rates on dividends apply only to qualified dividends paid on shares of corporate stock [IRC Section 1(h)(11)]. However, lots of payments that are commonly called *dividends* are not qualified dividends under the tax law. For instance,

- dividends paid on credit union accounts are really interest payments. As such, they are considered ordinary income and are therefore taxed at regular rates, which can be as high as 37%;
- dividends paid on some preferred stock issues that are actually publicly traded "wrappers" around underlying bundles of corporate bonds. So clients should not buy preferred shares for their taxable accounts without knowing exactly what they are buying;
- mutual fund dividend distributions that are paid out of the fund's short-term capital gains, interest income, and other types of ordinary income are taxed at regular rates. So, equity mutual funds that engage in rapid-fire trading of low-dividend growth stocks will generate payouts that are taxed at up to 37% rather than at the optimal 0%/15%/20% rates your clients might be hoping for;
- bond fund dividends are taxed at regular rates, except to the extent the fund is able to reap long-term capital gains from selling appreciated assets;
- mutual fund dividends paid out of (1) qualified dividends from the fund's corporate stock holdings and (2) long-term capital gains from selling appreciated securities are eligible for the reduced 0%/15%/20% rates;
- most REIT dividends are not eligible for the reduced rates. Why? Because the main sources of cash for REIT payouts are usually not qualified dividends from corporate stock held by the REIT or long-term capital gains from asset sales. Instead, most payouts are derived from positive cash flow generated by the REIT's real estate properties. So most REIT dividends will be ordinary income taxed at regular rates. As a result, clients should not buy REIT shares for their taxable accounts with the expectation of benefiting from the 0%/15%/20% rates; and
- dividends paid on stock in qualified foreign corporations are theoretically eligible for the reduced rates. Here is the rub: these dividends are often subject to foreign tax withholding. Under the U.S. foreign tax credit rules, individual investors may not necessarily receive credit for the full amount of withheld foreign taxes. So, investors can wind up paying the advertised 0%/15%/20% rates to the U.S. Treasury, plus some incremental percentage to some foreign country. The combined U.S. and foreign tax rates may exceed the advertised 0%/15%/20% rates. [See IRC Sections 1(h)(11)(c)(iv) and 904.]

The reduced rates do not apply to dividends earned inside tax-deferred retirement accounts (traditional IRA, Keogh, SEP, solo 401(k), and so on). Clients are taxed at their regular rates when dividends accumulated in these accounts are withdrawn as cash distributions. (Dividends accumulated in a Roth IRA are federal-income-tax-free as long as the client meets the requirements for tax-free withdrawals.).

Warning: To be eligible for the reduced 0%/15%/20% rates on qualified dividends earned in a taxable account, the stock on which the dividends are paid must be held for more than 60 days during the

---

120-day period that begins 60 days before the ex-dividend date (the day following the last day on which shares trade with the right to receive the upcoming dividend payment). Bottom line: When shares are owned only for a short time around the ex-dividend date, the dividend payout will count as ordinary income taxed at regular rates [IRC Section 1(h)(11)(B)(iii)].

The preferential 15% and 20% rates are increased by 3.8% when the NIIT applies, in which case the actual rates are 18.8% and 23.8%. In addition, the 25% and 28% rates can be increased by 3.8% when the NIIT applies.

Knowledge check

1. What are the current maximum federal income tax rates (not counting the potential impact of the NIIT) on an individual's IRC Section 1231 gains from selling depreciable real estate?

    a. 28%.
    b. 20% and 25%.
    c. 15%.
    d. 28.8%.

2. What is the current maximum federal income tax rate (not counting the potential impact of the NIIT) on qualified dividends earned in an individual's taxable account?

    a. 20%.
    b. 35%.
    c. 37%.
    d. 40.8%.

3. What is the current maximum federal income tax rate (not counting the potential impact of the NIIT) on recaptured IRC Section 1250 gains?

    a. 15%.
    b. 25%.
    c. 37%.
    d. 40.8%

Many individuals are eligible to pay 0% on investment profits

Long-term capital gains and qualified dividends earned in an individual's taxable retirement savings account are taxed at 0% when they fall within the 0% bracket for long-term gains and dividends. (The 0% brackets for 2019 long-term gains and dividends were shown earlier). Many more people than you might initially think are eligible for the 0% rate. Here are a few examples.

- Your married client files jointly and claims the $24,400 standard deduction for 2019. She could have up to $103,150 of adjusted gross income (including long-term capital gains and dividends) and still be within the 0% rate bracket for long-term gains and dividends. Her taxable income would be $78,750, which is the top of the 0% bracket for joint filers.
- Your divorced client uses head of household filing status, has two dependent kids, and claims the $18,350 standard deduction for 2019. He could have up to $71,100 of adjusted gross income (including long-term capital gains and dividends) and still be within the 0% rate bracket for long-term gains and dividends. His taxable income would be $52,750, which is the top of the 0% bracket for heads of households.
- Your single client has no kids and claims the $12,200 standard deduction for 2019. She could have up to $51,575 of adjusted gross income (including long-term capital gains and dividends) and still be within the 0% rate bracket for long-term gains and dividends. Her taxable income would be $39,375, which is the top of the 0% bracket for singles.

Key point: The adjusted gross income figures previously cited are after subtracting any above-the-line write-offs allowed on page 1 of the client's Form 1040. Among others, these write-offs include deductible retirement account contributions, health savings account (HSA) contributions, and self-employed health insurance premiums. So, if the taxpayer will have some above-the-line deductions, the adjusted gross income can be that much higher, and he or she will still be within the 0% bracket for long-term gains and dividends.

Tax-smart strategies for capital gain assets

Clients should try to satisfy the more-than-one-year holding period rule before selling appreciated investments held in taxable accounts. That way, they will qualify for the 0%/15%/20% long-term capital gains rates (plus the 3.8% NIIT when applicable). The higher the client's tax rate on ordinary income, the more this advice rings true. Of course, the client should never expose an accrued profit to great downside risk solely to be eligible for a lower tax rate. The client is always better off making a short-term profit and paying the resulting higher tax liability than hanging on too long and losing his or her profit altogether.

Clients should hold equity index mutual funds and tax-managed funds in taxable investment accounts. These types of funds are much less likely to generate ordinary income dividends that will be taxed at higher regular rates. Instead, these funds can be expected to generate qualified dividends and long-term capital gains that will be taxed at the reduced rates.

Clients should hold mutual funds that engage in rapid-fire asset churning in tax-advantaged retirement accounts. That way, the ordinary income generated by these funds will not cause any tax harm.

If the client insists on engaging in rapid-fire equity trading, he or she should confine that activity to the tax-advantaged retirement accounts where there is no tax disadvantage to lots of short-term trading.

Key point: Clients with an equity investing style that involves rapid-fire trading in stocks and ownership of quick-churning mutual funds should try to do this inside their tax-advantaged retirement accounts. Why? Because using this style in a taxable account generates ordinary income taxed at higher regular rates. Inside a tax-advantaged retirement account, however, there is no harm done. If the clients therefore devote most or all of their tax-advantaged retirement account balances to such rapid-fire equity trading, they might be forced to hold some or all of their fixed-income investments in taxable accounts. That is okay. Even though they will pay their higher regular rate on the ordinary income produced by those fixed-income assets, they should still come out ahead on an overall after-tax basis.

Broad-based stock index options

The current federal income tax rates on long-term capital gains are still pretty low, ranging from a minimum of 0% to a maximum of 20% depending on income (plus the 3.8% Medicare surtax which can affect higher-income taxpayers). But the rates on short-term gains are not so low. They will range from 22% to 37% for most investors (plus the 3.8% NIIT for higher-income investors). That is why, as a general rule, you should try to satisfy the more-than-one-year holding period requirement for long-term gain treatment before selling winner shares (worth more than you paid for them) held in taxable brokerage firm accounts. That way, the IRS won't be able to take more than a relatively modest bite out of your profits. However, the investment climate is not always conducive to making long-term commitments. But making short-term commitments results in short-term gains that may be taxed at high rates.

One popular way to place short-term bets on broad stock market movements is by trading in ETFs (exchange traded funds) like QQQ (which tracks the NASDAQ 100 index) and SPY (which tracks the S&P

500 index). Of course when you sell ETFs for short-term gains, you must pay your regular federal tax rate, which can be as high as 37%. The same is true for short-term gains from precious metal ETFs like GLD or SLV. Even long-term gains from precious metal ETFs can be taxed at up to 28%, because the gains are considered collectibles gains.

There is a way to play the market in a short-term fashion while paying a lower tax rate on gains. Consider trading in broad-based stock index options.

Favorable tax rates on short-term gains from trading in broad-based stock index options

The IRC treats broad-based stock index options, which look and feel a lot like options to buy and sell comparable ETFs, as *IRC Section 1256 contracts*. Specifically, broad-based stock index options fall into the non-equity option category of IRC Section 1256 contracts. [See IRC Section 1256(b)(1) and (g)(3) and IRS Publication 550 (Investment Income and Expenses) under the heading "Section 1256 Contracts Marked to Market."]

IRC Section 1256 contract treatment is a good deal for investors because gains and losses from trading in IRC Section 1256 contracts are automatically considered to be 60% long-term and 40% short-term [IRC Section 1256(a)(3)]. So your actual holding period for a broad-based stock index option doesn't matter. The tax-saving result is that short-term profits from trading in broad-based stock index options are taxed at a maximum effective federal rate of only 26.8% [(60% × 20%) + (40% × 37%) = 26.8%]. If you're in the top 37% bracket, that's a 27.6% reduction in your tax bill. The effective rate is lower if you're not in the top bracket. For example, if you're in the 24% bracket, the effective rate on short-term gains from trading in broad-based stock index options is only 18.6% [(60% × 15%) + (40% × 24%) = 18.6%]. That's a 22.5% reduction in your tax bill. (Of course, the 3.8% NIIT can potentially apply too, for higher-income individuals).

Key point: With broad-based stock index options, you pay a significantly lower tax rate on gains without having to make any long-term commitment. That's a nice advantage.

Favorable treatment for losses too

If an individual taxpayer suffers a net loss from IRC Section 1256 contracts, including losses from broad-based stock index options, an election can be made to carry back the net loss for three years to offset net gains from IRC Section 1256 contracts recognized in those earlier years, including gains from broad-based stock index options [IRC Section 1212I]. In contrast, garden-variety net capital losses can only be carried forward.

Year end mark-to-market rule

As the price to be paid for the aforementioned favorable tax treatment, you must follow a special mark-to-market rule at year end for any open positions in broad-based stock index options [IRC Section 1256(a)]. That means you pretend to sell your positions at their year-end market prices and include the resulting gains and losses on your tax return for that year. Of course, if you don't have any open positions at year end, this rule won't affect you.

Reporting broad-based stock index option gains and losses

According to IRS Publication 550, both gains and losses from closed positions in broad-based stock index options and year-end mark-to-market gains and losses from open positions are reported on Part I of Form 6781 (Gains and Losses from IRC Section 1256 Contracts and Straddles). The net short-term and long-term amounts are then transferred to Schedule D.

Finding broad-based stock index options

A fair number of options meet the tax law definition of broad-based stock index options, which means they qualify for the favorable 60/40 tax treatment. You can find options that track major stock indexes like the S&P 500 and the Russell 1000 and major industry and commodity sectors like biotech, oil, and gold. One place to identify options that qualify as broad-based stock index options is http://tradelogsoftware.com/resources/options/broad-based-index-options.

Although trading in these options is not for the faint-hearted, it's something to think about if you consider market volatility to be your friend.

Knowledge check

4. How are short-term profits from trading in broad-based stock index options taxed?

    a. As 40% long-term capital gain and 60% short-term gain.
    b. As short-term capital gains (that is, ordinary income).
    c. As 60% long-term capital gain and 40% short-term gain.
    d. As ordinary income.

Gifts of appreciated securities

High-bracket clients should consider gifting away appreciated securities to their low-bracket children and grandchildren (assuming the "kiddie tax" does not apply). For instance, if your client has an adult child. For 2019, the client can give the child up to $15,000 worth of appreciated securities without any adverse gift or estate tax consequences for the client. So can the client's spouse. The child can then sell the appreciated securities and pay 0% of the resulting long-term capital gains to the U.S. Treasury (assuming the child is in the 0% bracket for long-term capital gains and qualified dividends). The same 0% rate applies to qualified dividends collected from dividend-paying shares the child receives as gifts from the parents (again assuming the child is in the 0% bracket for long-term gains and dividends). For this idea to work, however, client and child must together hold the appreciated securities for more than one year. Beware: this strategy can backfire if the child is younger than age 24. Under the kiddie tax rules, some or all of the youngster's capital gains and dividends may be taxed at the rates that apply to estates and trusts. That would defeat the purpose of this strategy.

Selling the right losers

For year-end tax planning purposes, it is generally more advisable to sell short-term losers as opposed to long-term losers because short-term losses offset short-term gains that would otherwise taxed at ordinary income rates of up to 37%.

Knowledge check

5. For year-end tax planning purposes, why is it generally more advisable to sell short-term losers as opposed to long-term losers?

   a. Because short-term losses offset long-term gains that would otherwise be taxed at a maximum rate of 15% or 20%.
   b. Because short-term losses offset short-term gains that would otherwise be taxed at ordinary income rates of up to 37%.
   c. Because short-term losses can offset ordinary income without any limitation.
   d. Because the Investor Tax Credit can be claimed for short-term losses.

Tax-smart strategies for fixed-income investments

The federal income tax rate structure penalizes holding ordinary-income-producing investments in taxable account compared to stocks that the client expects to generate qualified dividends and long-term capital gains. Strategy: clients should generally put fixed-income assets that generate ordinary income (like Treasuries, corporate bonds, and CDs) into their tax-deferred retirement accounts. That way they will avoid the tax disadvantage.

The federal income tax rate structure also penalizes holding REIT shares in a taxable account compared to garden-variety corporate shares that the client expects to generate qualified dividends and long-term capital gains. As you know, REIT shares deliver current income in the form of high-yielding dividend payouts, plus the potential for capital gains, plus the advantage of diversification. These are all desirable attributes to have inside a tax-deferred retirement account. Inside a taxable account, however, REIT shares receive less-favorable treatment than garden-variety corporate shares because their dividend payments are not treated as qualified dividends. Strategy: the tax-deferred retirement account is now generally the best place to keep one's REIT stock investments.

Borrowing to buy dividend-paying stocks is usually inadvisable

Your individual client can borrow money to acquire dividend-paying stocks for taxable investment account. Then he or she can deduct the interest expense against an equal amount of ordinary income that would otherwise be taxed at up to 37%. Meanwhile, the client pays a reduced rate (0%/15%/20%) on all the qualified dividends and long-term capital gains thrown off by his or her savvy stock investments. Although this may seem like a good idea, let us take a closer look.

First, many individuals will find themselves unable to claim current deductions for some or all of the interest expense from borrowing to buy investments. Why? Because a loan used to acquire investment assets generates investment interest expense. Unfortunately, investment interest can only be deducted to the extent of the individual's net investment income for the year [IRC Section 163(d)]. Any excess investment interest is carried over to the next tax year and subjected to the very same net investment income limitation all over again.

Net investment income means interest, net short-term capital gains (excess of net short-term capital gains over net long-term capital losses), certain royalty income, and the like reduced by allocable investment expenses (other than investment interest expense). Investment income does not include net capital gains (excess of net long-term capital gains over net short-term capital losses). Under the current rules, investment income does not include qualified dividends either [IRC Section 163(d)(4)(B)].

Despite the preceding general rules, an individual can elect to treat specified amounts of net capital gain and qualified dividends as investment income in order to "free up" a bigger current deduction for investment interest expense. If the election is made, the elected amounts are treated as ordinary income and are taxed at regular rates [IRC Sections 1(h)(2) and 1(h)(11)(D)(i)]. So when the election is made, the increased investment interest deduction and the elected amounts of net capital gains and qualified dividends wind up offsetting each other at ordinary income rates. As a result, there is generally no tax advantage to borrowing in order to buy stocks. (The exact tax results of making or not making the election are explained in detail later in this chapter.) The big exception is when the individual can avoid making the election because he or she has sufficient investment income (generally from interest and short-term capital gains) to currently deduct all of the investment interest expense.

Even when the investment interest expense limitation can be successfully avoided, there is another tax law quirk to worry about. It arises when the client borrows to acquire stocks via the brokerage firm margin account. The brokerage firm can lend to short sellers shares held in the client's margin account worth up to 140% of the margin loan balance. As compensation, the client then receives payments in lieu of dividends. These payments compensate the client for dividends that would have otherwise been received from the shares that were lent out to short sellers. Unfortunately, these payments in lieu of dividends do not qualify for the reduced tax rates on dividends. Instead, the payments are considered to be ordinary income.

Key point: The tax planning solution is to keep dividend-paying stocks in a separate brokerage firm account that has no margin loans against it.

Variable annuities are damaged goods

Variable annuities are basically mutual fund investments wrapped up inside a life insurance policy. Earnings are tax-deferred, but they are treated as ordinary income when withdrawn. So the investor pays his or her regular tax rate at that time even if most or all of the variable annuity's earnings were from dividends and capital gains that would otherwise qualify for the reduced 0%/15%/20% rates. This factor, plus the high fees charged by insurance companies on variable annuities, makes these products very problematic. It can take many (too many) years for the tax deferral advantage to overcome the inherent disadvantages. If the investor ever catches up at all, that is.

Planning for mutual fund transactions

When clients are considering selling appreciated mutual fund shares near year-end, they should pull the trigger before that year's dividend distribution. That way, the entire gain—including the amount attributable to the upcoming dividend—will be taxed at the reduced 0%/15%/20% rates (assuming the shares have been held more than 12 months). In contrast, if the client puts off selling until after the "ex-dividend" date, he or she is locked into receiving the payout. Some of that will probably be taxed at ordinary rates. In other words, inaction can convert a low-taxed capital gain into an ordinary income dividend taxed at up to 37%.

For the same reason, it can pay to put off buying into a fund until after the ex-dividend date. If the investor acquires shares just before the magic date, he or she will get the dividend and the tax bill that comes along with it. In effect, the investor will be paying taxes on gains earned before buying in. Not a good idea.

To get the best tax results, the client should be advised to contact the fund and ask for the expected year-end payout amount and the ex-dividend date. Then transactions can be timed accordingly.

The good thing about equity mutual funds is they are managed by professionals. These taxpayers should be well-qualified to judge which stocks are most attractive, given the client's investment objectives. The bad thing about funds (besides the fees) is that the client has virtually no control over taxes.

The fund—not the client—decides which of its investments will be sold and when. If its transactions during the year result in an overall gain, the client will receive a taxable distribution (in other words, a dividend) whether he or she likes it or not. This is because funds are required to pass out almost all of their gains every year or pay corporate income tax. (The special federal income tax rules for mutual funds are found in IRC Section 852.) When the client gets a distribution, he or she will owe the resulting tax bill even though the fund shares may have actually declined because he or she bought in.

This *unwanted distribution* issue is less of a problem with index funds and tax-efficient (a.k.a., tax-managed) funds. Index funds essentially follow a buy-and-hold strategy, which tends to minimize taxable distributions. Tax-efficient funds also lean toward a buy-and-hold philosophy, and when they do sell securities for gains, they attempt to offset them by selling some losers in the same year. This approach also minimizes taxable distributions.

In contrast, funds that actively "churn" their stock portfolios in attempting (sometimes futilely) to maximize returns will usually generate hefty annual distributions in a rising market. The size of these payouts can be annoying enough, but it is even worse when a large percentage comes from short-term gains. They are taxed at the investor's ordinary rate (as high as 37%). Not good.

On the other hand, funds that buy and hold stocks will pass out distributions mainly taxed at the reduced rates for long-term gains.

The bottom line: If the client will be investing via taxable accounts, he or she should really look at what kind of *after-tax* returns various funds have been earning and use these figures in picking between competing funds.

Now, if the client is using a tax-deferred retirement account (IRA, 401(k), and so on) or a tax-free Roth IRA to hold the mutual fund investments, the client can focus strictly on total return and ignore all this stuff about tax woes from distributions.

With the basics behind us, let us cover some specifics about how mutual fund investments are taxed.

Identifying sale transactions

Like regular stock shares, mutual fund shares can be sold outright. The client can sell and get cash on the barrelhead. When this happens, the client is (hopefully) well aware that he or she must figure the capital gain or loss for tax purposes. Mutual fund companies allow investors to make other transactions that are also treated as taxable sales—or not, depending on the circumstances. The added convenience is fine and dandy, as long as the client understands the tax ramifications. Here are the three biggest problem areas:

- Client can write checks against his or her account with the cash coming from liquidating part of the investment in fund shares. When the client takes advantage of this arrangement, he or she has made a sale and must now calculate the taxable gain or loss on the deal.
- Client switches the investment from one fund in a mutual fund family to another. This is a taxable sale.
- Client decides to sell 200 shares in a fund for a tax loss. Because the client participates in the fund's dividend reinvestment program, he or she automatically buys 50 more shares in that same fund within 30 days before or after the loss sale. For tax purposes, the client made a wash sale of 50 shares. As a result, the tax loss on those shares is disallowed. However, the client does get to add the disallowed loss to his or her tax basis in the 50 shares acquired via dividend reinvestment.

Once it is determined that there has indeed been a taxable sale, the next step is to compute the capital gain or loss. For this, we need to know the tax basis of the shares that were sold.

Calculating mutual fund share basis

When blocks of fund shares are purchased at different times and prices, think of it as creating several layers—each with a different per-share price. When some of the shares are sold, we need some method to determine which layer those shares came from so we can figure their tax basis and calculate the capital gain or loss. Three methods are available.

1. First in, first out (FIFO)
2. Average basis
3. Specific identification

FIFO method

FIFO assumes the shares that are sold come from the layers purchased first. In rising markets, FIFO gives the worst tax answer because it maximizes gains. However, FIFO must be used unless the client acts to use the average basis or specific ID methods explained later.

Example 1-1

- Fred bought his first 200 shares in the SoSo Fund for $10 each (the first layer).
- Later, he bought another 200 shares at $15 (the second layer).
- He then sold 160 shares at $17.50.
  - Under FIFO, the client is considered to have sold his shares out of the first layer, which cost only $10 each. His capital gain is $1,200 ($2,800 proceeds, less $1,600 basis).

Average basis method

Using this method, the investor figures the average basis in fund shares any time a sale is made.

Example 1-2

- Assume the same situation as in the previous example, except Fred uses the average basis method to calculate his gain or loss.
- The average basis per share is $12.50 ($5,000 total cost divided by 400 shares).
  - Now the capital gain is only $800—$2,800 proceeds less basis of $2,000 (160 shares times $12.50 per share).

Most mutual funds report average basis information on transaction statements sent to investors. So there may be no need to make any calculations. However, the taxpayer must make the notation *average basis method* on the line of Schedule D where the gain or loss is reported. The taxpayer must then use the average basis method for all future sales of shares in that particular fund.

Specific ID method

Using this method, the client specifies exactly which shares to sell by reference to the acquisition date and per-share price. Most mutual funds require written instructions by letter or fax. According to the IRS guidelines, the fund or broker must then follow up by confirming the client's instructions in writing. The specific ID method allows the client to choose to sell the most expensive shares to minimize gain. Remember, the client must act at the time of the sale by giving instructions to the brokerage firm. If the client waits until tax return time to get interested in this idea, he or she will have missed the boat.

The client should receive a written or emailed confirmation of his or her instructions about which specific shares are being sold when the specific ID method is used. For online transactions, brokerage firms have procedures that allow you to choose to use the specific ID method to identify the shares you are selling.

Example 1-3

- Same situation as in the preceding examples, except Fred specifies he is selling 100 shares from the second block (costing $15 each) and 60 from the first (costing $10 each).
    - Using the specific ID method to calculate his gain or loss, the basis of the shares sold is $2,100 [(100 × $15) + (60 × $10)]. Now the capital gain is now only $700 – $2,800 proceeds, less basis of $2,100.

Mutual fund aggregate basis worksheet

The original cost (including brokerage fees, transfer charges, and load charges) of the shares is the starting point for keeping track of the aggregate tax basis of an investment in a particular mutual fund.

1. Enter the original cost amount.		
Now make the following adjustments:		
2. Increase basis by the amount of reinvested distributions.	+	
3. Increase basis by the amount of long-term capital gains retained by the fund, as reported on Form 2439 (this is fairly rare).	+	
4. Decrease basis by the amount of fund-level taxes paid on long-term gains retained by the fund, as reported on Form 2439 (again, fairly rare).	–	
5. Decrease basis by the amount of basis allocable to shares already sold. (See the following worksheet for the basis of shares sold using the average cost method.)	–	
6. The result is the aggregate tax basis of the remaining fund shares. If one sells one's entire holding in the fund, subtract this aggregate basis figure from the net sales proceeds to calculate the gain or loss. (If one sells some but not all of one's shares, see the following worksheet to figure the capital gain or loss.)	=	

Mutual fund capital gain or loss worksheet using average basis method

Use this worksheet to calculate gain or loss each time an investor sells some but not all of his or her shares in a particular fund for which the average basis method is used. (If the investor sells all of the shares in the same transaction, skip lines 2–4, and simply enter the amount from line 1 directly on line 5.)

1.	Aggregate basis of shares in this fund at the time of sale (from previous worksheet).	
2.	Number of shares owned just before selling.	
3.	Divide line 1 by line 2. This is the average basis.	
4.	Number of shares sold in this transaction.	
5.	Multiply line 3 by line 4. This is the basis of the shares that were sold, using the average basis method.	
6.	Total sales proceeds (net of commissions).	
7.	Subtract line 5 from line 6. This is the taxable capital gain or loss.	

Foreign taxes on international funds

If the client invests in international mutual funds, the year-end statements may reveal that some foreign taxes were paid. The client can either deduct the share of those taxes (on Schedule A) or claim a credit against his or her U.S. taxes. Generally, taking the credit is the best option. To take a credit more than $300 ($600 for a joint return), Form 1116 (Foreign Tax Credit) must be filed. If the client has smaller amounts of foreign taxes (no more than $300 or $600 if filing jointly) solely from interest and dividends (such as via international mutual funds), the credit can be entered directly on the appropriate line on page 2 of Form 1040 without filing Form 1116. (See IRS Publication 514, "Foreign Tax Credit for Individuals," for help in preparing Form 1116.)

Converting capital gains and dividends into ordinary income to maximize investment interest write-offs

Individuals incurring investment interest expense must include Form 4952 (Investment Interest Expense Deduction) with their returns. The form limits the itemized deduction for investment interest to the amount of "investment income" from interest, short-term capital gains, and so on. [IRC Section 163(d)]. If there is insufficient investment income, the taxpayer can elect to make up some or all of the difference by treating a designated amount of long-term capital gain or qualified dividends as investment income taxed at ordinary rates [IRC Section 163(d)(4)(B)].

The election is made by reporting the amount of long-term capital gain or qualified dividends to be treated as investment income on Form 4952 (the same number is then entered on Schedule D). The amount of gain or qualified dividends so treated can be as much or as little as the taxpayer wishes, but any gain must come from investment assets rather than business assets or rental real estate [IRC Section 163(d)(5)]. In other words, the gain cannot be IRC Section 1231 gain treated as long-term capital gain. The taxpayer then has that much more investment income, which allows the deduction of that much more investment interest expense.

If the election is made, capital gains qualifying for the 15% and 20% rates are converted before gains taxed at 28%. Most taxpayers will not actually have any 28% gains and gains qualifying for the 25% rate do not come into play here because they are from IRC Section 1231 property.

When 15% gains are converted, taxpayers in the 22% bracket essentially pay a 7% tax for the privilege of deducting more investment interest currently, those in the 24% bracket pay 9%, those in the 32% bracket pay 17%, and those in the 35% bracket pay 20%. Therefore, taxpayers in all these brackets will recognize a 15% net tax benefit from converting long-term gains into ordinary income.

Taxpayers in the top 37% bracket will pay 17% to convert gains that would otherwise be taxed at 20%. Therefore, taxpayers in the 37% bracket will recognize a net 20% tax benefit from converting long-term gains into ordinary income (37% deduction for the extra investment interest expense minus the 17% cost for converting).

How to make the election

The election is made by reporting the elected amount (that is, the amount of qualified dividend income or net capital gain to be treated as investment income taxed at ordinary rates) on line 4g of Form 4952. The elected amount is then "backed out" of the amounts eligible for preferential tax rates via calculations made on those fun-filled Schedule D worksheets.

According to the Form 4952 instructions, the elected amount indicated on line 4g is normally deemed to come first from the taxpayer's net capital gain from property held for investment (shown on line 4e), and then from qualified dividend income (shown on line 4b). However, per the instructions, the taxpayer can choose different treatment by making a notation on the dotted line to the left of the box on line 4e.

Key point: According to Regulation 1.163(d)-1, the election can be revoked only with IRS consent.

Election is not a no-brainer

The following examples illustrate that making the election is not always advisable.

Example 1-4

- Buck (a 35% bracket taxpayer) has $6,000 of 2018 investment interest expense, but his investment income from interest and short-term capital gains is only $2,500. He also has several significant 15% long-term capital gains from stock and mutual fund transactions.
  - Making the election to convert $3,500 of long-term capital gain into investment income lets Buck deduct all his investment interest. At a marginal rate of 35%, $1,225 comes off his 2018 tax bill ($3,500 × 35%).
  - But he would also pay an extra 20% on the $3,500 of converted long-term gain because that amount would be taxed at 35% instead of 15%. The extra tax would amount to $700 ($3,500 × 20%).
  - The net tax savings are $525 ($1,225 minus $700), so Buck realizes a net 15% tax benefit from the bigger deduction $525 ÷ $3500 = 15%). (He will realize a 15% tax benefit if his marginal federal income tax rate is 22%, 24%, 32%, or 35%.)

What to do (or not do) in this situation? Clients should consider passing on the election. The 2018 excess investment interest expense ($3,500 in Buck's case) will carry over into 2019 when he may have enough investment income to fully deduct the carryover, plus any investment interest incurred this year.

If his 2019 investment income is high enough, the client will realize a 22%, 24%, 32%, 35%, or 37% tax benefit from the carryover without paying any extra tax on his capital gains. Of course, there is a time value of money advantage to making the election and claiming a bigger 2018 investment interest expense deduction, but a bigger 2019 tax benefit might more than make up the difference.

Example 1-5

- Assume the same facts as example 1-4, except Buck carries over the $3,500 excess investment interest and deducts it in 2019. (Assume Buck already knows he will have plenty of 2019 investment income, because he has decided the stock market is overvalued and has therefore allocated a bigger percentage of his investment assets to fixed-income assets and dividend-paying stocks.)
  - Assuming the 35% marginal rate still applies to Buck in 2019, the $3,500 deduction for the investment interest expense carried over from 2018 saves him $1,225 on his 2019 federal income tax bill ($3,500 × 35%).

Of course, if the client cannot foresee having enough investment income anytime soon, he or she should make a current-year election to convert enough long-term capital gain to fully deduct the full amount of his or her current-year investment interest expense. This will result in only a 15% net tax benefit (if the client is in the 22%, 24%, 32%, or 35% marginal bracket) or a 20% net tax benefit (if the client is in the 37% marginal bracket), but that is better than waiting indefinitely for the write-off.

Planning for capital gain treatment for subdivided lot sales via IRC Section 1237 relief

When a landowner subdivides a parcel to sell off individual lots, he or she is generally considered a real estate dealer, and the lots represent inventory. As a result, gains from the lot sales are taxed as ordinary income.

Fortunately, IRC Section 1237 provides an exception to ordinary income treatment. Subject to the limitations explained in the following section, the seller will not be considered a dealer merely because the land has been subdivided into lots or because of advertising, promotion, selling activities, or the use of sales agents.

In other words, if the seller was holding the land for investment, subsequent subdividing and selling activities will not cause the property to be transformed into inventory, and the seller can still take advantage of the reduced 0%/15%/20% rates on long-term capital gains from sales of lots held more than 12 months. (The 3.8% NIIT can also apply to capital gains recognized by higher-income individuals.)

Restrictions on IRC Section 1237 relief

Needless to say, Congress has imposed some restrictions on the availability of IRC Section 1237 relief:

1. Relief is unavailable to taxpayers whose activities with respect to their other land holdings indicate they are real estate dealers [Regulation Section 1.237-1(a)].
2. Relief is generally unavailable to C corporation sellers [IRC Section 1237(a)]. However, it is available to individuals; partnerships; LLCs treated as partnerships for federal income tax purposes; and S corporations.
3. The seller must have held the property for at least five years unless it was inherited. However, under IRC Section 1223, the seller's holding period may include that of a previous owner in certain circumstances. [See examples in Reg. Sec. 1.1237-1(b) and (c).]
4. The land in question must be a *tract of real property* as defined by IRC Section 1237(c) and Reg. Sec. 1.1237-1(g).
5. The seller cannot have ever held any portion of the land for sale in the ordinary course of business (in other words, as inventory); and in the year of sale, the seller cannot hold any other real property primarily for sale in the ordinary course of business.
6. The seller cannot have made any substantial improvements that materially increased the value of the lots that are sold, nor can such improvements be made pursuant to the contract for sale between the seller and buyer. Improvements made by certain related parties (such as a controlled corporation) are considered made by the seller [IRC Section 1237(a)(2)(A) and Reg. Sec. 1.1237-1(c)].
7. After more than five lots from the same tract have been sold, gains from lot sales in the year the sixth lot is sold, and in later years, are ordinary income to the extent of 5% of the sales price for those lots [IRC Section 1237(b)].

For purposes of the preceding rules, the seller is treated as holding other real estate owned individually, jointly, indirectly as a member of a partnership or LLC, or indirectly as an S corporation shareholder [Reg. Sec. 1.1237-1(b)(3) and Committee Reports on IRC Section 1314 of Small Business Protection Act of 1996].

However, the seller is generally not treated as indirectly holding other real estate owned by family members, estates, trusts, or C corporations [Reg. Sec. 1.1237-1(b)(3)].

As stated in item 6, substantial improvements made by certain other parties (including the buyer if pursuant to the sales contract) are considered made by the seller and can disqualify the seller from IRC Section 1237 relief.

Example 1-6

- Wayne, who is not a real estate dealer, is a member of an LLC engaged in real estate development. Assume the LLC is a dealer because it holds real estate primarily for sale in its development business. During the year, Wayne subdivides a tract he has owned for many years and sells off four lots for large gains.
  - Unfortunately, Wayne is treated as an owner of the LLC's real estate and is therefore disqualified from IRC Section 1237 relief (see item 5). As a result, Wayne's lot sale gains will be taxed as ordinary income.
  - However, if the real estate development entity was a C corporation (rather than an LLC) and Wayne was a shareholder, his indirect ownership of the C corporation's real estate would not disqualify him from IRC Section 1237 relief. In this circumstance, Wayne could treat his lot sale gains as long-term capital gains subject to reduced tax rates, assuming he also meets all the other IRC Section 1237 requirements.

Example 1-7

- Belinda, who is a real estate dealer, sells four subdivided lots from a single tract she owns.
  - Because Belinda is a dealer during the year, she sells the lots, IRC Section 1237 relief is unavailable (see item 1). Accordingly, she will have to pay ordinary income rates on her lot sale gains.

Example 1-8

- Victoria's rich Uncle Dudley gave her a small but valuable real estate tract as a gift. Uncle Dudley made his millions as a real estate developer. He held the tract for four years and intended to subdivide the property and sell off lots in the ordinary course of his business.
- Victoria holds the tract for three years and then subdivides the parcel. She succeeds in selling three lots for large gains.
    - Under IRC Section 1223, Victoria's holding period for the property includes her Uncle Dudley's holding period because she received the tract as a gift. Victoria therefore meets the five-year rule.
    - However, the regulations say she is disqualified from IRC Section 1237 relief because of Uncle Dudley's motive for owning the property, unless Victoria can demonstrate that she did not also hold the tract primarily for sale in the ordinary course of business [Reg. Sec. 1.1237-1(b)(3)]. (Apparently, Victoria could prove this by showing she intended to hold the tract for investment for several years before later deciding to subdivide the property and sell it off as lots.)

Example 1-9

- Rhonda is a CPA who sometimes buys raw land for investment. She has no other activities that would indicate she is a real estate dealer. During the year, Rhonda sells three tracts acquired five years ago for substantial profits.
    - She can treat the gains as long-term capital gains and pay a reduced tax rate. She does not need IRC Section 1237 relief (nor does she qualify for it), because the tracts were investment property and were not subdivided and sold off as lots.
    - The same result would apply if Rhonda is considered a dealer in real estate, as long as she can prove her reason for holding the three tracts in question was for investment rather than primarily for sale in her business as a real estate dealer.

Definition of tract of real property

IRC Section 1237 relief is available only if the subdivided land constitutes a "tract of real property." (See item 4.) In general, this means a single piece of real estate. However, two or more pieces can qualify if at any time they were contiguous (that is, having a common boundary at one or more points) in the hands of the seller, or if the pieces would be contiguous but for a road, street, railroad, stream, and so on [IRC Section 1237(c) and Reg. Sec. 1.1237(g)(1)].

A tract of real property can be assembled from acquisitions at various times, and the seller can treat contiguous pieces as a single tract even though some pieces are owned individually; some jointly; and some indirectly as a partner, member of an LLC, or for tax years beginning after 1996 as an S corporation shareholder.

For counting purposes under the *five-lot rule* (see item 7), the remaining lots in a tract of real property constitute a new tract after one or more lots have been sold from the original tract and five years have passed since the last sale from the original tract.

Definition of substantial improvement

Per item 6, the lot seller cannot make *substantial improvements* that *substantially increase* the value of the lots. Similarly, such improvements cannot be made under the terms of the contract for sale between the seller and buyer. Improvements made by certain related parties (such as the seller's-controlled corporation) are considered made by the seller [IRC Section 1237(a)(2)(A) and Reg. Sec. 1.1237-1(c)(2)].

To restate the rule, improvements result in disqualification for IRC Section 1237 relief only if (1) they are substantial in character and (2) they substantially enhance the value of the lot that is sold.

Under the regulations, substantial improvements include commercial or residential buildings; hard surface roads; and sewer, water, gas, and electric lines. Examples of insubstantial improvements include a temporary structure used as a field office; surveying, filling, draining, leveling, and clearing operations; and minimum all-weather access roads, including gravel roads where required by the climate [Reg. Sec. 1.1237-1(c)(4)].

Even substantial improvements will not disqualify the seller from IRC Section 1237 relief for a particular lot sale unless it also directly and substantially enhances the value of that specific lot. What is *substantial*? According to Reg. Sec. 1.1237-1(c)(3), an increase of 10% or less is insubstantial, and when improvements increase value by more than 10%, all relevant factors should be examined to determine if the increase is substantial.

Under these rules, the values of particular lots could be substantially increased by improvements, but the values of other lots are not. Therefore, some lots may become ineligible for IRC Section 1237 relief, and certain other lots in the same tract still qualify.

 Example 1-10

- Vern made major improvements to a tract he had owned for two years. He then made a gift of the property to his son Delgado. Four years later, Delgado subdivided the tract and began selling off lots.
  - Vern's improvements substantially enhanced the value of the lots. Delgado is therefore ineligible for IRC Section 1237 relief because he is treated as having made the improvements that Vern paid for (see item 6).

Election to disregard substantial improvements

Individual taxpayers may be eligible for a special election to treat otherwise disqualifying improvements as not being substantial. The election is available if all the following requirements are met:

1. The seller agrees to not deduct the costs of the improvements or add the costs to the basis of the lot or lots sold.
2. The seller has held the property for 10 years (not counting ownership by the previous owner if the property was inherited).
3. The improvements are limited to roads (including hard surface roads), curbs, and gutters; and water, sewer, and drainage facilities (including both surface and subsurface facilities).
4. The IRS District Director is satisfied that the improvements are necessary to bring the fair market value (FMV) of the lot (or lots) up to the prevailing value for similar sites in the local area. The specifics on how to make this election are covered in Reg. Sec. 1.1237-1(d)(iii). Obviously, the election is advisable only when the tax savings from IRC Section 1237 relief outweigh the tax detriment of ignoring the improvement costs.

Situations where the election could make sense include the following:

1. The seller has capital loss carryovers that will shelter all or part of the capital gain from selling the lots (without IRC Section 1237 relief, capital loss carryovers would not shelter the lot sale gains because the gains would be ordinary income).
2. The gains are large in relation to the improvement costs and the tax savings from the reduced long-term capital gain tax rates outweigh the tax benefit from adding the improvement cost to the basis of the lots.

Keep in mind the election is available only when the improvements are necessary to bring the price of the lots up to the prevailing market. If the seller can get market price without the making the improvements, the election is not an option.

 Example 1-11

- Tom, who is in the 37% marginal tax bracket, owns a five-acre tract of unimproved land in a highly desirable residential area. Tom has owned the land for 14 years, and his basis is only $80,000. He wants to subdivide the property into five one-acre lots, in accordance with the local zoning restrictions.
- Unfortunately, Tom's land has some serious (but correctable) drainage problems and is therefore much less valuable than similar nearby unimproved sites. Tom recently received a written offer of $100,000 per acre for his parcel (total of $500,000). Similar nearby improved tracts (with road and drainage improvements) are selling for $200,000 per acre, and the improvements to these similar properties cost an average of about $50,000 per acre.
- According to the IRC Section 1237 regulations, this makes the prevailing market price for comparable unimproved acreage about $150,000 per acre ($200,000 less $50,000). Assume Tom can install a road and correct the drainage problems on all five lots for a total of $325,000. The lots could then be sold for around $200,000 each (total of $1,000,000).

Example 1-11 (continued)

- Tom's proposed improvements would clearly be substantial in character and result in a substantial increase in the value of the lots. However, based on the offer Tom received, the improvements are needed just to raise the value of the lots to the prevailing level. Therefore, Tom is eligible to make the election to treat the improvements as not substantial and ignore their cost in calculating his gain from sale.
  - If Tom makes the improvements for the expected cost, sells the lots for the expected price, and makes the election, he will have a long-term capital gain of $920,000 ($1m sales proceeds less $80,000 basis), and his federal income tax hit at 20% will be $184,000. (The 20% rate applies only because the election allows Tom to qualify for IRC Section 1237 relief.) In contrast, if Tom does not make the election, his gain will be only $595,000 ($1m sales proceeds less basis of $405,000, including the cost of improvements), but the tax on that amount at 37% is $220,150.
  - In this example, making the election saves the taxpayer $36,150 ($220,150 – $184,000) based on current tax rates. (This example ignores the potential impact of the 3.8% NIIT.)

The five-lot rule

Under the IRC Section 1237 rules, when more than five lots from the same tract of real property are sold, gains from lot sales in the year the sixth lot is sold and in later years are treated as ordinary income to the extent of 5% of the selling price for each affected lot [IRC Section 1237(b)].

Note that lot sales in tax years before the sale of the sixth lot are unaffected by this gain recharacterization rule, but if more than five lots are sold in the first year of sales, all sales are affected.

The amount of gain that is re-characterized as ordinary income is limited to the excess (if any) of 5% of the selling price over the selling expenses for the lot. [See Reg. Sec. 1.1237-1(e)(2) for examples of how this limitation is calculated.] The sale of two or more contiguous lots to the same buyer in the same transaction counts as only one lot sale for purposes of the five-lot rule [Reg. Sec. 1.1237(e)(2)].

In addition, the remaining lots in a particular tract of real property constitute a new tract after one or more lots have been sold from the original tract and five years have passed since the last sale from the original tract. Under this *fresh start* provision, the remaining lots need not still be contiguous to qualify as a single new tract [IRC Section 1237(c) and Reg. Sec. 1.1237(g)(2)].

Example 1-12

- Neville has owned a tract of raw land for six years. In 2019, he subdivides the property into 12 lots and immediately sells single lots to Horace, Evander, Desiree, and Dolly. At the same time, he also sells three contiguous lots to Emory.
  - Under the five-lot rule, Neville is treated as selling only five lots because the three contiguous lots sold to Emory count as only one. Assuming Neville meets all the other IRC Section 1237 requirements discussed earlier, his lot sale gains are all long-term capital gains eligible for preferential tax rates.
- Neville then waits for five years without selling any further lots.
  - His remaining five lots now constitute a new tract of real property for purposes of the six-lot rule (even if some 2019 sales caused the remaining lots to be noncontiguous). Neville can then sell the remaining lots without having to worry about the gain recharacterization rule.

Land is not always a capital asset

In two 2014 decisions, the Tax Court and a California District Court ruled that gains from land sales were high-taxed ordinary income rather lower-taxed long-term capital gains (*Cordell Pool,* TC Memo 2014-3 and *Frederic Allen*, 113 AFTR 2d 2014-2262, DC CA 05/28/2014). Here is the scoop on how to determine the federal income tax treatment of land sale gains.

Capital gains tax basics

Long-term gains recognized by individual taxpayers from the sale of capital assets are taxed at lower federal rates than ordinary income. The current maximum federal income tax rate on net long-term capital gains from most capital assets held for more than one year is "only" 20% (plus the 3.8% NIIT when applicable).

For real estate, long-term gains recognized by individual taxpayers that are attributable to depreciation are subject to a maximum federal rate of 25% (plus the 3.8% NIIT when applicable).

In contrast, the maximum federal rate on ordinary income recognized by individual taxpayers is 37% (plus the 3.8% NIIT when applicable or the 0.9% additional Medicare tax on salary and self-employment income when applicable).

Key point: Net short-term capital gains recognized by individual taxpayers are taxed at the same high rates as ordinary income and are also potentially subject to the 3.8% NIIT.

Land held as inventory is not a capital asset

Preferential tax rates apply only to long-term gains from dispositions of *capital assets*, which do not include property held by the taxpayer primarily for sale to customers in the ordinary course of the taxpayer's business. Such assets are commonly called *inventory*. In determining whether property is inventory (or not), the Tax Court and the Ninth Circuit Court of Appeals have identified the following five factors as relevant.

1. The nature of the acquisition of the property.
2. The frequency and continuity of property sales by the taxpayer.
3. The nature and the extent of the taxpayer's business.
4. Sales activities of the taxpayer with respect to the property.
5. The extent and substantiality of the transaction in question.

Key point: Taxpayers have the burden of proving that they fall on the right side of these factors. If they fail, the IRS wins the argument.

Tax Court decision

In a case decided in early 2014, Concinnity LLC (CL) was classified as a partnership for federal income tax purposes. CL was organized by Cordell Pool, Justin Buchanan, and Thomas Kallenbach (collectively, the taxpayers). These individuals also organized, incorporated, and owned Elk Grove Development Company (EGDC). CL acquired 300 undeveloped acres in Montana for $1.4m. At the time of the purchase, the land was already divided into four sections (phases 1–4). The land later became the Elk Grove Planned Unit Development (the PUD). CL contracted to give EGDC the exclusive right to purchase from CL phases 1, 2, and 3 which consisted of 300 lots in the PUD. On its 2005 Form 1065, CL reported long-term capital gains totaling $500,761 from two installment sales of the lots in phases 2 and 3. In turn, the three taxpayers (the CL partners) reported their passed-through shares of CL's gains as long-term capital gains on their respective 2005 Forms 1040. After an audit, the IRS claimed that CL's land sales produced ordinary income rather than long-term capital gains and asserted tax deficiencies against the three taxpayers. The unhappy taxpayers took their cases to the Tax Court where they claimed the land sales produced long-term capital gains because the land was held by CL for investment purposes. The Tax Court applied the five factors listed previously and found that none of them weighed in favor of the taxpayers. Therefore, the Tax Court agreed with the IRS that CL's land sale gains should have been reported as high-taxed ordinary income. Here are the details.

Factor no. 1 (nature of acquisition)

The IRS claimed that CL acquired the land which came to be included in the PUD to divide and sell lots to customers. Supporting this position was the fact that CL's 2000 Form 1065 identified its principal business activity as "development" and its principal product or service as "real estate." The Tax Court also believed that the record suggested that CL's purpose in acquiring the land was to develop and sell it. Therefore, the Tax Court concluded that evaluation of this factor failed to show that CL held the property for investment rather than as inventory for sale to customers.

Factor no. 2 (frequency and continuity of sales)

The Tax Court noted that frequent and substantial sales of real property indicate sales of inventory in the ordinary course of business; at the same time, infrequent sales indicate property held for investment. In this case, the record was not clear about the frequency and substantiality of CL's land sales. The Tax Court noted that CL's Forms 1065 reflected two installment sales of lots in phases 2 and 3 to EGDC, and an affidavit stated that CL had directly entered into agreements for the sale of 81 lots in phase 1 without the involvement of EGDC. However, the Tax Court believed that the record was insufficient to establish the overall extent of CL's land sale activities. Therefore, the Tax Court concluded that evaluation of this factor failed to show that CL's land sales were infrequent or insubstantial.

Factor no. 3 (nature and extent of business)

In evaluating this factor, the IRS claimed that that the only documents in the record indicated that CL brokered land sale deals, found additional investors for necessary development work, secured water and wastewater systems, and guaranteed that necessary improvements were made. The Tax Court agreed that the record showed that CL paid for certain water and wastewater improvements to the PUD and that this level of activity was more akin to a developer's involvement than to an investor's action to simply increase the value of the property. The Tax Court concluded that evaluation of this factor failed to show that CL held Elk Grove PUD land primarily for investment rather than as inventory for sale in the ordinary course of business.

Factor no. 4 (sales activities with respect to the property)

The record was unclear about whether CL sought out the 81 individual phase 1 lot buyers or whether those buyers sought out CL. Therefore, the Tax Court concluded that evaluation of this factor failed to show that CL did not spend significant time actively participating in selling lots.

Factor no. 5 (extent and substantiality of transaction)

EGDC agreed to buy the land in phases 2 and 3 from CL at prices that appeared to be inflated. According to the Tax Court, this indicated that CL did not make bona fide arm's-length sales to EGDC, which was also owned by the three taxpayers. Instead, indications were that EGDC was formed by the taxpayers for tax avoidance reasons: to buy the lots from CL and then sell them to customers in order to avoid the appearance that CL was itself in the business of selling lots to customers. Therefore, the Tax Court concluded that the taxpayers were on the wrong side of this factor.

Bottom line

Because the taxpayers were not found to be on the right side of any of the five factors, the Tax Court agreed with the IRS that CL held the PUD lots as inventory for sale to customers in the ordinary course of business. Therefore, CL's land sales generated high-taxed ordinary income rather than lower-tax, long-term capital gains. (See *Cordell Pool*, TC Memo 2014-3.)

District court decision

In *Allen*, a California District Court held that a joint-filing married couple was required to recognize ordinary income rather than long-term capital gain when they received a payment pursuant to a land sale agreement. Factually, Frederic Allen and his wife Phyllis (collectively, the taxpayers) went to District Court seeking a refund of federal income tax assessed by the IRS on $63,662 of income from the sale of 2.63 acres of undeveloped land. The taxpayers claimed that the income was long-term capital gain from selling property held for investment. The IRS said it was ordinary income from the sale of inventory. Allen purchased the land in 1987 and initially testified that that he intended to develop it and sell it himself. He later testified that he bought the land as an investment. Ultimately, he admitted that between 1987 and 1995, he attempted to develop the property by himself. In so doing, he paid for engineering plans and took out a second mortgage. From 1995-1997, he attempted to find investors or partners to help develop and sell the property. In 1999, Allen finally sold the property to Clarum Corporation, a real estate development outfit, in an installment sale deal that was later renegotiated. In 2004, the taxpayers received from Clarum a final installment payment of $63,662, and Clarum issued a Form 1099-MISC to the taxpayers to report the payment. In 2007, the taxpayers finally filed their Form 1040 for 2004, but the return did not report the $63,662 from Clarum. In 2008, they filed an amended return that reported the $63,662 as long-term capital gain.

Using the five-factor analysis explained earlier, the District Court decided that the property was inventory in the taxpayers' hands, because two factors favored that treatment while the other three factors were inconclusive. Therefore, the District Court granted summary judgment in favor of the IRS. So the $63,662 was high-taxed ordinary income rather than lower-taxed long-term capital gain. [See *Frederic Allen*, 113 AFTR 2d 2014-2262 (DC CA 2014).]

Tax planning implications

In the *Pool* case, better advance planning would have allowed CL's land sale profits to be properly characterized as lower-taxed long-term capital gains. To achieve this result, the taxpayers should have limited CL's activities to acquiring the property and subsequently making just a few land sales to the development entity—EGDC. The taxpayers failed to prove: (1) that CL did not perform significant development work itself and (2) that CL was not involved in selling lots to customers.

In the *Allen* case, the taxpayers' fate may have been sealed on day one because the first factor (nature of the acquisition), which is arguably the single most important factor, weighed decisively against them. But if Allen had taken pains at the beginning to establish that the land was held for investment (which it pretty clearly was not in this case), the outcome could have been different.

Beneficial capital gain treatment allowed for sale of right to buy land and build condo project

In a decision rendered in late 2014, the 11th Circuit Court of Appeals concluded that an individual's $5.75m in proceeds from selling rights to buy land and build a luxury condo project was properly characterized as long-term capital gain rather than ordinary income. The decision reversed an earlier Tax Court opinion. [See *Philip Long*, 114 AFTR 2d 2014-6657 (11th Cir. 2014).]

Case facts

Philip Long was a real estate developer who operated his business as a sole proprietorship. In 2006, he received $5.75m in exchange for selling contract rights that he had obtained as a successful plaintiff in a lawsuit. The lawsuit involved the rights to buy a parcel of land in Fort Lauderdale, Florida and build a luxury condominium tower on the parcel. After auditing the Long's 2006 Form 1040, the IRS issued a notice of deficiency indicating that Long had taxable income of $4,145,423 in 2006 and owed $1,430,743 of federal income tax for that year. Among other things, the IRS claimed that the $5.75m received by Long was in lieu of future ordinary income payments and should therefore be counted as ordinary income under the "substitution for ordinary income doctrine."

Long claimed that the $5.75m should be taxed as long-term capital gain. Thanks to the lawsuit, he owned an option to buy the land underlying the condo project along with the right to build the condo tower itself. He had been working on this project for some 13 years. The IRS rejected his claim. The unhappy taxpayer took his case to the Tax Court.

Unfortunately for Long, the Tax Court agreed with the IRS that the $5.75m constituted ordinary income because, according to the Tax Court, Long intended to sell the land underlying the condo project land to customers in the ordinary course of his business.

11th Circuit reverses Tax Court

The 11th Circuit's decision starts off by noting that gain from selling a *capital asset* that the taxpayer has held for more than a year constitutes long-term capital gain that is taxed at preferential rates. In contrast, ordinary income is taxed at higher rates. The term *capital asset* means property held by the taxpayer (whether or not connected with his or her business) but does not include property held by the taxpayer primarily for sale to customers in the ordinary course of his or her business. In certain circumstances, contract rights can qualify as capital assets.

The 11th Circuit then pointed out that the Tax Court had erred by mistakenly concluding that Long sold the land underlying the condo project for the $5.75m. In fact, he never owned the land. What he actually sold was the right to purchase the land pursuant to the terms of the condo development agreement and the associated right to build the condo tower. As stated earlier, he won these rights in a legal judgment rendered by a Florida court. Therefore, the real issue was whether Long held the contract rights primarily for sale to customers in the ordinary course of his business. The 11th Circuit found no such evidence. Instead the court ruled that the evidence showed that Long had always intended to develop the condo project himself, until he ultimately decided to sell his contract rights.

The 11th Circuit also rejected the government's argument that the $5.75m received by Long was in lieu of future ordinary income payments and should therefore be counted as ordinary income under the "substitution for ordinary income doctrine." According to the court, the rights that Long sold only represented the potential to earn future income based on the owner's future actions and on future events that could not necessarily be fully anticipated. Rights to earn future undetermined income (as opposed to rights to receive income that has already been earned) constitute a capital asset.

Finally, the 11th Circuit concluded that Long had owned the contract rights for more than one year because they resulted from a lawsuit that was filed in 2004. Because the contract rights constituted a capital asset that Long had owned for more than one year (he sold the rights in 2006), he was entitled to treat the $5.75m in proceeds from selling the rights as long-term capital gain. The Tax Court's earlier decision to the contrary was reversed.

Conclusion

It is almost always better to be able to characterize taxable income as capital gain rather than ordinary income. As the 11th Circuit decision summarized in this analysis illustrates, capital gain treatment may be available in somewhat surprising circumstances.

Escape taxable gains altogether with like-kind exchanges

Clients who are serious real estate investors periodically adjust their portfolios by getting rid of some properties and acquiring new ones. Unfortunately, selling appreciated properties results in a current tax hit—something real estate investors hate, especially when they intend to simply "roll over" their sales proceeds by purchasing new properties.

The good news is IRC Section 1031 allows taxes to be deferred if a like-kind exchange can be arranged. Deferral is mandatory, rather than elective, when IRC Section 1031 applies.

IRC Section 1031 says taxable gains are deferred when buyers and sellers swap properties that are similar in nature, except to the extent cash or dissimilar property (*boot*) is received in the transaction. If a party to the transaction receives boot, gain is currently recognized in an amount equal to the lesser of the total gain or the boot's FMV [IRC Section 1031(b)].

Even deferred like-kind exchanges can qualify for the gain deferral privilege [IRC Section 1031(a)(3)]. This is very important, because it is usually difficult for a seller who wants to make a like-kind exchange to locate another party who has suitable replacement property and who also wants to make an exchange rather than a cash sale. As you will see, under the deferred exchange rules, the seller need not make a direct and immediate exchange of one property for another. The seller can, in effect, sell for cash and then locate the replacement property a little bit later. And the owner of the replacement property can actually sell for cash without spoiling the first party's ability to defer taxable gain.

Warning: Thanks to a change included in the TCJA, tax-deferred Section 1031 treatment is no longer allowed for exchanges of personal property that are completed after December 31, 2017. This is a permanent change. However, the prior-law rules, which allowed Section 1031 treatment for properly structured exchanges of personal property, still apply to such exchanges if one leg of the exchange was completed as of December 31, 2017, but one leg of the exchange was still open on that date. The TCJA did not change the rules for Section 1031 exchanges of real property.

Like-kind exchange basics

Under IRC Section 1031, mandatory nonrecognition of gains (and losses) applies when *like-kind* properties are exchanged in what would otherwise be a taxable sale transaction.

To qualify, both the property given up by the seller and the property received must be investment property or business property in the seller's hands. Note that investment property can be swapped for other like-kind investment property or for like-kind business property, and vice versa. From the perspective of either party to the exchange transaction, it does not matter whether or not the other party qualifies under IRC Section 1031 (Rev. Rul. 75-292).

Like-kind means similar in general nature or character. The regulations give a liberal interpretation to this standard. For example, Reg. Sec. 1.1031(a)-1 says improved real estate can be swapped for unimproved real estate, a strip shopping center can be traded for an apartment building, a marina can be swapped for a golf course, and so on. However, real property cannot be traded for personal property and personal property cannot be exchanged for personal property after December 31, 2017. Finally, property held for personal use (such as a home or a boat), inventory, partnership interests, and investment securities do not qualify for IRC Section 1031 treatment.

The majority of IRC Section 1031 exchanges involve only real estate.

Realized versus recognized and receipt of boot

When two parties wish to make an IRC Section 1031 exchange of properties with differing FMVs, the party with the less valuable property must add additional consideration to equalize the values. This is called *boot*. Boot can actually be in the form of cash or dissimilar property, or a mixture of both.

In analyzing an IRC Section 1031 transaction, the first step is determining the amount of realized gain (or loss) for each party. Realized gain equals

1. FMV of property (including any noncash boot) plus any cash boot received, minus
2. the tax basis of the property given up (including any noncash boot) plus any cash boot given.

In contrast to the realized gain, the *recognized* gain is the amount that must be currently reported under the federal income tax rules (not to exceed the realized gain). As explained earlier, a party to an IRC Section 1031 exchange generally has no recognized gain unless boot is received. If boot is received, the recognized gain is the lesser of

1. the realized gain, or
2. the FMV of the boot.

 Example 1-13

- Huck and Buck trade undeveloped agricultural acreage in an IRC Section 1031 like-kind exchange.
- Huck's land has FMV of $50,000 and tax basis of $30,000. Buck's land is worth only $43,000, and his basis is $8,000.
- To equalize the trade, Buck gives Huck $7,000 worth of manure.
  - Huck's realized gain is $20,000 ($43,000 + $7,000 − $30,000); however, he currently recognizes only $7,000 (lesser of the $20,000 realized gain or the $7,000 worth of boot received).
  - Buck's realized gain is $35,000 ($50,000 − $8,000 − $7,000), but he has no recognized gain on the land swap, because he receives no boot.

Any loss realized in an IRC Section 1031 exchange cannot be recognized currently. As shown in example 1-23, the realized loss becomes *built-in* to the basis of the like-kind property received.

If a party to the exchange gives only cash boot plus like-kind property and receives only like-kind property in return, he or she will not have any recognized gain.

However, if the transferor gives *dissimilar property* as boot, he or she recognizes gain or loss equal to the difference between its FMV and tax basis, as if it were sold for FMV [Reg. Sec. 1.1031(d)-1(e)]. For instance, if in example 1-13 Buck's basis in the manure was $4,000, he would recognize no gain on the land swap, but he would recognize a $3,000 gain on the manure part of the deal.

Basis and holding period for like-kind property received

In effect, the tax basis of the like-kind property received is adjusted down or up for any unrecognized gain or loss attributable to the like-kind property given up [IRC Section 1031(d)]. Therefore, the tax basis of the like-kind property received equals the following:

	1.	The tax basis of the like-kind property given up
+	2.	Gain recognized (if any) on like-kind property given up
+	3.	FMV of boot given up (if any)
−	4.	FMV of boot received (if any)

The holding period for the new like-kind property received includes the holding period of the old like-kind property given up [IRC Section 1223(1)].

As for any noncash boot received, its tax basis will always be equal to FMV, because it's received in a fully taxable transaction. Therefore, as of the transaction date, a new holding period begins for the noncash boot.

 Example 1-14

- Assume the same facts as in example 1-13.
  - Huck's basis in the like-kind property received is $30,000 ($30,000 + $7,000 + $0 − $7,000). This makes sense because the property Huck now holds has an FMV of $43,000.
  - In effect, the $13,000 unrecognized gain from the old property has become a $13,000 built-in gain in the new property (FMV of $43,000 less tax basis of $30,000).
  - Buck's basis in his new like-kind property is $15,000 ($8,000 + $0 + $7,000 − $0). Again, this makes sense because the property Buck now holds has an FMV of $50,000.
  - Buck's $35,000 unrecognized gain from the old property has become a $35,000 *built-in* gain in the new property (FMV of $50,000 less tax basis of $15,000).

Example 1-15

- Assume the same facts as in example 1-13, except Buck's basis in his original piece of land was $45,000.
  - His basis in the new like-kind property becomes $52,000 ($45,000 + $0 + $7,000 − $0). This makes sense, because the $2,000 unrecognized loss from the original land has become a $2,000 *built-in* loss in the land Buck now holds ($50,000 FMV less $52,000 tax basis).

Effect of liabilities

In real life, most IRC Section 1031 real estate transactions involve properties burdened by mortgages. The impact of liabilities on realized and recognized gains and losses is explained in the following section.

Effect on realized gain computation

Under Reg. Sec. 1.1031(d)-2, the transferor's realized gain equals the following:

	1.	Gross amount of debt shifted to the transferee
+	2.	FMV of boot received in form of cash or dissimilar property (if any)
+	3.	FMV of like-kind property received
−	4.	Tax basis of like-kind property given plus any boot given
−	5.	Gross amount of liabilities taken on by transferor

Effect on recognized gain computation

The transferor's recognized gain equals the lesser of the realized gain (as explained earlier) or the boot received. When the transferee assumes a liability or takes property subject to a liability, this counts as boot received for purposes of computing the recognized gain. When both parties assume liabilities, or take property subject to liabilities, amounts are netted. For example, if the transferor takes on liabilities in excess of the amount shifted to the transferee, the transferor has *given* boot equal to the net amount, and the transferee has *received* boot in the same amount.

However, deemed net boot given from liabilities (excess of the line 5 amount over the line 1 amount) cannot be used to offset *actual* boot received in the form of cash or dissimilar property (the line 2 amount) [Reg. Sec. 1.1031(d)-2, example 2]. Put another way, the transferor must recognize gain equal to the lesser of the realized gain or the actual boot received (the line 2 amount), even when the transferor has given net boot attributable to liabilities.

When the transferor gives actual boot in the form of cash or dissimilar property (included in the line 4 amount), the actual boot given offsets any net boot received from liabilities (excess of line 1 amount over line 5 amount) [Reg. Sec. 1.1031(d)-(2), example 2]. Thus, if actual boot given exceeds the net boot received from liabilities transferred to the other party, there is no recognized gain.

 Example 1-16

- Rhonda owns Happy Acres (FMV of $4,000,000, mortgage of $3,400,000, and tax basis of $3,000,000). She swaps the property for Grumpy Hills (FMV of $3,600,000, mortgage of $3,500,000, and tax basis of $3,200,000), which is owned by Bill. Because Bill's equity in Grumpy Hills is only $100,000 versus Rhonda's $600,000 equity in Happy Acres, Bill tosses in $500,000 of cash to square the deal.
  - Rhonda's realized gain is

1.	$3,400,000	Happy Acres debt shifted to Bill
2.	500,000	FMV of boot received
3.	3,600,000	FMV of like-kind property received
4.	(3,000,000)	Tax basis of property given up
5.	(3,500,000)	Grumpy Hills debt assumed by Rhonda
	$1,000,000	

  - Rhonda's recognized gain is limited to $500,000, which equals the amount of actual boot received. Rhonda gets no "credit" for the $100,000 of net boot given from liabilities (excess of $3.5m she assumed over $3.4m she shifted to Bill). However, as seen in the following list item, the net boot given from liabilities increases Rhonda's tax basis in Grumpy Hills.
  - Rhonda's tax basis in Grumpy Hills is

1.	$3,000,000	Tax basis of Happy Acres
2.	100,000	Boot given from liabilities
3.	500,000	Gain recognized on disposition of Happy Acres
4.	(500,000)	Boot received (cash)
	$3,100,000	

  - Therefore, Rhonda has a *built-in* gain of $500,000 in Grumpy Hills (FMV of $3,600,000 less her basis of $3,100,000). This equals her realized gain of $1,000,000, less the $500,000 deferred by making the like-kind exchange.
  - Bill's realized gain on the disposition of Grumpy Hills is

1.	$ 3,500,000	Grumpy Hills debt shifted to Rhonda
2.	0	FMV of boot received
3.	4,000,000	FMV of like-kind property received
4.	(3,700,000)	Tax basis of property and boot given
5.	(3,400,000)	Happy Acres debt assumed by Bill
	$ 400,000	

  - Bill's recognized gain is $0, because he offsets the $100,000 of net boot received from liabilities with the $500,000 of actual boot given to Rhonda.

Example 1-16 (continued)

- Bill's basis in Happy Acres is

$3,200,000	Tax basis of Grumpy Hills
500,000	Boot given
0	Gain recognized on disposition of Grumpy Hills
(100,000)	Boot received (from liabilities)
$3,600,000	

- Therefore, Bill has a built-in gain of $400,000 in Happy Acres (FMV of $4,000,000 less his basis of $3,600,000). This equals his realized gain of $400,000 from Grumpy Hills, all of which was deferred by making the like-kind exchange.

Deferred like-kind exchanges

Although the tax advantages of making a like-kind exchange are considerable for both parties, it is usually difficult or impossible to locate another party who has suitable like-kind property and is willing swap (most sellers want cash or at least an installment sale arrangement). As a result, IRC Section 1031 exchanges are rarely accomplished by making a simultaneous exchange of like-kind properties.

Instead we see *deferred exchanges* (commonly called *Starker exchanges*, after a famous 1979 court case). The qualification rules for deferred exchanges are found in Reg. Sec. 1.1031(k)-1. Deferred exchanges come in two flavors: three-party deals and four-party deals.

Deferred three-party exchanges

In this type of transaction, the transferor (the *first* party) trades his or her property to the *second* party, who then promises to find and buy replacement property from a *third* party.

The second party places the sales proceeds that would otherwise go to the first party in escrow. The funds are then used by the second party to purchase replacement property from a third party.

Finally, the replacement property is transferred by the second party to the first party. This completes the like-kind exchange.

Because the first party never actually gets his or her hands on any cash and ends up with like-kind property, the transaction is considered an IRC Section 1031 exchange from his or her perspective.

Deferred four-party exchanges

When the second party cannot or will not acquire replacement property to swap with the first party—or cannot be trusted to do so—a four-party exchange is required. These are more common than the three-party variety described earlier.

Here, the transferor (the *first* party) transfers his or her property to a qualified intermediary (the *fourth* party).

The intermediary's role is simply to facilitate a like-kind exchange for a fee.

The first party's property is transferred to a cash buyer (the *second* party).

The intermediary then uses the resulting sales proceeds to buy suitable replacement property (which has been previously identified by the first party) from a *third* party.

Finally, the intermediary transfers the replacement property to the first party to complete the like-kind exchange.

From the first party's perspective, this whole series of transactions qualifies as a like-kind exchange because he or she ends up with like-kind replacement property (supplied by the third party) rather than cash. The second party ends up paying cash for the original property (supplied by the first party). The third party ends up having sold his or her property for cash (supplied by the second party).

Naturally, qualified intermediaries charge for their services, usually based on a sliding scale according to the value of the deal. In percentage terms, the fees are generally quite nominal.

Rules for tax-free deferred exchanges

IRC Section 1031(a)(3) and Reg. Sec. 1.1031(k)-1 supply the two basic rules for deferred exchanges:

- Replacement property must be identified before the end of a 45-day *identification period*.
- Replacement property must be transferred to the seller before the end of the *exchange period*, which can extend up to 180 days.

The identification period commences when the first party transfers the original property (in other words, the closing date for that transaction). During the 45-day period, the replacement property must be unambiguously identified or actually received by the first party. This rule is satisfied if the replacement property is specified in a written document signed by the first party and sent to (1) the party who is to supply the replacement property or (2) another party, such as a qualified intermediary, escrow agent, or title company. In the document, the first party can list up to three properties considered suitable as replacement property. However, the aggregate FMV of the three cannot exceed 200% of the FMV of the original property.

The exchange period also commences when the first party transfers the original property. The exchange period ends on the *earlier* of (1) 180 days thereafter or (2) the due date (with extensions) of the first party's federal return for the tax year that includes the date of transfer. When the 180-day period straddles year-ends and would be cut short by the original due date of the return for the year of the transfer, obtaining an extension restores the full 180-day period. However, an extension must actually be obtained in order for this provision to come into play.

Avoiding constructive receipt problems with escrow arrangements

When the first party transfers property in exchange for the buyer's promise to purchase and transfer suitable replacement property (or the qualified intermediary's promise), the first party will naturally want assurance that the remaining legs of the transaction will be accomplished. Therefore, the buyer's promise to acquire and transfer replacement property is generally secured by placing the sales price in an escrow account. Alternatively, the funds may be placed in escrow with the qualified intermediary hired to facilitate the exchange.

The potential problem with escrow accounts is that the IRS may claim the first party was in constructive receipt of the sales proceeds. This would unravel the intended like-kind exchange and result in a taxable sale transaction. However, Reg. Sec. 1.1031(k)-1(g) provides safe harbor rules for escrow accounts. If these are met, constructive receipt problems are avoided.

Under the safe harbor rules, the first party will not have constructive receipt of cash or cash equivalents placed in a *qualified escrow account* if

- the escrow holder is not a *disqualified person* (various parties related to the first party and parties considered agents of the first party), and
- the escrow agreement expressly limits the first party's right to receive, borrow, pledge, or otherwise obtain the benefits of the assets held in the escrow account.

Despite the second rule, the first party is not prohibited from being credited with interest on funds held in a qualified escrow account [Reg. Sec. 1.1031(k)-1(g)(5), (g)(6), and (h)].

 Example 1-17 Deferred three-party exchange

- Melinda (the first party) owns Halfacre, which is worth $2,000,000 and has a tax basis of $500,000. Second-party Harold (unrelated to Melinda) wants to buy the parcel for development. However, Melinda insists on a like-kind exchange in order to avoid any current tax liability.
- Ultimately Melinda agrees to transfer Halfacre in exchange for Harold's promise to acquire and transfer suitable replacement property. In accordance with the agreement, Melinda transfers Halfacre to Harold on December 1, 2018. Harold's promise is secured by $2,000,000 of cash placed in a qualified escrow account.
- Within the 45-day identification period, Melinda sends Harold a signed document designating Pineland—currently owned by Vanessa (the third party) and having an FMV of $1,600,000—as suitable replacement property.

Example 1-17 Deferred three-party exchange (continued)

- On March 19, 2019, Harold buys Pineland from Vanessa for $1,600,000 cash. On the same day, he transfers Pineland to Melinda along with the $400,000 balance from the escrow account.
  - In this example, both the 45-day identification period rule and 180-day exchange period rule are met (the starting point for both periods is the December 1, 2018, closing date for the transfer of Halfacre to Harold).
  - Accordingly, this deal qualifies as a deferred three-party exchange for Melinda. On March 19, 2019, she recognizes a $400,000 taxable gain—lesser of $400,000 boot received or realized gain of $1.5m. [See Reg. Sec. 1.1031(k)-1(g)(8), example 1 and Reg. Sec. 1.1031(k)-1(j)(2)(vi), example 1.]

Note: The escrow arrangement must be a *qualified escrow account*, in order to avoid any risk of Melinda being considered in constructive receipt of the entire $2,000,000 as of December 1, 2018.

Deferred four-party exchanges

In real life, second parties are often unwilling or unable to acquire title to the replacement property or are not considered trustworthy enough to be relied upon. In such cases, the solution is using a qualified intermediary to conduct a four-party exchange.

Under the IRC Section 1031 regulations, the qualified intermediary is not considered the agent of the first party, even though the intermediary actually functions in that capacity. Accordingly, the first party can transfer his or her property to the qualified intermediary and instruct the intermediary to sell the property for cash. The first party will not be considered in constructive receipt of the sales proceeds received by the qualified intermediary [Reg. Sec. 1.1031(b)-2(a)]. (If the intermediary does not meet the qualified intermediary definition, there will generally be an agency relationship for tax purposes, and the first party will have a constructive receipt problem.)

Reg. Sec. 1.1031(k)-1(g)(4) defines a qualified intermediary as a person who is not the taxpayer or a *disqualified person* and who, pursuant to a written *exchange agreement* with the taxpayer,

- acquires the original property from the taxpayer;
- transfers the taxpayer's property to the buyer;
- acquires replacement property from the seller; and
- transfers the replacement property to the taxpayer.

Disqualified persons are defined in Reg. Sec. 1.1031(k)-1(k) and include certain parties automatically considered to be the taxpayer's agent (taxpayer's employee, attorney, and so on) and certain parties related to the taxpayer under IRC Sections 267(b) or 707(b), as modified.

In real estate transactions, qualified intermediaries may be unwilling to actually hold title to the original and replacement properties – however briefly – because of environmental liability issues. Therefore, Reg. Sec. 1.1031(k)-1(g)(4)(v) says the qualified intermediary is deemed to accomplish the previous title transfers via written assignments of contract rights. Actual title transfers are not necessary. Example 1-18 illustrates the rules that must be satisfied to accomplish a successful deferred four-party exchange.

Example 1-18 Deferred four-party exchange

- Assume the same facts as in example 1-17, except, for the reason previously discussed, Harold refuses to have even momentary ownership of Pineland, because of potential exposure to environmental liabilities for any owner in the chain of title. Therefore, Melinda engages a qualified intermediary—We Do Swaps—to facilitate a deferred four-party exchange.
- On December 1, 2018, Melinda contracts to sell Halfacre to Harold for $2m cash. The closing date is to be January 15, 2019. On or before that date, Melinda enters into a written exchange agreement with We Do Swaps to function as a qualified intermediary (assume We Do Swaps is also unwilling to hold actual title to the properties involved in the transaction).
- Before title to Halfacre is actually transferred to Harold, Melinda assigns in writing to We Do Swaps her contract rights to sell the property (this is pursuant to the exchange agreement between Melinda and We Do Swaps). Melinda also notifies Harold of the assignment in writing before transferring Halfacre to him. Melinda then transfers title to Halfacre directly to Harold on January 15, 2019. This is called a *direct deed* transaction, because the title to Halfacre actually bypasses We Do Swaps. At closing, Harold transfers $2,000,000 to a qualified escrow account set up at the local bank (or the payment could go into an account controlled by We Do Swaps).
- Melinda now locates Pineland (owned by Vanessa) and contracts to purchase it as replacement property for $1,600,000. The scheduled closing date for this transaction is March 19, 2019. Before that date, Melinda assigns in writing to We Do Swaps her contract rights to buy Pineland and notifies Vanessa of this assignment in writing. On March 19, 2019, the escrow agent releases $1,600,000 to Vanessa to close on Pineland. On the same date, Vanessa direct deeds Pineland to Melinda. Melinda also receives the remaining $400,000 from the escrow account.
  - All legs of the deferred exchange are now complete. The 45-day and the 180-day rule are both met (the starting point for both periods is the January 15, 2019 closing date for the Halfacre transaction). By entering into the exchange agreement with We Do Swaps and assigning her purchase and sale contract rights, Melinda is deemed to have made a like-kind exchange with We Do Swaps. As a qualified intermediary, We Do Swaps is deemed to have acquired and transferred both Halfacre and Pineland.
  - Accordingly, on March 19, 2019, Melinda recognizes a $400,000 taxable gain. As can be seen, these are exactly the same tax results as in example 1-17, which involved a three-party exchange. [See Reg. Sec. 1.1031(k)-1(g)(8), Example 4 and Reg. Sec. 1.1031(k)-1(j)(2)(vi), Example 2.]

Variation

The tax results would also be the same if pursuant to the exchange agreement with Melinda, We Do Swaps takes actual title to Halfacre and Pineland before transferring them to Harold and Melinda, respectively. [See Reg. Sec. 1.1031(k)-1(g)(8), Example 3.]

Watch out

If Melinda fails to transfer her Halfacre contract rights to We Do Swaps on or before direct deeding Halfacre to Harold, she is not considered to have engaged in a like-kind exchange with We Do Swaps. The unfortunate result is that Melinda is now treated as having made a taxable sale of Halfacre to Harold, followed by a taxable purchase of Pineland through her agent, We Do Swaps. [See Reg. Sec. 1.1031(k)-1(g)(8), Example 5.]

Reverse Starker exchanges

As explained earlier, deferred exchanges where the replacement property is identified and acquired after the "relinquished property" (the property originally held by the taxpayer seeking IRC Section 1031 exchange treatment) has effectively been sold are often called Starker exchanges. As discussed, regulations permit properly structured Starker exchanges to fall under the IRC Section 1031 rules which can yield tremendous tax deferral advantages for real estate clients.

However, the tax treatment of reverse Starker exchanges has been left unclear for many years. In a reverse Starker exchange, the replacement property is acquired before the relinquished property is unloaded. In other words, the taxpayer has identified a property he or she wishes to acquire in an IRC Section 1031 exchange but has not yet identified the property to be given up in exchange. The regulations cited earlier in this chapter did not provide any guidance regarding such reverse Starker exchanges.

In Rev. Proc. 2000-37 (as modified by Rev. Proc. 2004-51), the IRS finally addressed this longstanding question. Rev. Proc. 2000-37 provides safe harbor treatment (meaning IRC Section 1031 treatment will be deemed to apply) for reverse Starker exchanges that are conducted via "qualified exchange accommodation arrangements" (QEAAs).

A QEAA is considered to exist if

1. to facilitate the exchange, the legal titles to (or attributes of beneficial ownership in) both the replacement and relinquished properties are transferred to an "exchange accommodation titleholder" (as defined by Rev. Proc. 2000-37) (Once the exchange accommodation titleholder acquires title to (or attributes of beneficial ownership in) the replacement and relinquished properties, the exchange accommodation titleholder must continue to hold the properties until the replacement property is ultimately transferred to the taxpayer and the relinquished property is ultimately transferred to its new owner.);
2. at the times the replacement property and the relinquished property are transferred to the exchange accommodation titleholder, the taxpayer (the party seeking IRC Section 1031 treatment for the deal) must have a bona fide intent to exchange said properties in a transaction that qualifies for nonrecognition treatment (in whole or in part) under IRC Section 1031;
3. within five business days after the date of transfer of title to (or attributes of beneficial ownership in) the replacement or relinquished property to the exchange accommodation titleholder, the taxpayer and the exchange accommodation titleholder must agree in writing that said property is being held to facilitate an IRC Section 1031 exchange under Rev. Proc. 2000-37 and that the tax reporting rules established by Rev. Proc. 2000-37 will be respected by both parties;
4. within 45 days after the transfer of title to (or attributes of beneficial ownership in) the replacement property to the exchange accommodation titleholder, the taxpayer must identify the relinquished property in a manner consistent with Reg. Sec. 1.1031(k)-1(c) (Alternative or multiple properties may be identified.);
5. within 180 days after the transfer of title to (or attributes of beneficial ownership in) the replacement property or relinquished property to the exchange accommodation titleholder, the replacement and relinquished properties must be transferred to their respective new owners; and
6. the combined time period that the replacement and relinquished properties are held by the exchange accommodation titleholder cannot exceed 180 days.

The exchange accommodation titleholder fulfills the same role as a qualified intermediary in a "regular" four-party deferred exchange, as explained in example 1-18. The taxpayer should take pains to ensure that the exchange accommodation titleholder meets the definition of a qualified intermediary.

In essence, the exchange accommodation titleholder is simply a transient owner (or beneficial owner) of the relinquished property and the replacement property. However, the exchange accommodation titleholder is treated for tax purposes as the legitimate legal owner solely in order for IRC Section 1031 treatment to apply to the exchange.

The taxpayer and the exchange accommodation titleholder can engage in certain commercially necessary transactions in order to accomplish the desired property exchange. For example, the taxpayer can loan the exchange accommodation titleholder the money needed to acquire the replacement property, or the taxpayer can guarantee debt incurred by the exchange accommodation titleholder to do so. The taxpayer can also indemnify the exchange accommodation titleholder against costs incurred in the transaction. The taxpayer can even lease the replacement property from the exchange accommodation titleholder. And the taxpayer can manage the replacement property and supervise improvements to it while it is held by the exchange accommodation titleholder. (See IRC Section 4.03 of Rev. Proc. 2000-37.)

However, the IRS admits that some reverse Starker exchanges that fall outside the Rev. Proc. 2000-37 guidelines may still qualify for IRC Section 1031 treatment, presumably based on consideration of all facts and circumstances. (See Sections 3.02 and 3.04 of Rev. Proc. 2000-37.) In other words, the rules under Rev. Proc. 2000-37 are intended only as a safe harbor for reverse Starker exchanges, as opposed to absolute standards that must be followed in order for IRC Section 1031 treatment to apply.

For example, the IRS has allowed IRC Section 1031 treatment for a direct reverse Starker exchange. (See Ltr. Rul. 9823045.)

On the other hand, the IRS has disallowed IRC Section 1031 treatment for other reverse Starker exchanges for various reasons. [See TAM 200039005 and *Donald DeCleene, et ux. v. Commissioner*, 115 TC No. 34 (November 17, 2000).]

Observation: As a practical matter, taxpayers seeking IRC Section 1031 treatment for reverse Starker exchanges would be crazy not to comply with the safe harbor guidelines of Rev. Proc. 2000-37 (as modified by Rev. Proc. 2004-51).

Example 1-19

Assume the same essential facts as in example 1-18, except this time Melinda identifies the replacement property before she identifies the property she wishes to relinquish in a reverse Starker exchange. Melinda engages a qualified intermediary—We Do Swaps—to function as the exchange accommodation titleholder in what ultimately turns out to be a four-party reverse Starker exchange with Vanessa and Harold.

On December 1, 2018, Melinda contracts with Vanessa to purchase Pineland as the replacement property for $1,600,000. The scheduled closing date for this transaction is January 15, 2019. Before that date, Melinda assigns in writing to We Do Swaps her contract rights to buy Pineland. This is pursuant to the exchange agreement between Melinda and We Do Swaps. Melinda also notifies Vanessa of this assignment in writing. Melinda then loans We Do Swaps the $1,600,000 needed to buy Pineland. Assume We Do Swaps is unwilling to hold actual legal title to the properties involved in the exchange for liability reasons. Melinda, Vanessa, and We Do Swaps agree in writing that Pineland will be beneficially owned (albeit only momentarily) by We Do Swaps to facilitate an IRC Section 1031 exchange under the Rev. Proc. 2000-37 guidelines. At the closing on January 15, 2019, Vanessa direct deeds Pineland to Melinda (that is, the actual legal title to Pineland bypasses We Do Swaps and goes directly to Melinda), and We Do Swaps releases the $1,600,000 to Vanessa.

On January 20, 2019, Melinda finally identifies Halfacre as the property she wishes to relinquish in exchange for Pineland. On that same date, she contracts to sell Halfacre to Harold for $2m cash. The closing date is March 19, 2019. On or before that date, Melinda enters into a written exchange agreement with We Do Swaps to function as a qualified intermediary.

Melinda assigns in writing to We Do Swaps her contract rights to sell Halfacre to Harold. Melinda also notifies Harold of the assignment in writing. Melinda, Harold, and We Do Swaps agree in writing that Halfacre will be beneficially owned (albeit only momentarily) by We Do Swaps to facilitate an IRC Section 1031 exchange under the Rev. Proc. 2000-37 guidelines. At the closing on March 19, 2019, Melinda direct deeds Halfacre to Harold; he transfers $2,000,000 to We Do Swaps; and We Do Swaps transfers the $2,000,000 to Melinda. The $2,000,000 represents a return of the $1,600,000 loan from Melinda to We Do Swaps plus the $400,000 difference between the sale price for Halfacre ($2,000,000) and the purchase price for Pineland ($1,600,000).

All legs of the reverse Starker exchange are now complete. The 45-day and the 180-day rule are both met (the starting point for both periods is the January 15, 2019, closing date for the Pineland transaction). By entering into the exchange agreement with We Do Swaps and assigning her purchase and sale contract rights, Melinda is deemed to have made a like-kind exchange with We Do Swaps. (For this purpose, the transactions with Vanessa and Harold are ignored.)

Accordingly, on March 19, 2019, Melinda recognizes a $400,000 taxable gain. This is the amount of taxable cash boot that she received when all was said and done. As can be seen, these are exactly the same tax results as in example 1-18, which involved a "regular" Starker exchange.

Example 1-19 (continued)

Variation

The tax results would be the same if pursuant to the exchange agreement with Melinda; We Do Swaps takes actual legal title to Pineland and Halfacre before transferring them to Melinda and Harold, respectively. [See Reg. Sec. 1.1031(k)-1(g)(8), Example 3.]

Watch out

If Melinda fails to transfer her Halfacre contract rights to We Do Swaps on or before direct deeding Halfacre to Harold, she is not considered to have engaged in a like-kind exchange with We Do Swaps. The unfortunate result is that Melinda is now treated as having made a taxable purchase of Pineland through her agent, We Do Swaps, followed by a taxable sale of Halfacre to Harold. [See Reg. Sec. 1.1031(k)-1(g)(8), Example 5.]

Knowledge check

6. What is the difference between the amount of gain realized in an IRC Section 1031 like-kind exchange and the amount of gain recognized?

    a. The amount realized includes both the amount of gain taxed currently and the amount of gain deferred for tax purposes, and the amount recognized is the currently taxed portion of the gain.
    b. The amount realized is the amount the taxpayer knows he or she actually owes tax on, and the amount recognized is the lesser amount he or she is actually willing to pay tax on.
    c. There is no difference. Realized gain and recognized gain are just two ways to say the same thing.
    d. The amount realized equals the total sale price and the amount recognized equals the amount of sale price that has been collected so far.

7. In the context of an IRC Section 1031 like-kind exchange, what is a qualified intermediary?

    a. A consultant hired by one side to negotiate the best possible deal terms for that side.
    b. A tax expert hired to structure the best possible tax results for whichever party hires him.
    c. A party hired to facilitate a deferred exchange.
    d. A party hired to appraise the value of the properties involved in the exchange.

8. Under the federal income tax rules for deferred IRC Section 1031 exchanges, which is correct?

    a. Only Starker exchanges are allowed.
    b. Both Starker and reverse Starker exchanges are allowed.
    c. Neither Starker nor reverse Starker exchanges are allowed.
    d. IRC Section 1031 exchanges are fully taxable.

Primer on the 3.8% net investment income tax

The IRS calls the 3.8% Medicare surtax on investment income the net investment income tax, or NIIT. We will adopt that terminology. The NIIT was established by Section 1411 of the IRC, which was added as part of the 2010 healthcare legislation. The NIIT is effective for tax years beginning after December 31, 2012. Therefore, it is effective for 2013 and beyond for calendar-year taxpayers, which include almost all individual taxpayers.

In late 2013, the IRS released a batch of final NIIT regulations and a batch of proposed regulations as well. These regulations are generally effective for tax years beginning after December 31, 2013 [Regulation 1.1411-1(f)].

NIIT basics

For individuals, trusts, and estates, the following types of income and gain (net of related deductions) are generally included in the definition of net investment income and thus potentially exposed to the NIIT [IRC Section 1411(c)].

- Gains from selling assets held for investment – including gains from selling investment real estate and the taxable portion of gains from selling personal residences.
- Capital gain distributions from mutual funds.
- Gross income from dividends.
- Gross income from interest (not including tax-free interest such as municipal bond interest).
- Gross income from royalties.
- Gross income from annuities.
- Gross income and gains from passive business activities (meaning business activities in which the taxpayer does not materially participate) and gross income from rents. Gross income from non-passive business activities (other than the business of trading in financial instruments and commodities) is excluded from the definition of net investment income for NIIT purposes, and so is gain from selling property held in such activities [IRC Section 1411(c)].
- Gains from dispositions of passive ownership interests in partnerships and S corporations.
- Gross income and gains from the business of trading in financial instruments or commodities (even if the activity is non-passive).

Impact on individual taxpayers

An individual is hit with the NIIT only when modified adjusted gross income (MAGI) exceeds $200,000 for an unmarried taxpayer, $250,000 for a married joint-filing couple or a qualifying widow or widower, or $125,000 for taxpayers who use married filing separate status. These MAGI thresholds are fixed by statute and will not be adjusted for inflation in future years. The amount subject to the NIIT is the *lesser* of (1) net investment income or (2) the amount by which MAGI exceeds the applicable threshold.

For this purpose, MAGI is defined as (1) regular AGI from the bottom of page 1 of Form 1040 plus (2) certain excluded foreign-source income of U.S. citizens and residents living abroad net of certain deductions and exclusions [IRC Section 1411(d)]. Relatively few taxpayers will be affected by this add-back. Non-resident aliens are not subject to the NIIT [IRC Section 1411(e)].

Impact on trusts and estates

Trusts and estates can also be hit with the NIIT [IRC Section 1411(a)(2)]. For them, the NIIT applies to the lesser of (1) the trust or estate's undistributed net investment income or (2) the trust or estate's AGI in excess of the threshold for the top trust federal income tax bracket. For 2017 and 2018, that threshold is only $12,500. As a result, many trusts and estates may be hit with the NIIT.

Tracking the various NIIT regulations and their effective dates

As mentioned earlier, we have both final and proposed NIIT regulations.

- For the final regulations issued in late 2013, see Regulations 1.1411-1, -2, -3, -4, -5, -6, -8, -9, and -10, and 1.469-11 (found in TD 9644). With the exception of Regulation 1.1411-3(d), which deals with charitable remainder trusts (CRTs) and applies to CRT tax years beginning after December 31, 2012, the final regulations apply to tax years beginning after December 31, 2013. [See Regulation 1.1411-1(f) and (g) and Regulation 1.1411-3(f).]
- For the proposed regulations issued in late 2013, see Proposed Regulations 1.1411-3, 1.1411-4, and 1.1411-7 (found in REG-130843-13). These proposed regulations are generally effective for tax years beginning after December 31, 2013. However, if the final regulations include stricter rules than these proposed regulations, the stricter rules will not be effective until they are issued as final regulations. (See the Preamble to REG-130843-13.) [See Regulation 1.1411-1(f) and (g).]

Quick guide to NIIT regulations

Here is where to find guidance on specific subjects in the NIIT regulations.

General rules

For the general NIIT rules and definitions, see Final Regulations 1.1411-1 and -2.

Trusts and estates

For the rules applicable to trusts and estates, see Proposed Regulation 1.1411-3 and Final Regulation 1.1411-3. Note that special rules apply to certain types of trusts such as electing small business trusts; tax exempt trusts (such as charitable trusts and retirement plan trusts); grantor trusts that are ignored for federal income tax purposes; and trusts that are not classified as trusts for federal income tax purposes (such as REITs).

Net gains

For the rules on how to calculate net gains that must be included in net investment income and the impact of capital losses and other property disposition losses, see Proposed Regulation 1.1411-4 and Final Regulation 1.1411-4.

Passive versus non-passive businesses

For the rules on determining whether business income and gains are passive or non-passive, see Final Regulations 1.1411-4 and -5. This is an important distinction, because income and gains from non-passive business activities are generally exempt from the NIIT.

Trading in financial instruments or commodities

For the rules applicable to the business of trading in financial instruments or commodities, see Final Regulation 1.1411-5. Note that such income and gains must be included in net investment income even if the trading activity is non-passive.

Portfolio income

For the rules applicable to portfolio income, see Final Regulation 1.1411-5.

Rental activities and passive business activities

For the rules applicable to income and gains from rental activities and passive business activities, see Final Regulations 1.1411-5 and 1.469-11.

Business working capital

For the treatment of income and gains from the investment of business working capital, see Final Regulation 1.1411-6.

Allocable deductions

For the rules on determining allowable allocable deductions when calculating net investment income, see Final Regulation 1.1411-4(f). These rules also cover the impact of personal deduction disallowance rules in determining allowable allocable deductions when calculating net investment income.

Dispositions of non-passive partnership and S corporation ownership interests

For special rules on the NIIT treatment of gains and losses from dispositions of non-passive partnership and S corporation ownership interests, see Proposed Regulation 1.1411-7 (found in REG-130843-13).

Distributions from tax-favored retirement plans

For the NIIT exemption for distributions from tax-favored retirement plans and accounts, see Final Regulation 1.1411-8.

Self-employment income

For the NIIT exemption for income and deductions considered in calculating net self-employment income, see Final Regulation 1.1411-9.

CFCs and PFICs

For the NIIT treatment of income from controlled foreign corporations (CFCs) and passive foreign investment companies (PFICs), see Final Regulation 1.1411-10.

Calculating net investment income

For purposes of determining the NIIT, net investment income is calculated in two steps.

Step 1

Add up the following:

- Gains from dispositions of assets that are considered held for investment – including stocks, bonds, mutual fund shares, investment real estate, and the taxable portion of gains from selling personal residences.
- Capital gain distributions from mutual funds.
- Gross income from dividends.
- Gross income from interest (not including tax-free interest such as municipal bond interest).
- Gross income from rents.
- Gross income from royalties.
- Gross income from annuities.
- Gross income and gains from passive business activities (as opposed to non-passive business activities in which the taxpayer materially participates), including gains from dispositions of passive ownership interests in partnerships and S corporations (Final Regulations 1.1411-4 and -5, and Proposed Regulation 1.1411-7).
- Gross income and gains from the business of trading in financial instruments or commodities – even if the activity is non-passive [Regulation 1.1411-5(c)].

Step 2

Reduce the total from Step 1 by deductions properly allocable to the types of income listed in Step 1. The result is the net investment income amount. Examples of potentially allocable deductions include investment interest expense, investment advisory fees, brokerage fees, expenses related to rental and royalty income, state and local income taxes, tax preparation fees, and fiduciary expenses of trusts and estates [Regulation 1.1411-4(f)].

Key point: These calculations are made on IRS Form 8960 (NIIT – Individuals, Estates, and Trusts).

Income that is exempt from the NIIT

The following categories of income, among others, are exempt from the NIIT (Final Regulations 1.1411-4, -5, -8, and -9).

- Wages and self-employment income.
- Operating income from non-passive business activities and businesses.
- Distributions from tax-favored retirement plans and accounts such as 401(k) plans, pension plans, traditional IRAs, and Roth IRAs. (These plans and accounts are described in IRC Sections 401(a), 403(a), 403(b), 408, 408A, and 457(b).]
- Social Security benefits.
- Tax exempt interest, unemployment compensation, alimony, and Alaska Permanent Fund Dividends.

Gains from selling personal residences

Gain from selling a principal residence is federal-income-tax-free to the extent of the allowable IRC Section 121 home sale gain exclusion (up to $250,000 for an unmarried taxpayer and up to $500,000 for a married joint-filing couple). Such tax-free principal residence gains are exempt from the NIIT. However, to the extent a principal residence gain exceeds the exclusion, the excess is considered investment income that is potentially subject to the NIIT. Gain from selling a vacation property is also considered investment income that is potentially subject to the NIIT. (See the examples later in this section.)

Individual taxpayer examples

Here are some general examples that illustrate how the NIIT can affect individual taxpayers.

 Example 1-20

Floyd files as an unmarried individual. He has $300,000 of MAGI, which includes $90,000 of net investment income. He owes the 3.8% NIIT on all of his net investment income (the lesser of his excess MAGI of $100,000 or his net investment income of $90,000).

 Example 1-21

Gerald and Gloria file jointly. They have $300,000 of MAGI which includes $110,000 of net investment income. They owe only the 3.8% NIIT on $50,000 (the lesser of their excess MAGI of $50,000 or their net investment income of $110,000).

 Example 1-22

Heidi files as an unmarried individual. She has $199,000 of MAGI. She is completely exempt from the 3.8% NIIT, because her MAGI is less than the $200,000 threshold for unmarried individuals. Therefore, it doesn't matter how much net investment income she has.

 Example 1-23

Ingrid and Irving file jointly. They have $249,000 of MAGI. They are completely exempt from the 3.8% NIIT, because their MAGI is less than the $250,000 threshold for joint filers. Therefore, it doesn't matter how much net investment income they have.

Example 1-24

Jack is an unmarried individual. In the current year, he sold his highly appreciated principal residence, which he had owned for 30 years, for a $550,000 gain. Thanks to the Section 121 IRC principal residence gain exclusion break, his taxable gain for federal income tax purposes is "only" $300,000 ($550,000 gain – $250,000 exclusion for unmarried taxpayers). Unfortunately, the entire $300,000 gain counts as investment income for purposes of the 3.8% NIIT.

To keep things simple, assume Jack has no other investment income and no capital losses. But he does have $125,000 of MAGI from other sources (salary, self-employment income, taxable Social Security benefits, whatever).

Due to the big home sale gain, Jack's net investment income is $300,000 (all from the home sale), and his MAGI is $425,000 ($300,000 from the home sale plus $125,000 from other sources).

Jack owes the NIIT on $225,000 (the lesser of: (1) his net investment income of $300,000 or (2) his excess MAGI of $225,000 ($425,000 – $200,000 threshold for singles). The NIIT amounts to $8,550 (3.8% × $225,000).

Example 1-25

Ken and Kylee file jointly. In the current year, they sold their greatly appreciated vacation home, which they had owned for 25 years, for a $600,000 gain. That profit is fully taxable, and it is also treated as investment income for purposes of the 3.8% NIIT.

To keep things simple, let's stipulate that the couple has no other investment income and no capital losses. But they do have $125,000 of MAGI from other sources (pension income, taxable Social Security benefits, taxable retirement account withdrawals, whatever).

Due to the big vacation home profit, their net investment income is $600,000 (all from the vacation home sale), and their MAGI is $725,000 ($600,000 from the vacation home plus $125,000 from other sources). They owe the NIIT on $475,000 (the lesser of (1) their net investment income of $600,000 or (2) their excess MAGI of $475,000 ($725,000 – $250,000 threshold for joint-filing couples). The NIIT amounts to $18,050 (3.8% × $475,000).

Planning to minimize or avoid the NIIT

This analysis covers some planning strategies that individuals can use to minimize or avoid exposure to the 3.8% NIIT.

Identifying affected individuals

You are exposed to the NIIT only if your MAGI exceeds the applicable threshold of $200,000 if you are unmarried, $250,000 if you are a married joint-filer or qualifying widow or widower, or $125,000 if you use married filing separate status.

The amount subject to the NIIT is the lesser of: (1) your net investment income or (2) the amount by which MAGI exceeds the applicable threshold. For this purpose, MAGI is defined as regular AGI from the bottom of page 1 of Form 1040 plus certain excluded foreign-source income net of certain deductions and exclusions (relatively few individuals are affected by this add-back).

NIIT avoidance strategies must aim at the proper target

Because the NIIT hits the lesser of: (1) your net investment income or (2) the amount by which your MAGI exceeds the applicable threshold, planning strategies must be aimed at the proper target to have the desired effect of avoiding or minimizing your exposure to the NIIT.

If exposure mainly depends on net investment income level

If your net investment income amount is significantly less than your excess MAGI amount (the amount by which MAGI exceeds the applicable threshold), your exposure to the tax mainly depends on your net investment income level. Therefore, you should focus first on strategies that will reduce net investment income. Of course, some strategies that reduce net investment income will also reduce MAGI. If so, that cannot possibly harm your situation.

If exposure mainly depends on excess MAGI level

On the other hand, if your excess MAGI amount is significantly less than your net investment income amount, your exposure to the tax mainly depends on your MAGI level. Therefore, you should focus first on strategies that will reduce MAGI. Of course, some strategies that reduce MAGI will also reduce net investment income. If so, that cannot possibly harm your situation.

Example 1-26

Randy will file as an unmarried individual. Unless something changes, he will have $375,000 of MAGI which will include $100,000 of net investment income. He will owe the NIIT on all $100,000 of his net investment income (the lesser of Randy's excess MAGI of $175,000 or his net investment income of $100,000). Without some effective tax planning, the NIIT hit will amount to $3,800 (3.8% × $100,000).

As you can see, Randy's exposure to the NIIT mainly depends on his net investment income level. Therefore, he should focus first on strategies that will reduce net investment income. For instance, he could sell loser securities from his taxable brokerage firm accounts to offset earlier gains from those accounts. Additional strategies to reduce net investment income are explained in the following example.

In contrast, strategies that would lower Randy's MAGI would not reduce his exposure to the NIIT unless those strategies reduce his MAGI by a whole lot. For instance, making an additional $15,000 deductible contribution to his tax-favored retirement account would not by itself reduce Randy's exposure to the NIIT.

 Example 1-27

Sandy and Ted will file jointly. Unless something changes, they will have $375,000 of MAGI which will include $160,000 of net investment income. They will owe the NIIT on $125,000 (the lesser of their excess MAGI of $125,000 or their net investment income of $160,000). Without some effective tax planning, the NIIT hit will amount to $4,750 (3.8% × $125,000).

As you can see, this couple's exposure to the NIIT mainly depends on their MAGI level. Therefore, Sandy and Ted should focus first on strategies that would reduce MAGI. For instance, making $25,000 of additional deductible contributions to their tax-favored retirement accounts would reduce their MAGI by $25,000 and significantly reduce the NIIT hit. Selling loser securities from their taxable brokerage firm accounts to offset earlier gains from those accounts would also reduce MAGI. Additional strategies to reduce MAGI are explained in the next section.

In contrast using a method that allocates some additional deductions to offset their investment income would not reduce this couple's NIIT bill, unless the method reduces their net investment income amount by a big number (not likely).

👆 Example 1-28

In 2019, Vern and Wanda will file jointly. In that year, they expect to sell their greatly appreciated vacation home, which they have owned for many years, for a whopping $650,000 gain. That profit will be fully taxable for federal income tax purposes and it will also count as investment income for purposes of the NIIT. To keep things simple, assume Vern and Wanda will have no other investment income and no capital losses for 2019. However, they will have $175,000 of MAGI from other sources (salary, bonuses, self-employment income, and so forth).

Due to the big vacation home profit, the couple's 2019 net investment income—unless something changes—will be a whopping $650,000 (all from the vacation home sale) and their MAGI will be an even-more-whopping $825,000 ($650,000 from the vacation home plus $175,000 from other sources). Without some effective tax planning, Vern and Wanda will owe the NIIT on a whopping $575,000 (the lesser of (1) net investment income of $650,000 or (2) excess MAGI of $575,000 ($825,000 − $250,000 threshold for joint-filing couples). The NIIT hit would amount to $21,850 (3.8% × $575,000).

In this example, the sole source of exposure to the NIIT is the big gain from selling the vacation home which pushed their excess MAGI way over the applicable threshold. Vern and Wanda should consider the following strategies:

- Sell the vacation home on the installment plan to spread the big gain over several years and thus minimize or maybe even eliminate exposure to the NIIT.
- If possible, swap the vacation home in an IRC Section 1031 like-kind exchange, which would defer the big gain and completely eliminate exposure to the NIIT until further notice.
- Failing the previous steps, Vern and Wanda should take steps to reduce their 2019 MAGI, which would reduce their exposure to the NIIT. Some MAGI-reduction strategies are explained in the following section.

Seven strategies to reduce current-year net investment income

1. Sell loser securities held in taxable brokerage firm accounts to offset earlier gains from such accounts. (This will also reduce MAGI.)
2. Gift soon-to-be-sold appreciated securities to children or grandchildren and let them sell them to avoid including the gains on your return. (This will also reduce MAGI.) But beware of the kiddie tax, which can potentially apply until the year a child or grandchild turns age 24.
3. Instead of cash, donate appreciated securities to IRS-approved charities. That way, the gains will not be included on your return. (This will also reduce MAGI.)
4. Select a method for determining deductions allocable to gross investment income that will maximize such deductions and thereby reduce net investment income (see the discussion earlier in this chapter).
5. If possible, become more active in rental and business activities (including those conducted through partnerships and S corporations) to "convert" them from passive to non-passive by meeting one of the material participation standards. That would make income from the activities exempt from the NIIT, because the NIIT does not apply to income from non-passive business activities (including rental activities that rise to the level of non-passive business activities).

6. To facilitate the preceding strategy, consider taking advantage of the one-time opportunity to regroup activities for purpose of applying the passive activity rules.
7. If possible, defer gains subject to the NIIT by making installment sales or IRC Section 1031 like-kind exchanges. (These steps will also reduce MAGI.)

Five strategies to reduce current-year MAGI

1. Sell loser securities held in taxable brokerage firm accounts to offset earlier gains in such accounts. (This will also reduce net investment income.)
2. Gift soon-to-be-sold appreciated securities to children or grandchildren and let them sell them to avoid including the gains on your return. (This will also reduce MAGI.) But beware of the kiddie tax, which can potentially apply until the year a child or grandchild turns age 24.
3. Instead of cash, donate appreciated securities to IRS-approved charities. That way, the gains will not be included on your return. (This will also reduce net investment income.)
4. Maximize deductible contributions to tax-favored retirement accounts such as 401(k) accounts, self-employed SEP accounts, and self-employed defined benefit pension plans.
5. If you are a cash-basis self-employed individual, take steps to defer business income into the next year and accelerate business deductions into the current year.

Five longer-term strategies to minimize or avoid NIIT in future years

The following moves might not do much to reduce or eliminate exposure to the NIIT in the current year, but they could help a lot over the long run.

1. Convert traditional retirement account balances to Roth accounts, but watch out for the impact on MAGI in the conversion year. The deemed taxable distributions that result from Roth conversions are not included in net investment income, but they increase MAGI – which may expose more of your investment income to the NIIT in the conversion year. Over the long haul, however, income and gains that build up in a Roth IRA will usually be bullet-proof with respect to the NIIT, because qualified Roth distributions are tax-free for both regular income tax and NIIT purposes. Because qualified Roth distributions are not included in MAGI (unlike the taxable portion of distributions from other types of tax-favored retirement accounts and plans), qualified Roth distributions will not increase your exposure to the NIIT by increasing your MAGI.
2. Invest more taxable brokerage firm money in tax exempt bonds. This would reduce both net investment income and MAGI. Use tax-favored retirement accounts to invest in securities that are expected to generate otherwise-taxable gains, dividends, and interest.
3. Invest in life insurance products and tax-deferred annuity products. Life insurance death benefits are generally exempt from both the federal income tax and the NIIT. Earnings from life insurance contracts are not taxed until they are withdrawn. Similarly, earnings from tax-deferred annuities are not taxed until they are withdrawn.
4. Invest in rental real estate and oil and gas properties. Rental real estate income is offset by depreciation deductions, and oil and gas income is offset by deductions for intangible drilling costs and depletion. These deductions can reduce both net investment income and MAGI.
5. Invest taxable brokerage firm account money in growth stocks. Gains are not taxed until the stocks are sold. At that time, the negative tax impact of gains can often be offset by selling loser securities held in taxable accounts. In contrast, stock dividends are taxed currently, and it may not be so easy to take steps to offset them.

Conclusion

Some of the strategies explained here are double tax-savers because they can reduce both your regular federal income tax (FIT) bill and your NIIT bill. If you are self-employed, some of the strategies are triple tax-savers because they can reduce your FIT bill, your NIIT bill, and your self-employment tax bill. Finally, these strategies might reduce your state income tax bill as well. However, some of these strategies take time to implement. So, get started on identifying strategies that can help your clients before it is too late to implement them.

Knowledge check

9. The NIIT is never imposed on

    a. Income and gains from the investment of business working capital.
    b. Passed-through income and gains from partnerships and S corporations.
    c. Income and gains accumulated in tax-favored retirement accounts such as 401(k) accounts and IRAs.
    d. Income from rental activities.

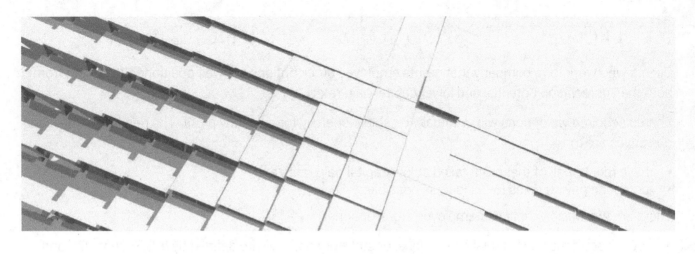

Chapter 2

Planning for Employer Stock Options, Employer Stock Held in Retirement Accounts, and Restricted Stock

Learning objectives

- Identify ways to advise clients on how to minimize taxes on employer stock options and employer stock held in qualified retirement plan accounts.

- Differentiate between incentive stock options (ISOs) and nonqualified stock options (NQSOs).

Introduction

This chapter covers several easy to implement tax-saving ideas for employer stock options, employer stock held in qualified retirement plan accounts, and restricted employer stock.

Employer stock options: Tax implications

Clients who work for a company that grants employee stock options are well-positioned to benefit from both the appreciation potential and lower capital gain rates.

Shares acquired via options will eventually be sold, hopefully for a healthy profit. The general tax planning objectives are to

- have most or all of that profit taxed at low capital gain rates and
- postpone paying taxes for as long as possible.

There are two basic varieties of employee stock options:

- ISOs (sometimes called qualified options, or statutory options) are defined by IRC Section 422 and are entitled to preferential tax treatment. But ISOs are also subject to some special restrictions and unfavorable handling under the alternative minimum tax (AMT) system.
- Nonqualified stock options, or NQSOs, are not subject to such restrictions, but they also confer no special tax breaks on their owners beyond deferring income recognition.

Knowledge check

1. With employer stock options, one usual tax planning objective is to
    a. Put off paying taxes.
    b. Accelerate the taxable event in order to qualify for lower long-term capital gains tax rates.
    c. Maximize the pre-tax profit.
    d. Minimize risk.

Regular tax rules for ISO and ISO shares

An option must meet certain rules (set forth in IRC Section 422 and related regulations) upon issuance to qualify as an ISO. The single most important rule is the requirement that the exercise price cannot be less than the stock's market value at the time the employee receives the option.

For regular tax purposes, ISOs deliver two major league advantages (the not-so-favorable AMT situation is explained later):

- First, when the option is exercised, the excess of market value over exercise price (the bargain element) goes untaxed at that time.
- Second, when ISO shares are sold, the entire profit (excess of sale price over exercise price) can qualify for the reduced federal income tax rates on long-term capital gains. However, to qualify for reduced rates, the date of sale for ISO shares must be
    - more than two years after the option grant date (when the employee was given the option) and
    - more than 12 months after the shares are purchased (by exercising the option).

If the preceding two holding-period rules are satisfied, the employee can achieve the twin goals of having the entire profit taxed at the lowest possible rate and delaying the tax bill until shares are sold and the employee has the cash to pay the tax.

Example 2-1

- On March 1, 2017, Elvette was granted an ISO allowing her to buy 200 shares of company stock at $25 at any time before January 1, 2020. On October 1, 2017, she exercised when the stock was trading at $34. On May 1, 2019, the shares were trading at a lofty $52, and she cashed in her chips.
  - Elvette met the ISO requirements because the sale date was more than two years after the March 1, 2017, grant date and more than 12 months after the October 1, 2017, exercise date. So her entire $5,400 profit ($27 per share) counts as a 2019 long-term capital gain eligible for reduced tax rates.
  - As always with stock, the insatiable appetite for tax savings must be balanced against the risk of a price decline if the shares are held long enough to qualify for the reduced rates.
- What if Elvette's luck was not so good and she sold her company shares for less than their value on the exercise date ($34), or, even worse, less than her exercise price ($25)? Elvette's per-share tax basis equals the exercise price. Therefore, if she sells for more than $25, she still would have a capital gain taxed at reduced rates. If the sale price is less than $25, she has a capital loss.

Key point: This example ignores the potential impact of the 3.8% NIIT.

AMT rules for ISOs and ISO shares

Unfortunately, the bargain element on the exercise date counts as a *positive adjustment* for AMT purposes (positive for the Treasury, negative for the employee) in the year of exercise [IRC Section 56(b)(3)]. The adjustment increases AMT income, which may cause the AMT to exceed the regular tax bill. If so, the taxpayer must pay the higher amount. (If not, the adjustment does no harm.)

If the taxpayer does end up owing AMT, he or she may be entitled to an AMT credit, which can be used to reduce the regular tax bill in a later year. Use Form 6251 (Alternative Minimum Tax—Individuals) to see if the taxpayer owes AMT in the year of exercise. If so, Form 8801 (Credit for Prior Year Minimum Tax) should be completed when preparing the following year's return to see if there is a credit.

In some cases, *staggering* the exercise of ISOs can avoid triggering the AMT with a big bargain element number in a single year. Unfortunately, this does not work too well when the stock continues to rise. As it increases, the bargain element on the remaining unexercised ISO shares gets bigger, which can defeat the staggering strategy.

However, staggering can make sense near year-end.

For example:

- The taxpayer can exercise some ISOs in December of the current year and the rest early in the following year.
- Assuming the stock does not rise much between the two exercise dates, this could avoid AMT in both years.

Another strategy is to simply exercise the ISOs before the stock price advances much beyond the exercise price. Then the bargain element is minimal, and the AMT bill may fade into oblivion. Of course, to use this *exercise early* technique, the taxpayer must come up with the money to pull the trigger, so he or she should be confident the stock will rise enough to justify the investment.

When ISO shares are sold, the gain or loss must be calculated under the AMT rules. The AMT basis equals the market price on the exercise date (not the lower exercise price, which is the regular tax basis). The higher AMT basis shows up as a *negative adjustment* on Form 6251 in the year of sale. So, if the taxpayer sells for more than the market price on the exercise date, there is a gain for both AMT and regular tax, but the AMT number will be lower. If the sale price is less than market price on the exercise date but more than the exercise price, there is an AMT loss and a regular tax gain. In either case, if the AMT credit was earned in the year of exercise and has not yet been used, the taxpayer can likely use the credit in the year of sale.

Key point: The Tax Cuts and Jobs Act (TCJA) retains the individual AMT, but AMT exemption deductions are significantly increased and phased out at much higher income levels for 2018–2025. For many individuals, AMT exposure under prior law was caused by high itemized deductions for state and local taxes and multiple personal and dependent exemption deductions, as well as by exercises of in-the-money ISOs as discussed here. Itemized deductions for state and local taxes are disallowed under the AMT rules. With the TCJA limits on deductions for state and local taxes, the elimination of personal and dependent exemption deductions, and liberalized AMT exemptions, many individuals who owed the AMT under prior law will be off the hook in 2018–2025. Others who owed the AMT under prior law may still owe it but will likely owe less.

 Example 2-2

- Under the same facts as in example 2-1, Elvette would have done her 2017 AMT bookkeeping by entering a $1,800 positive adjustment (the $9 per share bargain element) on Form 6251 filed with her 2017 return. Her per-share AMT basis becomes $34 (market value at exercise).
- In preparing her 2018 return, she completed Form 8801 to see if she ran up an AMT credit from the 2017 exercise. Assume she did. If she owes regular tax in 2018, she can use the credit to reduce her regular tax, at least to the point where it equals her 2018 AMT number.
  - On Elvette's 2019 Form 6251, she will report a $1,800 negative adjustment when she sells her shares for $52 each, so her AMT gain will be only $3,600, compared to $5,400 for regular tax purposes.
  - If Elvette has any leftover AMT credit, she can probably use it to reduce her 2019 regular tax bill.

Key point: This example ignores the potential impact of the 3.8% NIIT.

Regular tax rules for disqualifying dispositions of ISO Shares

If the taxpayer sells ISO shares within two years of the grant date or one year of the exercise date, it is too soon according to the tax law. The seller has made a *disqualifying disposition.* This will not get the taxpayer into any trouble with the government, but it will hike the tax bill. Nevertheless, it is sometimes smart to make a disqualifying disposition, for the reason explained later in this section.

When the sale price exceeds the exercise price, there is of course a regular tax gain. Gain up to the amount of the bargain element (spread between market value and exercise price on the exercise date) is considered compensation income in the year of sale. So that piece gets taxed at regular rates (up to 37%). However, no employment taxes are due, and no income tax withholding is necessary. Any additional profit is capital gain.

The tax rate on the *capital gain piece* depends on how long the shares were owned (ownership starts on the exercise date).

For example: If there is a disqualifying disposition because the sale date is less than two years after the grant date, but the sale date is more than a year after the exercise date, the capital gain piece is taxed at the reduced rates for long-term gains.

Obviously, disqualifying dispositions have the negative effect of causing all or part of the profit to be taxed at higher ordinary income rates. But the key word here is *profit*. If the stock is diving, holding on too long may simply erase the taxpayer's gain. Until our tax rate reaches 100%, people are better off taking the gain early with a disqualifying disposition and paying a bit more in taxes.

If someone is unlucky (or stubborn) enough to hold onto ISO shares until they fall to less than the exercise price, there is a regular tax capital loss on a disqualifying disposition.

AMT rules for disqualifying dispositions of ISO shares

Now let us look at the AMT rules for disqualifying dispositions. If the exercise and disqualifying disposition occur in the same year, there is no AMT impact. However, if exercise and disqualifying disposition occur in two different years, the positive adjustment for the bargain element may cause an AMT liability in the exercise year, as explained earlier. Hopefully, that will generate an AMT credit which can be used in the year of sale, when the seller is entitled to a negative adjustment for the basis difference.

Observation: Notice that all the AMT damage (if any) is over and done with in the year the ISO is exercised. After that, taxpayers should just pay attention to the regular tax consequences of either hanging onto the ISO shares long enough to have the entire profit taxed at reduced rates or prudently bailing out early with a disqualifying disposition.

Year-end strategy: Making disqualifying disposition to avoid AMT hit

If your client exercised some ISOs earlier this year, he or she could be facing a big AMT liability. This is because, as explained earlier, the bargain element (difference between market value and exercise price on the exercise date) is a positive AMT adjustment in the year of exercise. So far, so bad; but it can get worse—much worse.

Say the client's ISO shares have now plummeted in value to less than the exercise price. Does the current-year AMT liability go away? Unfortunately, it won't, unless he acts before the end of the year of exercise.

If the client does nothing, he or she will still owe the AMT—on value that has now evaporated—when he or she files the 1040 for the year of exercise. So what can your client do?

Well, he or she can solve the AMT problem by selling the ISO shares before year-end. As was just explained, this is a disqualifying disposition, which sounds bad. But in your client's situation, it may be the best thing to do. When the client makes a disqualifying disposition in the same year the ISO is exercised, the AMT adjustment disappears. So, the AMT liability disappears. Now your client simply has a garden-variety short-term capital loss on the sale of the ISO shares. For both regular tax and AMT purposes, that loss equals the difference between the net sale price and the exercise price.

If the client has capital gains from other current-year transactions, he or she can use the capital loss to offset the gains.

If the client already has an overall current-year capital loss, he or she just adds the loss from the disqualifying disposition to the total. He or she can then deduct a maximum of $3,000 of capital losses against the taxable income from all other sources ($1,500 if he or she is married and filing separately). Of course, if his or her current-year capital loss exceeds the $3,000 (or $1,500) limit, the excess is carried over to next year. That's still a whole lot better than paying an unfair AMT bill for the current year.

But watch out for this

If your client wants to buy back company shares after selling his ISO shares in a disqualifying disposition, he or she should wait at least 31 days to do so. This advice applies whether the client will incur a loss from the disqualifying disposition, or break even on the deal, or even generate a taxable gain.

Why? Because a little-known provision in the regulations dealing with ISO shares says the tax results are truly horrific when employer shares are reacquired within 30 days of a disqualifying disposition of ISO shares. According to the rule, the disqualifying disposition would trigger ordinary income (for both regular tax and AMT purposes) equal to the full amount of the bargain element that existed at the time of exercise. That income is then added to the employee's basis in the ISO shares, which means the disqualifying disposition will result in a big capital loss. Triggering ordinary income and an offsetting capital loss is bad enough. Even worse, the capital loss will then be disallowed under the IRC Section 1091(a) wash sale rule. [See Regulation 1.422-1(b)(2)(ii) and (b)(3), Example 3.]

Key point: Don't let this happen to your client. Advise your client to wait at least 31 days after making a disqualifying disposition of ISO shares before reacquiring any company stock.

Knowledge check

2. With incentive stock options (ISOs), making a disqualifying disposition is

   a. Always a terrible idea from a federal income tax perspective.
   b. Advisable if the option stock is expected to continue to decline in value.
   c. Not allowed under the federal income tax rules.
   d. Not allowed under SEC rules.

Tax rules for nonqualified stock options (NQSOs) and NQSO shares

As mentioned earlier, employer stock options that do not qualify as ISOs are NQSOs. This discussion does not cover special rules that apply to *restricted stock* acquired with NQSOs. (An example of restricted stock is the situation in which ownership of the shares vests over a period of time provided the employee is still working for the company. The rules under IRC Section 83 apply to restricted stock.)

The tax rules for NQSOs are less favorable than for ISOs, but NQSOs have one huge advantage. They can be issued with an exercise price less than the stock's current market value. Because they can be delivered with a nice *built-in gain*, NQSOs are what corporate executives typically get. (However, whenever an option exercise price is set to less than a stock's current market value, at the date of the option's issuance, any impact of IRC Section 409A should be evaluated, which could potentially be triggered, resulting in an acceleration of the recognition of deferred income along with related imputed interest income and penalties.)

When an NQSO is exercised, the bargain element (difference between market value and exercise price at the time of exercise) is generally taxed at ordinary income rates in that year's tax return. (In unusual cases where NQSOs are publicly traded, tax may accrue on the grant date.)

Basis in the shares equals market price on the exercise date. Any subsequent appreciation is capital gain taxed when the shares are sold, and that amount is eligible for the reduced long-term gain rates if the shares are held over 12 months. If the stock goes down and is sold for less than the market price on the exercise date, there is a capital loss. This is simple enough, and you will be pleased to know there are no special AMT rules for NQSOs.

Example 2-3

- Assume the same facts as in example 2-1, except now Elvette's option is an NQSO issued when the price of the stock was $29. As before, the exercise price is $25, and Elvette exercised in 2017 when the market price was $34. Because the option is an NQSO, Elvette paid 2017 tax on the $1,800 bargain element at her ordinary rate (say $504 at a 28% marginal rate). Her per-share basis is $34, and her holding period began on October 2, 2017.
    - When she sells on May 1, 2019, for $52 per share, Elvette has a $3,600 long-term capital gain taxed at a reduced rate, say 15%. When all is said and done, she netted an after-tax profit of $4,356 ($1,800 + $3,600 − $504 − $540).
    - If Elvette could have exercised earlier when the stock was worth less than $34, she could have cut her tax bill for the year of exercise and increased the gain taxed later at only 15%. This is now the "conventional wisdom" for NQSOs: exercise early to minimize the current tax hit and maximize the amount treated as long-term capital gain when the option shares are sold.

Key point: This example ignores the potential impact of the 3.8% NIIT.

Strategy: Hold that option version 1

Here is another option strategy worth considering for both ISOs and NQSOs: instead of spending cash to exercise the option, the taxpayer can use the same amount to buy shares of company stock at market. The taxpayer can then hold those shares until he or she has a significant gain eligible for the reduced long-term gain rates. The shares can then be sold and the 15% (or whatever rate applies) tax paid, with the after-tax proceeds then used to exercise the option. The taxpayer can then immediately sell the NQSO shares. This results in tax at the ordinary rate on the entire profit from the option shares, but the taxpayer can still come out ahead because there are two gains instead of one.

Example 2-4

- Assume the same facts as in example 2-1, except Elvette buys 147 shares in 2017 at $34 with the same $5,000 needed to exercise her ISO for 200 shares at $25. She could then sell the 147 shares at $52 in 2019 to net a $2,249 profit after paying 15% tax on the $2,646 gain. She then spends $5,000 to exercise her option on the 200 shares in 2019 and immediately sells the option shares for $10,400.
    - Because this is a disqualifying disposition, Elvette owes tax in 2019 at her regular rate of say 24% on the $5,400 profit from selling the ISO shares, so she pays another $1,296 to Uncle in 2019 and collects an after-tax profit of $4,104 ($5,400 − $1,296). However, Elvette's after-tax profit from the two sales is $6,353 ($2,249 + $4,104) versus only $4,356 on the same $5,000 investment that would have been needed just to exercise the ISO.

Key point: This example ignores the potential impact of the 3.8% NIIT.

Strategy: Hold that option version 2

Although the preceding strategy of holding the option and investing the exercise price in additional company shares is fine, taxpayers may be well advised to instead hold the option and spend the same amount on other attractive equity investments. This results in a more diversified portfolio and avoids the risk that the employer stock may not perform as well as other equity alternatives.

Eventually, the taxpayer can sell the other equities, pay the 15% or 20% federal income tax (or whatever the preferential long-term capital gains rate happens to be at the time) and use the money to exercise the company stock option before it expires. Then taxpayer can sell the company shares immediately if he or she wishes. Again, this strategy can be pursued with both NQSOs (see example 2-5) and ISOs (see example 2-6).

Example 2-5

- Oswald has an NQSO to buy 500 company shares at $25 (the stock is currently worth $30). Instead of spending $12,500 to exercise immediately, he invests the same amount in several other stocks in different industries.
- Four years later, it is time to exercise the option because it is about to expire. Oswald's company stock and the other equities have all appreciated 10% annually. So he sells the other shares and pays 15% on the $5,801 gain to net an after-tax profit of $4,931 (.85 × $5,801). He then takes $12,500 and exercises the option on the 500 company shares, which are now worth $21,962. Oswald sells those immediately and pays 35% (his marginal rate) on the entire $9,462 profit, resulting in an after-tax take of $6,150 (.65 × $9,462). So Oswald has an after-tax profit of $11,081 ($4,931 + $6,150) from the two deals even after cutting in the government for its exorbitant share.
- If he had simply exercised his option when the stock was at $30, Oswald would have paid Uncle $875 in year 1 (35% of the $2,500 spread) plus another $1,044 when he sold [15% × ($21,962 − $15,000)]. His after-tax take would be only $7,543 ($21,962 − $12,500 − $875 − $1,044), compared to the $11,081 from holding the option and investing the exercise price. (Oswald comes out even better if his marginal tax rate is lower than the assumed 35%.)

Key point: This example ignores the potential impact of the 3.8% NIIT.

Example 2-6

- Assume the same facts as in example 2-5, except Oswald's option is now an ISO to buy 500 company shares at $30 (the current market price). Instead of spending $15,000 to exercise the ISO, Oswald again invests the exercise price in several other stocks in different industries.
    - Four years later, it is time to exercise the option. The company stock and the other equities have all appreciated 10% annually, so Oswald sells the other shares and pays his 15% on the $6,962 gain to net $5,918 (.85 × $6,962). He then takes $15,000 and exercises the option on the 500 company shares, which are now worth $21,962. If he sells those immediately and pays 35% on the entire $6,962 profit, his after-tax take is still $4,525. So Oswald bags an after-tax profit of $10,443 from the two deals ($5,918 + $4,525).
    - If he had simply exercised his ISO when the stock was at $30, Oswald would owe $1,044 when he sold [15% × ($21,962 − $15,000)], and his after-tax take would be only $5,918 ($6,962 − $1,044).

Key point: This example ignores the potential impact of the 3.8% NIIT.

Federal employment tax implications

Nonqualified options

When an employee exercises an NQSO, the bargain element (difference between exercise price and FMV on the date of exercise) is treated as ordinary income from compensation. The income is therefore subject to federal income tax withholding and the Social Security, Medicare, and Federal Unemployment Tax Act (FUTA) taxes (see Revenue Rulings 67-257 and 79-305) and should be reported on the employee's Form W-2 [Regulation Section 1.83-6(a)]. From the employee's perspective, the federal employment tax impact is usually only 1.45% (from the Medicare tax) if his or her compensation exceeds the Social Security tax ceiling before considering the income from exercising the NQSO. However, this additional tax cost should be considered in analyzing NQSO strategies.

Additional 0.9% Medicare tax

Before 2013, the Medicare tax on employee compensation (including the bargain element from exercising an NQSO) was 1.45%. Starting in 2013, an extra 0.9% Medicare tax is charged on taxable employee compensation greater than $200,000 for an unmarried individual, $250,000 for a married joint-filing couple, and $125,000 for those who use married filing separate status. These thresholds are not adjusted for inflation. [See IRC Section 1401(b)(2).] Employers must withhold the additional 0.9% Medicare tax from employee paychecks. That results in a current maximum Medicare tax withholding rate of 2.35% (1.45% + 0.9%).

Knowledge check

3. When an NQSO is exercised,

    a. The transaction is exempt from federal income tax withholding and exempt from Social Security and Medicare taxes.
    b. With respect to the bargain element treated as compensation, withholding of federal income tax is required and the Social Security and Medicare taxes apply.
    c. There are no immediate tax consequences.
    d. The bargain element is treated as long-term capital gain.

ISOs

For many years, it was clear that no Social Security or Medicare taxes (collectively referred to as federal employment taxes for purposes of this discussion) were triggered by exercising an ISO. This made sense only because, under IRC Section 421(a), exercising an ISO is not a taxable event for regular federal income tax purposes, even when there is a positive "spread" between the exercise price and the market value of the underlying shares on the date of exercise. [However, the "spread" is considered income for AMT purposes per IRC Section 56(b)(3).]

Similarly, it was clear that no federal employment or FUTA taxes were triggered by a *disqualifying disposition* of employer shares acquired by exercising an ISO. Nor was any Federal Income Tax withholding required. This was the case even though part or all of the taxable income triggered by a disqualifying disposition income can be treated as compensation income taxed at ordinary rates.

These taxpayer-friendly rules were originally courtesy of Revenue Ruling 71-52. In IRS Notice 87-49, the government announced it would continue its favorable policy regarding federal employment taxes on disqualifying dispositions of ISOs. Notice 87-49 also announced that Revenue Ruling 71-52 was under reconsideration, and that things could eventually change. Thankfully, however, the status quo will continue to prevail for the foreseeable future.

Per IRS Notice 2002-47, the IRS will not assess federal employment or FUTA taxes on (1) the "spread" from exercising ISOs, or (2) taxable income triggered by disqualifying dispositions of shares acquired by exercising ISOs. Furthermore, the IRS will not impose FIT withholding on (1) the exercise of ISOs, or (2) taxable income triggered by disqualifying dispositions of shares acquired by exercising ISOs.

The American Jobs Creation Act made this favorable treatment statutory and eliminated any lingering uncertainty on the subject.

How to handle employer stock received in a qualified retirement plan distribution

In general, retiring employees are well advised to roll over their distributions from company qualified retirement plan accounts into IRAs. This avoids an immediate tax impact and allows the taxpayer to continue to benefit from tax-deferred earnings until withdrawals are actually needed to finance living costs.

Withdraw shares and hold in taxable account

However, when a qualified retirement plan account holds appreciated employer stock, the taxpayer may be better off withdrawing the shares and holding them in a taxable account rather than rolling the shares over into an IRA.

As long as the shares are part of what qualifies as a lump-sum distribution from the taxpayer's qualified plan accounts, only the amount of the plan's cost basis for the shares (generally the FMV of the shares when they were acquired by the plan) is taxed currently [IRC Section 402(e)(4)(B)]. (Everything else received in the lump-sum distribution can, and generally should, be rolled over into the IRA.)

If the shares have appreciated substantially over the years, the cost basis could be a relatively small percentage of the shares' value on the distribution date (remember, however, that the cost basis number will not necessarily be an insignificant amount).

If the taxpayer is under age 59½, the 10% *premature distribution* penalty tax will also apply, but it will apply only to the cost basis amount rather than to the full FMV of the stock [IRC Section 72(t)(1)].

The tax on the cost basis is at the taxpayer's ordinary rate, but here are the offsetting benefits:

- The net unrealized appreciation when the shares are distributed (the difference between FMV on the distribution date and the plan's cost basis for the shares) qualifies for the reduced long-term capital gain tax rates. (See IRS Notice 98-24.)
- The capital gains tax on that unrealized appreciation is deferred until the shares are sold.
- Any post-distribution appreciation (after the shares come out of the qualified plan account) also qualifies for the reduced long-term capital gain tax rates if the shares are sold more than 12 months after the taxpayer's holding period begins [Regulation Section 1.402(a)-1(b)(1)(i)]. For this purpose, the taxpayer's holding period commences on the day after the shares are delivered by the plan to the transfer agent with instructions to reissue the shares in the employee's name (Revenue Ruling 82-75).
- If the taxpayer dies while still owning the shares, the heirs get a basis step-up for the post-distribution appreciation [IRC Section 1014(a) and (c)]. However, the heirs will owe tax on the unrealized appreciation amount, at the preferential rates for long-term capital gains, under the *income in respect of a decedent* rule (Revenue Ruling 75-125).

Rollover into IRA

In contrast, if the shares are rolled over into an IRA, there is no tax until money is withdrawn from the account. However, all the unrealized appreciation and all the post-distribution appreciation will wind up being taxed at ordinary rates. In addition, if the shares are still in the IRA at death, the taxpayer's heirs will owe tax at ordinary rates on their withdrawals from the IRA—including amounts attributable to unrealized appreciation and post-distribution appreciation.

 Example 2-7

- Bruce retires from a large corporation at age 62. As part of a lump-sum distribution from several retirement plan accounts, he receives 1,000 shares of employer stock with a cost basis to the plan of $10,000. The current FMV of the shares is $40,000, and Bruce expects the stock to continue to appreciate.
- Instead of rolling the shares into an IRA, Bruce heeds the advice of his CPA and holds the stock in a taxable account. (He rolls over everything else.) He pays tax at his ordinary rate of 24% on the $10,000 cost basis. Years later, Bruce passes on when the shares have appreciated to a value of $100,000.
    - Bruce's heirs receive a basis step-up equal to the post-distribution appreciation ($60,000 in this case assuming the current basis step-up rule continues). When they sell the stock, they will owe capital gain tax (at an assumed rate of 20%) on the unrealized appreciation (the $30,000 difference between the plan's $10,000 cost basis in the shares and the $40,000 FMV as of the distribution date) plus any appreciation that occurs after Bruce's death up to the date of sale.
    - If there is no further appreciation and the 20% rate applies, the total tax paid on the $100,000 worth of stock will be only $8,400 [$2,400 by Bruce in the year of the distribution plus $6,000 (20% of the $30,000 unrealized appreciation) by the heirs when the stock is sold].
    - In contrast, if Bruce had rolled the shares into an IRA, his heirs would owe tax at their ordinary rates on the entire $100,000 when the IRA is liquidated. In all likelihood, their taxes would total at least $25,000.

Warning

- The preceding tax treatment applies only to shares received as part of a lump-sum distribution.
- If the shares are distributed from a qualified retirement plan and are not part of a lump-sum distribution, the tax consequences of not rolling the shares over into an IRA are much less favorable.
- Specifically, the full FMV of the shares will be taxed as ordinary income, except to the extent of any nondeductible employee contributions plus the unrealized appreciation attributable to such nondeductible contributions [IRC Section 402(e)(4)(A)].
- However, post-distribution appreciation will still qualify for preferential long-term capital gains rates if the shares are held over 12 months before they are sold.

Restricted stock: Tax implications

According to some reports, restricted stock awards are replacing stock option grants as the most common form of equity-oriented executive compensation. The reason: stock options can lose most or all of their value if the underlying stock goes down in price. In contrast, restricted stock awards usually retain significant value as long as the underlying stock retains significant value. If the stock price goes down, additional restricted stock easily can be awarded to adjust for the decrease.

This analysis explains the federal income and employment tax impact of restricted stock awards.

Restricted stock basics

In a typical restricted stock arrangement, an executive receives company stock subject to one or more restrictions. The most common restriction is a requirement for continued employment through a designated date. Often, the stock is transferred at no cost or minimal cost to the executive. The right to keep the restricted shares is forfeited if the executive fails to fulfill the terms of the restricted stock program.

Tax-wise, the executive's recognition of taxable income and the employer's right to claim the related compensation deduction are both generally deferred until vesting occurs (meaning when the executive's ownership of the stock is no longer restricted) pursuant to the IRC Section 83 rules.

However, if the executive makes an IRC Section 83(b) election (explained later) to recognize taxable income at the time the restricted stock award is received, the tax effects are accelerated for both the executive and the employer.

Key point: IRC Section 409A provides that compensation that is deferred under certain deferred compensation arrangements must be recognized currently for federal income and employment tax purposes unless certain requirements are met. However, a restricted stock award that is taxed under the IRC Section 83 rules is generally not subject to the IRC Section 409A rules [Regulation 1.409A-1(b)(6)].

Weighing tax deferral versus preferential long-term capital gain treatment

When no IRC Section 83(b) election is made, the recipient executive is not taxed upon the receipt of restricted stock. Instead, the stock's value (including any subsequent appreciation) less the amount paid (if any) for the stock is recognized as taxable compensation income for federal income and employment tax purposes when the restrictions lapse (that is, when the stock becomes fully vested). Therefore, any stock price appreciation that occurs between the date the restricted stock is awarded and the date the restrictions lapse is treated as high-taxed ordinary income from compensation (the current maximum federal income tax rate on ordinary income is 37%).

Alternatively, the executive can choose to make an IRC Section 83(b) election to be taxed when the stock is awarded. If the election is made, the executive is taxed on the stock's date-of-award value (even though ownership has not yet vested) less the amount paid (if any) for the stock. Any subsequent appreciation is treated as capital gain which will qualify for preferential long-term gain tax rates if the stock is held for more than one year. (The current maximum federal income tax rate on long-term capital gain is 20% which is obviously much lower than the current 37% maximum rate on ordinary income from compensation.) The downside of making the IRC Section 83(b) election is that the executive must recognize taxable income at the time of the restricted stock award even though the restricted stock may later be forfeited or decline in value.

Requirements for restricted stock treatment

For federal income and employment tax purposes, stock is considered to be restricted (meaning not vested) when both of the following conditions are met [IRC Section 83(a)]:

1. The stock is subject to a substantial risk of forfeiture.
2. The stock is not freely transferable.

Subject to a substantial risk of forfeiture

This condition is met if full ownership of the stock depends on the future performance, or refraining from the performance, of substantial services by the recipient executive [IRC Section 83(c) (1)].

Not freely transferable

This condition is met if upon any transfer by the recipient executive of any interest in the stock to any person or entity other than the employer, the new holder's rights to the stock are still subject to the same substantial risk of forfeiture [IRC Section 83(c) (2)].

For instance, stock meets the not-transferable requirement if the recipient executive can sell the stock, but the new holder must still forfeit the stock upon the occurrence of the event causing the substantial risk of forfeiture (typically premature termination of the executive's employment). To ensure that the non-transferable requirement is met, restricted shares are commonly stamped with a legend that discloses the restriction(s) placed on them or indicating that they are not transferable. That way, any subsequent holder of the restricted shares is made aware of the restriction(s).

Definition of substantial risk of forfeiture

Stock is subject to a substantial risk of forfeiture if the rights to full ownership depend (directly or indirectly) on either of the following [Regulation 1.83-3(c)]:

- The requirement for future performance of substantial services by the recipient executive.
- The occurrence of a condition related to the purpose of the restricted stock grant. An example of such a condition is the requirement that the recipient executive must obtain an advanced educational degree, or a specified professional designation, or attain a certain job status within the company for the restricted stock to become vested.

Example 2-8

On March 31, 2019, your employer transfers 10,000 shares of company stock to you. You are not required to pay anything for the shares. The stock is worth $25 per share on the date of the transfer. Under the terms of the deal, you must forfeit all the shares back to your employer if you leave the company for any reason before March 31, 2023. If you sell the shares, whoever buys them must also forfeit them back to your employer if you leave the company for any reason before the magic date. Because you must perform substantial services over the next four years to gain full ownership of the stock, the shares are considered subject to a substantial risk of forfeiture. Therefore, the shares are considered restricted stock and are subject to the tax considerations explained in analysis.

The following are examples of restrictions that generally do not constitute a substantial risk of forfeiture [Regulation 1.83-3(c)(2)]:

- The risk that the value of the stock will decline.
- A non-lapse restriction placed on the stock (as subsequently explained).
- A requirement that the stock be returned to the employer if the executive is discharged for cause or for committing a crime.
- A requirement that the stock be returned if the executive accepts a job with a competing firm (unless the facts indicate that the executive could realistically obtain such other employment and that the covenant not to compete would actually be enforced).
- A requirement that the stock be returned if a retiring executive does not render consulting services upon the request of his or her former employer (unless he or she is expected to perform substantial services).

Non-lapse restrictions do not cause substantial risk of forfeiture

Restrictions that will never lapse are termed *non-lapse restrictions*. Such restrictions place a permanent limitation on the stock's transferability. [See Regulation 1.83-3(h).] However, such restrictions are not considered to cause the stock to be subject to a substantial risk of forfeiture. [See Regulation 1.83-3(c)(1).] On the other hand, non-lapse restrictions are considered in determining the stock's value on the transfer date [Regulation 1.83-5(a)].

Examples of non-lapse restrictions include the requirement for the recipient taxpayer to surrender his or her stock if he or she ever leaves the company and the existence of a permanent right of first refusal for the company to buy back the shares for a formula price. However, an obligation to sell back shares at FMV is not considered a non-lapse restriction [Regulation 1.83-3(h)].

Example 2-9

Same basic facts as example 2-8, but this time assume that as a condition of the stock transfer, you must offer the shares back to your employer at a price determined by a formula based on book value if you ever decide to sell the stock. In addition, you must offer the stock back to your employer at the formula price when you retire, and your estate must do the same if you die while still owning the shares. These restrictions are non-lapse restrictions that are ignored in determining whether the stock qualifies as restricted stock for federal tax purposes. However, these non-lapse restrictions are considered in determining the stock's value on the date of transfer and on the vesting dates.

Temporary limits on transferability do not cause substantial risk of forfeiture

In some cases, stock may be transferred to an executive with temporary limitations on transferability. This will not cause the stock to be considered subject to a substantial risk of forfeiture. In *Gudmundsson*, the taxpayer received stock subject to limitations imposed by both securities laws and agreements. For a short period of time, the taxpayer could not sell the stock on a public exchange and could transfer it only to a limited number of recipients. Although this affected the marketability of the stock, it was not a permanent restriction on the transferability of the stock. Therefore, the stock was not considered to be restricted stock for tax purposes. [See *Sally Gudmundsson*, 107 AFTR 2d 2011-852 (2nd Cir. 2011).]

Timing of executive's income recognition

When restricted stock is received, the recipient executive recognizes income for federal tax purposes as follows.

Without IRC Section 83(b) election

The restricted stock award results in the recognition of ordinary compensation income in the year the restriction causing the substantial risk of forfeiture lapses. The amount included in compensation income is the excess of the stock's value when the restriction lapses over the amount paid for the stock (if any). Federal income tax and federal employment taxes must be withheld and paid on the amount treated as compensation (Revenue Rulings 67-257, 78-185, and 79-305).

With IRC Section 83(b) election

As explained earlier, an executive who receives restricted stock can make an IRC Section 83(b) election to recognize income on the date the restricted shares are received. Making the election results in the immediate recognition of ordinary compensation income equal to the excess of the stock's value on that date over the amount paid for the stock (if any). Federal income tax and federal employment taxes must be withheld and paid on the amount treated as compensation income. The IRC Section 83(b) election must be made either before the share transfer or within 30 days after the share transfer.

Employer's compensation deduction

Assuming the income related to the transfer of restricted stock is timely reported to the recipient executive on a Form W-2 or 1099 (whichever is required), the employer is allowed a compensation deduction equal to the income included in the executive's income (without regard to what amount, if any, the executive actually reports as income) for the employer's tax year in which or within which the executive's tax year of inclusion ends [IRC Section 83(h) and Regulation 1.83-6(a)(1)]. The employer's failure to withhold FIT or pay Social Security and Medicare taxes or FUTA tax on the compensation income does not preclude the deduction. However, this rule acts only to insulate the employer's deduction. It does not relieve the employer of liability for any federal employment taxes that are due.

If a Form W-2 or 1099 is not timely furnished, the employer's position is less clear. The regulations state that the employer's deduction equals the amount included in the employee's income. In *Venture Funding*, the court found this to mean the corporation can deduct only what it can demonstrate the executive actually included in income [*Venture Funding Ltd*, 110 TC 236 (Tax Ct. 1998)]. However, in *Robinson*, the court held that an employer's deduction should be based on the amount legally required to be included in the employee's income, regardless of the amount actually included or whether a Form W-2 or Form 1099 was issued [*James Robinson*, 92-AFTR 2d 2003-5349 (Fed. Cir. 2003)].

Conclusion

The federal tax rules for restricted stock are fairly straightforward. The major tax planning consideration for the executive is deciding whether or not to make an IRC Section 83(b) election. In many cases, the risks of making the election will be perceived as greater than the potential tax-saving benefit, so tax advisers should be well versed in the area to help counsel executives who are considering making that call.

Chapter 3

Maximizing Tax Benefits for Personal Residence Transactions

Learning objectives

- Identify ways to advise clients on how to make the most of their home ownership experience, with tax issues (including the changes in the Tax Cuts and Jobs Act [TCJA]) in mind.

- Recognize the conditions taxpayers qualify for gain exclusion under IRC Section 121.

Introduction

Under the IRC Section 121 home sale gain exclusion rules, married couples can exclude from federal income tax gains up to $500,000, and singles can exclude gains up to $250,000. The first part of this chapter covers the twists and turns necessary to wring the maximum tax savings out of the home sale gain exclusion rules which are still very helpful to many folks—particularly those who have owned their homes for a long time and those who have benefited from the recent strong bounce back in real estate values in many areas.

This chapter also covers the tax rules that can apply when a residence is sold in a short sale (that is, for less than the outstanding mortgage(s) against the property) or is foreclosed by the lender. Such transactions are still relatively commonplace.

Finally, this chapter covers the confusing tax implications of converting a personal residence into a rental property.

Qualification rules for gain exclusion privilege

IRC Section 121 allows singles to exclude gains up to $250,000, and married couples filing jointly to exclude up to $500,000. The seller need not complete any special tax form to take advantage. As explained later, sales that are wholly or partly taxable are reported on Schedule D. If the sale is partially taxable due to business or rental use, Form 4797 must also be completed to account for all or part of the gain and determine how much is subject to the 25% maximum rate on unrecaptured IRC Section 1250 gains (gain attributable to depreciation deductions).

Key point: The stipulated 25% maximum rate on unrecaptured IRC Section 1250 gains ignores the potential impact of the 3.8% NIIT.

Key point: Proposed tax reform legislation would have tightened the eligibility rules for the IRC Section 121 gain exclusion privilege, but none of the proposed changes made it into the actual TCJA legislation. As a result, the IRC Section 121 gain exclusion remains unchanged.

Ownership and use tests

The primary limitation rule is that the property must have been

- owned as the seller's principal residence for at least two years out of the five-year period ending on the sale date; and
- used as the seller's principal residence for at least two years out of the five-year period ending on the sale date.

Key point: Periods of ownership and use need not overlap.

Knowledge check

1. Under the IRC Section 121 principal residence gain exclusion rules, what happens when the taxpayer's periods of ownership of the property and periods of use of the property as a principal residence do not overlap?

    a. Only overlapping periods of ownership and use count toward passing the two-out-of-five-years ownership and use tests.
    b. It doesn't matter if they overlap or not.
    c. The periods must overlap for sellers who use married filing separate status. For all other sellers, there is no requirement that the periods overlap.
    d. The periods must overlap for joint-filing married couples. For all other sellers, there is no requirement that the periods overlap.

What is a principal residence?

The regulations say all facts and circumstances must be evaluated to determine whether or not a property is the taxpayer's principal residence for gain exclusion purposes. When several residences are occupied during the same year, the general rule is that the principal residence for that particular year is the one where the majority of time is spent during that year. Other relevant factors can include, but are not limited to, the following:

- Where the taxpayer works
- Where family members live
- The address shown on income tax returns, driver's licenses, and auto registration and voter registration cards
- The mailing address for bills and correspondence
- Where bank accounts are maintained
- Where memberships and religious affiliations are maintained [See Regulation 1.121-1(b)(2).]

Example 3-1

Melynda, an unmarried individual, owns one home in New Jersey and other in Arizona. During 2014–2018 (five years), she spends seven months each year in the New Jersey home and the remaining five months in the Arizona home. Melynda then sells both properties on January 1, 2019. Barring unusual circumstances, the New Jersey home is considered her principal residence, and she can claim the gain exclusion privilege only for that property.

Even though Melynda owned and used the Arizona home as a residence for an aggregate of 25 months during the five-year period ending on the sale date, she cannot claim the gain exclusion privilege for that property because it was not her principal residence at any time during the five-year period [Regulation 1.121-1(b)(4), Example 1]. However, see the next example.

The regulations confirm it is possible for two residences to simultaneously pass the gain exclusion ownership and use tests, as illustrated by the following example.

Example 3-2

Milton, an unmarried individual, owns one home in Vermont and another in Florida. During 2015 and 2016, he lives in the Vermont home. During 2017 and 2018, he lives in the Florida home. Under these facts, Milton would qualify for the gain exclusion privilege if either home is sold in 2019, because the two-out-of-five-years ownership and use tests would be passed for both homes. However, if both homes are sold in 2019, Milton cannot claim gain exclusions for both sales. That is prohibited by the anti-recycling rule explained later. [See Regulation 1.121-1(b)(4), Example 2.]

The requirements to (1) own the property for at least two years during the five-year period ending on the sale date, and (2) use the property as a principal residence for at least two years during the same five-year period are completely independent. In other words, periods of ownership and use need not overlap. For this purpose, *two years* means periods aggregating 24 months or 730 days. [See Regulation 1.121-1(c)(1) and (2).]

Example 3-3

Kirsten, a single individual, rents a condo and uses it as her principal residence for all of 2015 and 2016. On January 1, 2017, she purchases the condo and rents it out to others for all of 2017 and 2018. Early in 2019, Kirsten sells the property. Under these facts, Kirsten passes the two-out-five-years ownership and use tests, even though her periods of ownership and use are not concurrent. [See Regulation 1.121-1(c)(4), Example 3.]

In determining whether the two-out-of-five-years use test is passed, only periods during which the property is actually occupied by the taxpayer generally count. However, short temporary absences (such as for vacations) also count as periods of use. This is true even when the property is rented out during those short absences.

Example 3-4

Kris, a single individual, purchases a home on January 1, 2017. He uses it as his principal residence for all of 2017 and 2018. However, he vacations away from the property for two months during both of those years. On February 1, 2019, Kris sells the home.

Under these facts, Kris passes both the ownership and use tests, even though his actual periods of occupancy aggregate to only 21 months (25 months minus 4 months away on vacation). Why? Because short temporary absences count as periods of occupancy, and the regulations specifically indicate that a two-month vacation is a short temporary absence.

So Kris is deemed to have used the property as his principal residence for 25 months during the five-year period ending on the sale date. Kris is, therefore, entitled to a $250,000 gain exclusion. [See Regulation 1.121-1(c)(4), Example 5.]

Variation: The results would be the same if Kris rented out his home during his vacation absences [Regulation 1.121-1(c)(2)].

Gain exclusion rules for married couples

To qualify for the $500,000 joint return exclusion, (1) one or both spouses must pass the ownership test with respect to the property, and (2) both spouses must pass the use test [IRC Section 121(b)(2)(A)]. When only one spouse passes both tests, the maximum gain exclusion is generally only $250,000

[Regulation 1.121-2(a)(3)(ii)]. However, see the later explanation of how the prorated (reduced) gain exclusion privilege can potentially apply to the spouse who fails to pass both tests.

Example 3-5

Fritz and Stella are married after a whirlwind romance that began on a cruise ship. Immediately following the marriage, Fritz sells his valuable home for a $600,000 gain. Fritz had owned and used the home as his principal residence for many years before he met Stella. The couple files a joint return for the year of sale. Unfortunately, they do not qualify for the $500,000 joint return exclusion, because Stella does not pass the use test with respect to the property. Therefore, Fritz and Stella must report a whopping $350,000 taxable gain on their joint return ($600,000 − $250,000). [See Regulation 1.121-2(a)(4), Example 4.]

Strategy: Instead of selling immediately, the couple should live together in Fritz's home for at least two years after their marriage. That way, they will qualify for the full $500,000 joint return exclusion (Fritz will pass the ownership test, and both Fritz and Stella will pass the use test).

When a joint return is filed, it is also possible for the spouses to individually pass the ownership and use tests for two separate residences. In such case, a separate $250,000 exclusion is potentially available to each spouse [IRC Section 121(d)(1)]. Each spouse's eligibility for the $250,000 exclusion is determined separately, as if the couple were unmarried. For this purpose, however, a spouse is considered to individually own a property for any period the property is actually owned by *either* spouse. [See Regulation 1.121-2(a)(3)(ii).]

Example 3-6

Wilma and Fred have a commuter marriage. Wilma works in San Francisco and lives most of the time in the couple's condo there. Fred works in Baltimore and lives in the couple's townhouse there. On some weekends, one spouse flies to the other's city, and they both stay in their abode in that location. Under these facts, the $500,000 joint return exclusion is not available for either home. Why? Because both spouses must pass the use test in order for a residence to qualify for the larger exclusion.

However, separate $250,000 exclusions are potentially available for each residence. Assume both homes have been owned jointly by the couple for five years and that Wilma passes the use test for the San Francisco home, and Fred passes the use test for the Baltimore home.

Under these facts, Wilma would qualify for a $250,000 exclusion if the San Francisco home is sold, and Fred would qualify for a separate $250,000 exclusion if the Baltimore home is sold. [See Regulation 1.121-2(a)(4), Examples 3 and 4.] Because each spouse's eligibility for a $250,000 exclusion is determined separately, the San Francisco and Baltimore homes could be sold within two years of each other (or even in the same year) without violating the anti-recycling rule explained later. In other words, two separate $250,000 exclusions could be claimed in Wilma and Fred's joint return (or on separate returns), even if the two sales are close together in time.

Example 3-6 (continued)

Key point: If one spouse does not fully use his or her $250,000 exclusion, the other spouse cannot use the "leftover" exclusion amount so shelter gain from that person's home sale.

Variation: The results would be the same even if Fred separately owns the San Francisco home and Wilma separately owns the Baltimore home. Why? Because, under the joint return rules, Wilma is considered to own any home actually owned by Fred, and Fred is considered to own any home actually owned by Wilma [Regulation 1.121-2(a)(3)(ii)]. That means Wilma would still pass the ownership and use tests for the San Francisco home, and Fred would still pass the ownership and use tests for the Baltimore home.

Knowledge check

2. Can getting married allow the taxpayer to qualify for the $500,000 joint return gain exclusion though the taxpayer's home was owned prior to the marriage?

    a. Yes, if at least one spouse passes the use test.
    b. Yes, if a special election is made prior to getting married.
    c. Yes, it at least one spouse passes the ownership test.
    d. Only if the couple has been married for at least five years as of the sale date.

3. When both spouses qualify for separate $250,000 gain exclusions, what is the maximum amount of one spouse's "leftover" exclusion that can be used to shelter gain from the other spouse's home?

    a. $250,000.
    b. $125,000.
    c. $100,000.
    d. $0.

Special exception for unmarried surviving spouses may permit larger $500,000 gain exclusion

An unmarried individual can potentially exclude from federal income taxation up to $250,000 of gain from selling a principal residence under IRC Section 121. Married joint filers can potentially exclude up to $500,000. However, if your client is a surviving spouse, he or she is not allowed to file a joint return for years after the year in which the spouse dies (unless your client remarries). Before legislation enacted in 2007 fixed this problem, an unmarried surviving spouse could not take advantage of the larger $500,000 home sale gain exclusion if he or she sold a principal residence in a year after the year when the spouse died. Instead, the surviving spouse was limited to the smaller $250,000 exclusion.

Thankfully, the 2007 legislation corrected this unfair situation. Therefore, an unmarried surviving spouse can now claim the larger $500,000 gain exclusion for a principal residence sale that occurs within two years after the spouse's death, assuming all the other requirements for the $500,000 exclusion were met immediately before that person died. [See IRC Section 121(b)(4), as amended.]

Key point: The two-year eligibility period for the larger exclusion begins on the date of the deceased spouse's death. Therefore, a sale that occurs in the second calendar year following the year of death but more than 24 months after the deceased spouse's date of death will not qualify for the larger $500,000 gain exclusion.

Anti-recycling rule

As mentioned earlier, the other big qualification rule for the home sale gain exclusion privilege goes like this. The exclusion is generally available only when the taxpayer has not excluded an earlier gain within the two-year period ending on the date of the later sale [IRC Section 121(b)(3)]. In other words, the gain exclusion privilege generally cannot be "recycled" until two years have passed since it was last used.

The $500,000 joint return exclusion is available only when neither spouse excluded a gain from an earlier sale within the two-year period [IRC Section 121(b)(2)(A)(iii)]. If one spouse did, and the other did not, the gain exclusion is generally limited to $250,000.

All the discussion earlier in this section assumes the anti-recycling rule is met. If the rule is violated, the taxpayer is ineligible to claim a gain exclusion unless

1. a prorated (reduced) gain exclusion is available, under rules explained later; or
2. the taxpayer "elects out" of the gain exclusion privilege for the earlier sale, under rules explained later.

 Example 3-7

Murph, a single individual, sold his original principal residence on July 1, 2017, and excluded the gain. Before selling that home, Murph purchased another property and began using it as his new principal residence on January 1, 2017 (six months earlier). Murph then decides to sell the latest home on March 1, 2019, thinking he will qualify for the gain exclusion break on that sale too.

Although Murph passes the two-out-of-five-years ownership and use tests with flying colors, he violates the anti-recycling rule. Therefore, Murph is ineligible to exclude any gain from his 2019 sale, unless one of the two circumstances listed immediately above applies. [See Regulation 1.121-2(b).]

Prorated (reduced) gain exclusion loophole for "premature" sales

What happens when the taxpayer fails to meet the basic gain exclusion timing requirements? For example, the taxpayer might sell the home for a healthy profit after living there only 18 months instead of the required two years. Or the taxpayer might sell his or her current home less than two years after excluding gain from the sale of a previous residence. Must the taxpayer pay tax on the entire gain when he or she makes such a "premature" sale? Not necessarily. Under the regulations, taxpayers can often avoid any federal tax by claiming a prorated (reduced) gain exclusion (a fraction of the $250,000 or

$500,000 amount that would ordinarily apply). However, when the seller is ineligible for this prorated exclusion loophole, the entire profit is taxed. Fortunately, the regulations make it pretty easy to qualify for the prorated gain exclusion, as you are about to see.

Assuming the seller is eligible (more on that later), the prorated gain exclusion amount equals the full $250,000 or $500,000 figure (whichever would otherwise apply) multiplied by a fraction. The numerator is the shorter of (1) the aggregate period of time the property is owned and used as the principal residence during the five-year period ending on the sale date, or (2) the period between the last sale for which an exclusion was claimed and the sale date for the home currently being sold. The denominator is two years, or the equivalent in months or days. [See IRC Section 121(c)(1) and Regulation 1.121-3(g).]

Example 3-8

Chuck and Donna are married and file jointly. They owned and used a home as their principal residence for 11 months. Chuck and Donna are entitled to a prorated gain exclusion of $229,167 on their joint return ($500,000 × 11 ÷ 24). That should be more than enough to avoid any federal tax hit from prematurely selling their home.

Example 3-9

Draco is unmarried. He sold his previous home 15 months ago and excluded the gain. Now he is about to sell his current home, which he has owned and used as his principal residence for 21 months. He bought the current property and occupied it for six months before selling the previous home. Draco is entitled to a prorated gain exclusion of $156,250 ($250,000 × 15 ÷ 24). That should be more than enough to avoid any federal tax bill from prematurely selling his current home. (The gain exclusion that Draco claimed on the sale of his previous home is completely unaffected by all this.)

When the seller qualifies for the prorated exclusion, it will almost certainly be big enough to shelter the entire gain from making a premature sale. However, the prorated exclusion loophole is available only when the premature sale is primarily due to

- a change of place of employment,
- health reasons, or
- unforeseen circumstances.

Premature sale due to employment change

Under the regulations, the taxpayer is eligible for the prorated gain exclusion privilege whenever a premature home sale is primarily due to a change in place of employment for any qualified individual. *Qualified individual* means the taxpayer, his spouse, any co-owner of the home, or any other person whose main residence is within the taxpayer's household. [See Regulation 1.121-3(c).]

A premature sale will automatically be considered primarily due to a change in place of employment if any qualified individual passes the following distance test. The new place of employment or self-employment must be at least 50 miles farther away from the former residence (the property that is being sold) than was the former place of employment or self-employment from the former residence.

 Example 3-10

Susan runs her sole proprietorship business exclusively out of her home. She decides to sell the home, which she has owned and used as her principal residence for only 19 months. Susan then buys a new home 65 miles away. She again runs her business exclusively out of the new home.

Under these facts, Susan passes the 50-mile test. Why? Because her new place of self-employment (the new house) is 65 miles farther away from her former home than was her old place of self-employment (the old house which was, obviously, zero miles away from itself).

Therefore, Susan automatically qualifies for the prorated gain exclusion. If she is married, the prorated exclusion is $395,833 ($500,000 × 19 ÷ 24). If she is single, the prorated exclusion is $197,917 ($250,000 × 19 ÷ 24). Susan will almost certainly be able to avoid any federal tax bill from prematurely selling her home. Well, not quite. She will be taxed on any gain attributable to depreciation from post-5/6/97 business or rental usage of her home, as explained later.

 Example 3-11

Assume the same basic facts as in example 3-10, except this time let us say Susan's husband was the self-employed person who worked out of the home. Because he is a qualified individual who passes the 50-mile test, Susan automatically qualifies for the prorated gain exclusion privilege on her joint return. The prorated exclusion amount is $395,833 ($500,000 × 19 ÷ 24).

What happens when no qualified individual passes the 50-mile test? The taxpayer is still eligible for the prorated gain exclusion break if the facts and circumstances show his premature home sale was primarily due to a qualified individual's change in place of employment.

 Example 3-12

Dante is married and files jointly with his wife, Clara. She is an emergency room physician. Because Clara must live close to the hospital where she works, the couple's home is only three miles away. Now assume Clara becomes employed by a different hospital. As a result, the home is sold. However, it was owned and used as the principal residence for only 22 months. Dante and Clara then rent a townhouse that is only five miles away from her new job location. Assume her new job is 42 miles away from the old residence.

Example 3-12 (continued)

Dante and Clara fail the 50-mile test, because Clara's new job is only 39 miles farther away from the old home than was her old job (42 miles versus three miles). However, due to the nature of Clara's work, she must live close to her place of employment. In this case, the facts and circumstances clearly show the premature sale of the former home was primarily due to a change in the place of Clara's employment.

Therefore, Dante and Clara are eligible for the prorated gain exclusion privilege on their joint return. The prorated exclusion amount is $458,333 ($500,000 × 22 ÷ 24). [See Regulation 1.121-3(c)(4), Example 4.]

Key point: When the 50-mile test cannot be passed, obtain documentation showing the premature home sale was, nevertheless, primarily due to a qualified individual's change in place of employment (assuming the facts so indicate). That should preserve the client's eligibility for the prorated gain exclusion loophole.

Premature sale due to health reasons

Under the regulations, the home seller is also eligible for the prorated gain exclusion privilege whenever a premature sale is primarily due to health reasons. This test is passed whenever the seller must move to

- obtain, provide, or facilitate the diagnosis, cure, mitigation, or treatment of disease, illness, or injury of a qualified individual; or
- obtain or provide medical or personal care for a qualified individual who suffers from a disease, illness, or injury.

For this purpose, *qualified individual* means (1) the taxpayer, (2) his or her spouse, (3) any co-owner of the home, or (4) any person whose principal residence is within the taxpayer's household. In addition, almost any close relative of a person listed in (1)–(4) also counts as a qualified individual. Finally, any descendent of the taxpayer's grandparent (such as a first cousin) also counts as a qualified individual. [See Regulation 1.121-3(f)(1)-(5).]

A premature sale will automatically be considered primarily for health reasons whenever a doctor recommends a change of residence for reasons of a qualified individual's health (meaning to obtain, provide, or facilitate, as previously explained). Otherwise, the facts and circumstances must indicate that the premature sale was primarily for reasons of a qualified individual's health.

The prorated gain exclusion cannot be claimed for a premature sale that is merely beneficial to the general health or well-being of a qualified individual. [See Regulation 1.121-3(d).]

Key point: Whenever possible, the seller should obtain a doctor's recommendation in writing to prove the seller is entitled to the prorated gain exclusion, because the premature sale was primarily for reasons of a qualified individual's health. The doctor's note should be kept with the seller's tax records.

Premature sale due to other unforeseen circumstances

Regulation 1.121-3(e) provides that, in general, a premature sale is by reason of unforeseen circumstances if the primary reason for the sale is the occurrence of an event that the taxpayer could not have reasonably anticipated before purchasing and occupying the residence.

However, a premature sale that is primarily due to a preference for a difference residence or an improvement in financial circumstances will not be considered to be by reason of unforeseen circumstances, unless the safe-harbor rule subsequently explained applies. [See Regulation 1.121-3(e)(1) and (e)(4), Examples 7, 8, and 10.]

Under a regulatory safe-harbor rule, a premature sale will automatically be deemed to be by reason of unforeseen circumstances if any of the following events occur during the taxpayer's ownership and use of the property as the taxpayer's principal residence:

- Involuntary conversion of the residence
- A natural or manmade disaster or acts of war or terrorism resulting in a casualty to the residence
- Death of a qualified individual
- A qualified individual's cessation of employment making him or her eligible for unemployment compensation
- A qualified individual's change in employment or self-employment status that results in the taxpayer's inability to pay housing costs and reasonable basic living expenses for the taxpayer's household
- A qualified individual's divorce or legal separation under a decree of divorce or separate maintenance
- Multiple births resulting from a single pregnancy of a qualified individual

For purposes of this safe-harbor rule, a qualifying individual is defined by Regulation 1.121-3(f) as (1) the taxpayer, (2) taxpayer's spouse, (3) a co-owner of the residence in question, or (4) a person whose principal place of abode is in the same household as the taxpayer.

Key point: When none of the preceding safe-harbor events occur, the taxpayer can still qualify for the reduced gain exclusion privilege if the facts and circumstances indicate the primary reason for the premature home sale was the occurrence of an event that the taxpayer could not have reasonably anticipated before purchasing and occupying the residence. The regulations include three examples of non-safe-harbor situations that seem to indicate the IRS will be fairly liberal in this area. [See Regulation 1.121-3(e)(4), Examples 4, 6, and 9.]

Key point: The IRS can also designate other events as unforeseen circumstances in published guidance of general applicability (such as revenue rulings) or in rulings addressed to specific taxpayers (such as private letter rulings). In the latter case, however, the guidance applies only to the specific taxpayers to whom the guidance is directed. [See Regulation 1.121-3(e)(3).]

Premature sales in other situations

As explained earlier, when the taxpayer's premature sale does not qualify for any of the regulatory safe-harbor rules previously explained, the reduced gain exclusion break can still be claimed if the taxpayer can establish, based on facts and circumstances, that the primary reason for the premature sale was one of the three statutory circumstances [Regulation 1.121-3(b)].

Factors that may be relevant in determining the primary reason for a premature sale include, but are not limited to, the following [Regulation 1.121-3(b)]:

- Whether the premature sale and the circumstances giving rise to the sale are proximate in time
- A material change in the suitability of the property as the taxpayer's principal residence
- A material change in the taxpayer's financial ability to maintain the property
- Whether the taxpayer actually uses the property as a residence during the taxpayer's ownership period
- Whether the circumstances giving rise to the premature sale were reasonably foreseeable when the taxpayer began using the property as a principal residence
- Whether the circumstances giving rise to the premature sale actually occurred during the period when the taxpayer owned and used the property as a principal residence

Excluding gain from sale of land next to residence

The IRC Section 121 regulations also allow taxpayers to use the gain exclusion break to shelter profit from selling vacant land next to the principal residence. The taxpayer can even sell the parcel with the home and the surrounding vacant land in completely separate transactions. Naturally, there are some ground rules:

- The vacant land must be sold within two years before or after the sale of the parcel containing the house. (Separate sales of the parcel containing the house and the adjacent vacant land within this four-year window will not be considered to violate the anti-recycling rule.)
- The sale of the parcel containing the house must itself qualify for the gain exclusion.
- The vacant land must be adjacent to the parcel containing the house.
- The vacant land must have been owned and used as part of the taxpayer's principal residence, and the two-out-of-five-years ownership and use tests must be passed for the vacant land.

When all these tests are passed, the seller can use his or her gain exclusion privilege to avoid any federal tax on up to $250,000—or $500,000 for a joint filer—of combined profits from selling the parcel containing the house and the adjacent vacant land. [See Regulation 1.121-1(b)(3).]

For instance, an example in the regulations says the taxpayer can sell a one-acre parcel with his or her home in one transaction and a 29-acre adjacent parcel of vacant land in a separate transaction and use his or her gain exclusion to shelter the combined profits from the two sales. Presumably, the same favorable result would apply if the vacant land is sold in several separate transactions.

What happens when the adjacent vacant land is sold in advance of the parcel containing the house? Good question. If the parcel with the house is not sold until after the due date of the return for the year of the land sale, the seller must report the land sale gain on his return for that year. Then, after the parcel containing the residence is sold, the seller can file an amended return to exclude the earlier land sale gain. The seller generally has three years from the date the original return for the year of the land sale is filed to file an amended return (assuming the original return was filed on time). (See IRC Sections 6511 and 6513.)

Knowledge check

4. When the taxpayer sells vacant land adjacent to his or her principal residence and then later sells the parcel containing the residence in a separate transaction, what is the maximum combined amount of gain from the two sales that can be excluded under the principal residence gain exclusion privilege?

    a. $250,000, if the taxpayer is unmarried or $500,000 on a joint return.
    b. $500,000, if the taxpayer is unmarried or $1m on a joint return.
    c. Gain from selling the land can never be sheltered with the IRC Section 121 exclusion.
    d. Under a special rule, an additional $100,000 of gain from the land sale can be sheltered under the IRC Section 121 gain exclusion rule if the land was acquired in the same transaction as the residence.

Excluding gains in marriage and divorce situations

Home sales will often occur in both marriage and divorce situations. Of course, the IRC Section 121 home sale gain exclusion break can come in very handy when an appreciated principal residence is put on the block.

Sale after marriage

Say a couple gets married. They each own separate residences from their single days. After the marriage, the pair files jointly. In this scenario, it is possible for each spouse to individually pass the ownership and use tests for their respective residences. Each spouse can then claim a separate $250,000 exclusion on the couple's joint return [IRC Section 121(d)(1)]. Put another way, each spouse's eligibility for a separate $250,000 exclusion is determined independently, as if the couple were still unmarried. [See Regulation 1.121-2(a)(3)(ii).]

 Example 3-13

Jack and Julie get married and decide to move into Jack's home. Neither party had lived in the other's home before the marriage. Immediately after the marriage, Julie sells her home. The couple can exclude up to $250,000 of gain from that sale on their joint return, provided Julie (1) owned and used the property as her principal residence for at least two years out of the five-year period ending on the sale date, and (2) did not exclude gain from any earlier sale within the preceding two years.

The couple may also decide to sell Jack' home. Once again, up to $250,000 of gain can also be excluded on the couple's joint return, assuming Jack meets the same requirements. It does not matter if the sale of Jack's home occurs within two years of the sale of Julie's home.

Variation: Assume the sale of Jack's home would trigger a $450,000 gain. In that case, Jack and Julie should (1) live together in Jack's home for at least two years, and (2) make sure at least two years have elapsed since the sale of Julie's property. Then the couple can sell Jack's home and claim the full $500,000 joint return exclusion. [See Regulation 1.121-2(a)(4), Example 3.]

Sale before divorce

Say a soon-to-be-divorced couple sells their principal residence. Assume they are still legally married as of the end of the year of sale because their divorce is not yet final. In this scenario, the splitting couple can shelter up to $500,000 of home sale profit in two different ways.

First, the couple could file a *joint return* for the year of sale. Assuming they meet the basic home sale gain exclusion timing requirements, they can claim the maximum $500,000 exclusion on their joint return.

Alternatively, the couple could file *separate returns* for the year of sale, using married filing separate status. Assuming the home is owned jointly or as community property, each spouse can then exclude up to $250,000 of his or her share of the gain on his or her separate return. To qualify for two separate $250,000 exclusions, each spouse must have (1) owned his or her part of the property for at least two years during the five-year period ending on the sale date, and (2) used the home as his or her principal residence for at least two years during that five-year period. [See IRC Section 121(a) and (b) and Regulation 1.121-2(a).]

Key point: In most cases, the preceding favorable rules will allow the splitting couple to convert their home equity into tax-free cash. They can generally divide up that cash any way they choose without any further federal tax consequences and go their separate ways [IRC Section 1041(a)].

Sale in year of divorce or later

When a couple is divorced as of the end of the year in which their principal residence is sold, they are considered divorced for that entire year. Therefore, they will be unable to file jointly for the year of sale. The same is true, of course, when the sale occurs after the year of divorce. Here is the home sale gain exclusion drill in these situations.

Say ex-spouse A winds up with sole ownership of the residence, which was formerly owned solely by ex-spouse B, in a tax-free divorce-related transfer [under IRC Section 1041(a)]. Under these facts, A is allowed to count B's period of ownership for purposes of passing the two-out-of-five-years ownership test when A eventually sells the property [IRC Section 121(d)(3) and Regulation 1.121-4(b)(1)]. A's maximum gain exclusion will be $250,000, because A is now single. However, if A remarries and lives in the home with the new spouse for at least two years before selling, A can qualify for the larger $500,000 joint return exclusion.

Now, let us say ex-spouse A winds up owning some percentage of the home, and ex-spouse B winds up owning the rest. When the home is later sold, both A and B can exclude $250,000 of their respective shares of the gain, provided each person (1) owned his or her part of the home for at least two years during the five-year period ending on the sale date, and (2) used the home as his or her principal residence for at least two years during that same five-year period. [See IRC Section 121(a) and (b)(1).]

Key point: Under the preceding rules, both ex-spouses will typically qualify for separate $250,000 exclusions when the home is sold soon after the divorce. However, when the property remains unsold for some time, the ex-spouse who no longer resides there will eventually fail the two-out-of-five-years use test and become ineligible for the gain exclusion privilege. Please keep reading for how to avoid that outcome.

When "nonresident ex" continues to own home long after divorce

In many cases, the ex-spouses will continue to co-own the former marital abode for a lengthy period after the divorce. Obviously, however, only one ex-spouse will continue to live in the home. After three years of being out of the house, the "nonresident ex" will fail the two-out-of-five-years use test. That means when the home is finally sold, the nonresident ex's share of the gain will be fully taxable. This is not good when your client is the nonresident ex. However, this undesirable outcome can be easily prevented with some advance planning.

Specifically, your client's divorce papers should stipulate that, as a condition of the divorce agreement, the client's ex-spouse is allowed to continue to occupy the home for as long as he or she wants, or until the kids reach a certain age, or for a specified number of years, or whatever the divorcing couple can agree on. At that point, the home can either be put up for sale with the proceeds split per the divorce agreement, or one ex-spouse can buy out the other's share for its current fair market value (FMV) at that time.

This arrangement allows the nonresident ex (your client in our scenario) to receive "credit" for the other party's continued use of the property as that person's principal residence. So when the home is finally sold, the nonresident ex will still pass the two-out-of-five-years use test and thereby qualify for the $250,000 gain exclusion privilege. [See Regulation 1.121-4(b)(2).]

The same strategy works when your client is the nonresident ex and he or she winds up with complete ownership of the home, and the client's ex-spouse continues to live there. Making the ex-spouse's continued residence in the home a condition of the divorce agreement ensures that your client (the nonresident ex) will still qualify for the $250,000 gain exclusion when the home is eventually sold.

 Example 3-14

Doug and Anne are divorced in 2013. Each party retained 50% ownership of the former marital abode. As a specific condition of the divorce agreement, the decree stipulated that Anne is allowed to continue to reside in the home for up to six years (until the youngest child reaches age 18). Then Anne must either buy out Doug's 50% interest (based on market value at that time) or cooperate in selling the home.

Assume the property is indeed sold six years after the divorce. With respect to his 50% interest, Doug still passes the two-out-of-five-years ownership and use tests even though he has not lived in the home for six years. Why? Because he made sure the divorce decree included the magic words (the provision specifically permitting Anne to continue to reside in the home as a condition of the divorce settlement). Therefore, Doug is allowed to count Anne's continued use of the property as her principal residence as continued use by him. That means Doug qualifies for the $250,000 gain exclusion privilege, which he can use to shelter his share of the home sale profit.

Of course, Anne also passes the ownership and use tests. So, she also qualifies for a separate $250,000 exclusion, assuming she remains single.

Example 3-14 (continued)

Variation: Now assume Anne remarries. She and her new husband live in the home for at least two years before the sale date. With respect to her share of the gain, Anne can qualify for the larger $500,000 joint-filer exclusion by filing a joint return with her new husband for the year of sale. With respect to his share of the gain, Doug still qualifies for a $250,000 exclusion, as previously explained.

Key point: If Doug's attorney fails to include the magic words in the divorce decree, Doug will be taxed on his share of the home sale gain.

 Example 3-15

Assume the same basic facts as the previous example, except this time assume Doug has 100% ownership of the former marital abode after the divorce. As a specific condition of the divorce agreement, the decree stipulates that Anne is permitted to continue to reside in the home for up to six years. After that, Doug can sell the home at any time by giving Anne three months' notice of his intent to sell.

Assume the property is sold six years and three months after the divorce. Under these facts, Doug still passes the two-out-of-five-years ownership and use tests even though he has not lived in the home for more than six years. So, Doug qualifies for the $250,000 gain exclusion privilege, which he can use to shelter his home sale profit.

Key point: If Doug's attorney fails to include the magic words in the decree, Doug will be taxed on his entire home sale gain.

Knowledge check

5. When an ex-spouse continues to own all or part of the former marital abode, but no longer lives there, what happens to his gain exclusion privilege with respect to that property?

   a. It automatically terminates on the day the divorce becomes final.
   b. He automatically continues to be eligible for the $250,000 exclusion with respect to his share of the gain whenever the home is sold.
   c. It automatically terminates three years after he or she moves out of the house, unless proper language is included in the divorce papers.
   d. It automatically terminates three years after he moves out of the house, unless proper language is included in the divorce papers.

"Electing out" of gain exclusion privilege

The home seller always has the option of "electing out" of the gain exclusion rules and reporting the home sale profit as a taxable gain [IRC Section 121(f)]. The "election out" is made by reporting an otherwise excludable gain in the year-of-sale return. No further action is required. [See Regulation 1.121-4(g).]

In addition, the seller can retroactively make an "election out" or revoke an earlier "election out" by filing an amended return at any time within the three-year period beginning with the filing deadline for the year-of-sale return (without regard to extensions). [See Regulation 1.121-4(g).]

An obvious circumstance where the "election out" can really pay off is when the taxpayer makes two principal residence sales within a two-year period, with the second sale producing a larger gain.

 Example 3-16

Claudia, a single individual, owns a home in Dallas and another in Beaver Creek, Colorado. She used the Beaver Creek property as her principal residence in 2015 and 2016, and she used the Dallas home as her principal residence in 2017 and 2018. On January 1, 2019, Claudia sells the Dallas property for a $50,000 gain and moves into a new home in Austin, Texas. On July 15, 2019, Claudia sells the Beaver Creek home for a $250,000 gain.

She meets the two-out-of-five-years ownership and use tests for both properties. However, the Beaver Creek property is sold less than two years after the Dallas sale. If Claudia claims the gain exclusion privilege for the Dallas sale, she will be prohibited from claiming any exclusion for the Beaver Creek sale (because that would violate the anti-recycling rule explained earlier).

Under these facts, Claudia should "elect out" of the gain exclusion privilege for the Dallas sale. She can then exclude the entire $250,000 gain from the Beaver Creek sale.

Key point: The "election out" is made by simply reporting the $50,000 profit from the Dallas sale on Claudia's 2019 Schedule D.

Knowledge check

6. Why would anyone choose to "elect out" of the principal residence gain exclusion privilege?

   a. They would not.
   b. To be eligible to exclude a bigger gain from a later sale.
   c. To exclude home price appreciation from the owner's taxable estate.
   d. To avoid divorce-related complications.

Sale of former principal residence "freed up" suspended PALs from rental period even though gain on sale was excluded

In Chief Counsel Advice (CCA) 201428008, the IRS addressed the following scenario. The taxpayer bought a home that he or she owned and used as his or her principal residence for two years. The taxpayer then converted the property into a rental. The rental comprised his or her only passive activity. During the time that the former principal residence was rented out, it produced tax losses that were suspended under the passive activity loss (PAL) rules because the taxpayer had no passive income. After renting out the property for fewer than three years, it was sold to an unrelated third party for a gain. The taxpayer excluded the gain in accordance with IRC Section 121(a). The two questions in this scenario were (1) whether the taxpayer had to reduce his suspended PALs by the amount of gain that was excluded under the IRC Section 121 rules; and (2) whether the sale of the property counted as a complete taxable disposition that would "free up" the suspended PALs from the period when the property was rented out. In CCA 201428008, the IRS gave taxpayer-friendly answers to both questions as explained in the following sections.

Passive activity loss basics

Under IRC Section 469, PALs can generally be deducted only to the extent the taxpayer has passive income or gains. Disallowed PALs are suspended and carried forward to future tax years and are subject to the same limitation in those years. Suspended PALs are "freed up" when there is either (1) sufficient passive income; or (2) a fully taxable disposition of the activity that produced the suspended PALs.

Principal residence gain exclusion basics

As explained earlier in this chapter, IRC Section 121 allows a taxpayer to exclude gain resulting from the sale of a property that has been owned and used as a principal residence for periods aggregating two or more years during the five-year period ending on the sale date. Unmarried taxpayers can exclude up to $250,000 of gain. Married couples can exclude up to $500,000 of gain.

Taxpayer-friendly conclusions from the IRS

The IRS concluded that the home sale gain in this case did not reduce the taxpayer's suspended PALs, because the gain was not passive in nature. Instead, it was attributable to the sale of a principal residence, which is a personal-use asset rather than a passive rental activity asset.

The IRS also concluded that the sale of the former principal residence to the unrelated third party counted as a complete taxable disposition of the property for purposes of "freeing up" the suspended PALs from the period when it was rented out. The IRS noted that IRC Section 121 is an exclusion provision for gain realized under IRC Section 1001(a) and recognized under IRC Section 1001(c), as opposed to a non-recognition provision. (IRC Section 1031 is an example of a non-recognition provision.) Because the gain on the sale of the property was recognized, the sale counted as a complete taxable disposition under IRC Section 469(g)(1)(A), even though the gain was ultimately excluded under the IRC Section 121 rules. Therefore, the sale of the property freed up the suspended PALs from the period when the property was rented.

Understanding the tax implications of personal residence short sales and foreclosures

You may have some clients who borrowed heavily to buy in at the top of the local real estate market. Or you may have some who overindulged on home equity loans while prices were still increasing. In either case, a client can wind up with mortgage debt in excess of the current value of the home. That is bad enough, but if the client has to sell, he or she might face income taxes too. Then again, maybe not, as you will see later in this section.

Short sales involving recourse debt

Real estate pros call a sale where the mortgage debt exceeds the net sale price (after subtracting commissions and other costs) a short sale. We will adopt that terminology here. The easiest way to explain the tax implications of a personal residence short sale is with some examples.

Example 3-17

Your client Frances paid $190,000 for a residence that she could currently sell for $250,000. However, the first and second recourse mortgages against the property total $280,000. If Frances sells, she will have a taxable gain of $60,000. Why? Because the sale price exceeds the property's tax basis ($250,000 sale price − $190,000 basis = $60,000 gain). Will the IRS cut her any slack because she is still $30,000 in the red ($280,000 of debt compared to $250,000 sale price)? Nope. The sad truth is that you can have a tax gain without actually having any cash to show for it. Recourse mortgage debt does not affect the gain or loss calculation.

The good news is that Frances can probably exclude the $60,000 gain for federal income tax purposes—thanks to the IRC Section 121 home sale gain exclusion break explained earlier in this chapter. An unmarried person can exclude gain of up to $250,000 while married joint filers can exclude up to $500,000. Assuming Frances qualifies for the exclusion, the $60,000 gain won't trigger any federal income tax bill. Depending on her state of residence, there may or may not be a state income tax bill.

Of course, it is also possible to have a short sale for less than what was paid for the property.

Example 3-18

Your client Walt paid $310,000 for a residence that he could now sell for only $250,000. The first and second mortgages recourse against the property total $280,000. Walt will have a $60,000 loss if he sells ($250,000 sale price − $310,000 basis = $60,000 loss). Does the IRS allow him to write off his loss? Sorry, but no. You can claim a tax loss only on investment property. A loss on a personal residence is generally considered a non-deductible personal expense. In most states, the same principle applies for state income tax purposes.

The next question is what happens with the $30,000 that is still owed to the mortgage lender in both of the preceding examples ($280,000 of debt versus $250,000 sale price)? Usually, the lender will not give your client any relief. He or she will have to pay off the $30,000, and you will not get any tax deductions for doing so.

However, if the lender decides to forgive some or all of the unpaid $30,000, the forgiven amount constitutes cancellation of debt (COD) income for federal income tax purposes.

Short sales involving nonrecourse debt

You might encounter a short sale where the mortgage loan is nonrecourse. In this case, the lender cannot go after the borrower for any deficiency (negative difference between the sale price and the mortgage loan balance). Nevertheless, the lender agrees to go along with the deal to collect what can be collected now, before the property's value declines any further.

When property subject to a nonrecourse loan is sold in a short sale, the transaction is apparently treated for federal income tax purposes as a sale for proceeds equal to the nonrecourse loan balance. The actual sale price is apparently irrelevant. [See *Tufts*, AFTR 2d 83-1132, Supreme Court (1983).]

There cannot be any COD income, because the borrower's nonrecourse mortgage obligation is deemed to be fully satisfied in the deal (that is, the lender's only remedy against the borrower is to take control of the property, and the lender gives up that right by agreeing to the short sale). Therefore, on the borrower's side of the deal, the short sale can result only in straightforward gain or loss. A tax gain will be triggered if the nonrecourse loan balance exceeds the property's basis. However, with a principal residence loan, the borrower can often exclude the entire gain under the IRC Section 121 home sale gain exclusion rules. If the property's basis exceeds the nonrecourse loan balance, the short sale will trigger a non-deductible loss in the case of a personal residence. In the case of a business or investment property, the loss will be a tax-favored IRC Section 1231 loss.

Tax rules for cancellation of debt income

The general rule says that COD income is a taxable item [IRC Section 61(a)(12)]. For the year COD occurs, the lender is supposed to report the income amount to the borrower (and to the IRS) on Form 1099-C (Cancellation of Debt). As stated earlier, the borrower generally must include the amount as income on that year's Form 1040. However, IRC Section 108 provides several exceptions to the general rule that COD income is taxable. The IRC Section 108 exceptions most likely to apply to personal residence mortgage debt are briefly explained in the following sections.

Bankruptcy exception

If the borrower is in bankruptcy proceedings when COD occurs, it is entirely excluded from taxation. In other words, it is tax-free. [See IRC Section 108(a)(1)(A).]

Insolvency exception

If the borrower is insolvent (meaning with debts in excess of assets), the COD income is entirely excluded from taxation as long as the borrower is still insolvent after the COD occurs. On the other hand, if the COD causes the borrower to become solvent, part of the COD income is taxable (to the extent it causes solvency), and the rest is tax-free. [See IRC Section 108(a)(1)(B).]

Deductible interest exception

To the extent COD income consists of unpaid mortgage interest added to the loan principal and then forgiven, the amount of COD income that consists of forgiven interest that the borrower could have deducted if he or she had actually paid it is tax-free. [See IRC Section 108(e)(2).]

Seller-financed debt exception

If COD income is from forgiven seller-financed debt (in other words, mortgage debt that was owed to the previous owner of the property), it is tax-free. However, the tax-free amount is then subtracted from the basis of the home. If the client later sells the property for a gain, the gain will be that much bigger. As mentioned earlier, however, the client can probably exclude the gain under the IRC Section 121 home sale gain exclusion rules. [See IRC Section 108(e)(5).]

Principal residence mortgage debt exception

This one is the most likely candidate to help your homeowner clients for COD that occurs in 2007–2017 (or later year if this break is extended). It is explained later in this section.

Key point: COD income does not qualify for the IRC Section 121 home sale gain exclusion. This fact was confirmed in a real-life case involving a personal residence short sale. See *Gale, Robert G.* (TC Summary Opinion 2006-152). Therefore, COD income from a principal residence mortgage will be taxable unless an IRC Section 108 exception applies.

Foreclosures

Up until now, this discussion has dealt only with short sales where the home is sold to a third party. But what happens if the mortgage lender forecloses?

A foreclosure occurs when a mortgage borrower defaults and the mortgage lender seizes the mortgaged property, to sell it before things get worse.

Deed-in-lieu-of-foreclosure

Sometimes the borrower and lender will mutually agree on a deed-in-lieu-of-foreclosure transaction. This is a voluntary deal on both sides, and it can be beneficial for both sides, because the legal costs of a full-fledged foreclosure are avoided. For the borrower, the tax consequences of a deed in lieu transaction and a regular foreclosure are the same.

More than one mortgage

When there are several mortgages against a property, any of the mortgage lenders can potentially initiate foreclosure proceedings.

 Example 3-19

Stuart's principal residence is burdened by a $300,000 first mortgage and a $100,000 home equity loan (second mortgage). Stuart is current on the first but has stopped paying the second. The second mortgage lender can initiate foreclosure proceedings, even though Stuart is current on the first mortgage.

In foreclosure, the second mortgage lender's rights are generally the same as the first mortgage lender's rights, with one big difference—the first mortgage generally must be paid in full before the second mortgage lender can collect anything. The two lenders may cooperate as they attempt to protect their respective interests. For example, the first mortgage lender could offer to buy the second mortgage (probably for less than the outstanding principal) and try to work things out with the borrower. If that effort fails, the first mortgage lender, who now owns both loans, could foreclose later on.

Recourse versus nonrecourse mortgages

The foreclosure transaction is not necessarily the end of the story if the mortgage is a recourse loan. With a recourse mortgage, the lender can pursue the borrower for any negative difference (deficiency) between the foreclosure sale proceeds and the loan balance plus foreclosure costs. It can potentially take many months, or even several years, before the borrower finally learns his fate.

In contrast, when a mortgage is a nonrecourse loan, the lender's only remedy is to seize the property and sell it. If there is a deficiency, it is the lender's problem, because the lender cannot go after the borrower to collect the deficiency.

In some states, first mortgages taken out to acquire principal residences are nonrecourse, but second mortgages are recourse. In this scenario, the second mortgage lender can initiate foreclosure proceedings and pursue the borrower for any deficiency on the second, but the first mortgage lender cannot pursue the borrower for any deficiency on the first.

Federal income tax impact of foreclosure on borrower

For the borrower, the most important variable in determining the federal income tax consequences of a foreclosure transaction (or deed in lieu of foreclosure transaction) is whether the mortgage is recourse or nonrecourse.

In the case of a recourse mortgage, the other important variable for the borrower is whether the foreclosed home is worth more or less than the loan balance.

In the case of a nonrecourse mortgage, the value of the foreclosed home is irrelevant, as you will see later on.

Recourse mortgage: Property worth less than loan balance

When the property's FMV is less than the recourse loan balance (sometimes referred to as "underwater"), the tax rules treat the foreclosure as a sale of the property for the FMV figure. [See Regulation 1.1001-2(c), Example 8 and Rev. Rul. 90-16.]

Therefore, a tax gain will be triggered if the property's FMV exceeds its basis. However, with a principal residence loan, the borrower can often exclude the entire gain under the IRC Section 121 home sale gain exclusion rules discussed earlier in this chapter.

If the property's basis exceeds the FMV, the foreclosure will trigger a non-deductible loss in the case of a personal residence. In the case of a business or rental property, the loss will be a tax-favored IRC Section 1231 loss.

If the lender then forgives all or part of the difference between the higher amount of the mortgage debt and the lower FMV figure, the forgiven amount constitutes COD income. As explained earlier, COD income counts as taxable gross income unless the borrower qualifies for an exception under the IRC Section 108 rules.

 Example 3-20

Teri borrowed heavily against the value of her home when real estate was booming in the local area. The property was burdened by a recourse first mortgage of $360,000 and a recourse second mortgage of $200,000 (total recourse debt of $560,000). When Teri stopped paying the second mortgage, the lender foreclosed. Assume the home's FMV was $500,000. The property's tax basis was $420,000. Assume the entire $360,000 first mortgage balance was paid off and $140,000 of the second mortgage was paid off when the property was sold. Teri scraped up $10,000 to pay off part of the remaining $60,000 second mortgage balance. The second mortgage lender then forgave the last $50,000.

The foreclosure triggers an $80,000 gain on sale ($500,000 FMV – $420,000 tax basis). The gain can be excluded under the IRC Section 121 home sale gain exclusion rules, assuming Teri qualifies.

 Example 3-21

The $50,000 forgiven by the second mortgage lender is COD income. Teri must report it as gross income unless she qualifies for an exception under the IRC Section 108 rules.

Variation: Assume the same basic facts, except now assume the second mortgage lender pursues Teri for the $50,000 deficiency. In this variation, there is no COD income until the lender ultimately decides to forgive some or all of the deficiency. That may or may not happen. Until it does happen, there is nothing to report on Teri's tax returns with respect to the deficiency.

Recourse mortgage: Property worth more than loan balance

When the property's FMV exceeds the recourse loan balance (a somewhat rare situation), the foreclosure is treated as a deemed sale of the property for a price equal to the loan balance, plus any additional proceeds received by the borrower from the foreclosure sale. [See Regulation 1.1001-2(a)(1).]

However, if the costs of the foreclosure proceedings and sale are large enough to result in a deficiency (that is, there is still an unpaid loan balance when all is said and done), the borrower falls back under the aforementioned rules that apply when the property is worth less than the loan balance. If the lender later forgives all or part of the deficiency, the forgiven amount constitutes COD income. (See example 3-21.)

Nonrecourse mortgage

When property subject to a nonrecourse loan is foreclosed by the nonrecourse lender, the foreclosure is treated for federal income tax purposes as a deemed sale of the property to the lender for proceeds equal to the nonrecourse loan balance. The property's FMV is irrelevant [*Tufts*, AFTR 2d 83-1132, Supreme Court (1983)], and the lender cannot pursue the borrower for any deficiency.

Because the taking of the property in foreclosure is deemed to fully satisfy the borrower's nonrecourse debt obligation, there cannot be any COD income for the borrower with respect to the nonrecourse debt.

There can only be gain or loss from the deemed sale. A tax gain is triggered if the nonrecourse loan balance exceeds the property's basis. However, with a principal residence loan, the borrower can often exclude the entire gain under the IRC Section 121 home sale gain exclusion rules discussed earlier in this chapter.

If the property's basis exceeds the nonrecourse loan balance, the foreclosure triggers a non-deductible loss in the case of a personal residence. In the case of a business or rental property, the loss will be a tax-favored IRC Section 1231 loss.

 Example 3-22

Steve borrowed heavily to acquire his principal residence a few years ago. Then, he thought he made a real killing when he found a lender willing to give him a big nonrecourse HELOC. When Steve stopped paying the HELOC, the lender foreclosed. At that time, the property was burdened by a $175,000 first mortgage balance and a $100,000 HELOC balance (total nonrecourse debt of $275,000). The property's tax basis was only $180,000. Under the aforementioned deemed sale treatment, the foreclosure triggered a $95,000 tax gain ($275,000 total nonrecourse debt balance − $180,000 tax basis; the property's FMV is irrelevant). Assume Steve can exclude the entire gain under the IRC Section 121 home sale gain exclusion rules. That is the end of the story for him, because the mortgage lenders cannot come after him for any deficiency.

Variation: Assume the same basic facts, except now assume Steve's property is a vacation home. The $95,000 gain will be a long-term capital gain that cannot be excluded under the IRC Section 121 rules. Therefore, Steve will pay tax on the whole gain unless he has some offsetting capital losses. The good news is the mortgage lenders cannot come after him for any deficiency.

Key point: Compared to what happens with recourse debt foreclosures, the deemed sale treatment for nonrecourse debt foreclosures can sometimes be unfavorable for borrowers. With recourse debt, a foreclosure may result in COD income that the borrower can exclude from gross income under one of the IRC Section 108 rules summarized earlier in this chapter. With nonrecourse debt, however, any gain that cannot be excluded under the IRC Section 121 rules may wind up being fully taxable, unless the debtor has losses to offset the gain.

Reporting and treatment of COD income arising from foreclosures

COD income after a foreclosure must be reported as taxable gross income on the borrower's federal income tax return unless the borrower qualifies for an exception under the IRC Section 108 rules explained earlier.

In theory, a recourse mortgage lender is supposed to report COD income to the borrower on a Form 1099-C (Cancellation of Debt) issued for the year during which the debt cancellation is deemed to occur. In the real world, however, Forms 1099-C are sometimes issued for the wrong year and reported COD amounts are sometimes wrong too.

For example, in *Gaffney*, a Tax Court Summary Opinion addressed a situation where the borrower's home was foreclosed by the recourse mortgage lender in 1994. The lender charged off the loan in 1995. In 2006, the lender finally got around to issuing a 1099-C, but it showed the wrong first name for the borrower and was sent to an address the borrower had not used for eight years (a comedy of errors). The Tax Court concluded there was no identifiable debt cancellation event in 2006, so the borrower did not have to report any COD income for that year (the wrong address was not relevant in this case). Obviously, the actual debt cancellation event had occurred long before 2006 in a tax year that was closed by the time the 1099-C was issued. Thus, the borrower was in the clear tax-wise. (See *Dennis Gaffney*, TC Summary Opinion 2010-128.)

For two other recent Tax Court decisions involving erroneous Forms 1099-C, see *Thomas Linkugel*, TC Summary Opinion 2009-180 and *William McCormick*, TC Memo 2009-239.

Exclusion for principal residence mortgage debt discharges might save the day (if it still exists)

As you have just seen, for federal income tax purposes, COD income is taxable unless a specific exception makes it tax-free. Legislation enacted in 2007, 2008, 2012, 2014, 2015, and 2018 created and extended an additional exception for qualifying discharges of home mortgage debt in 2007–2017. [See IRC Section 108(a)(1)(E) and IRS Publication 4681.]

Key Point: The Bipartisan Budget Act of 2018 extended the exclusion through the end of 2017. The extension also allowed for debt discharged after 2017 to be excluded from income if the taxpayer had entered into a binding written agreement before January 1, 2018. However, the exclusion expired at the end of 2017. Whether it will be resurrected for 2018 and beyond remains to be seen.

Under the exception, an individual taxpayer can exclude up to $2m of COD income from a discharge of "qualified principal residence indebtedness" which means debt that was used to acquire, build, or improve the taxpayer's principal residence (as defined under the IRC Section 121 home sale gain exclusion rules explained earlier in this chapter) and that is secured by that residence. Refinanced debt can qualify to the extent it replaces debt that was used to acquire, build, or improve the taxpayer's principal residence. The basis of the taxpayer's principal residence is reduced (but not less than zero) by the amount of COD income that is excluded under this rule.

Note that this exception is not available to taxpayers in Title 11 bankruptcy cases. Finally, an insolvent individual can elect to forego this exception and instead rely on the more general exception for insolvent taxpayers under IRC Section 108(a)(1)(B).

Key point: The exception applies only to COD income from debt used to acquire, build, or improve a principal residence. COD income from discharges of home equity loans used for other purposes will not qualify for the new exception, nor will COD income from discharges of vacation home loans. However other exceptions (under IRC Section 108) may allow clients to exclude COD income in these circumstances.

Tax angles when client converts personal residence into rental property

You may have clients who are thinking about converting their principal residences into rental properties—especially if they have already bought another home and are now paying two mortgages, two property tax bills, and so forth. However, converting a former principal residence into a rental has some tricky tax implications.

Basis for loss and depreciation purposes depends on market value

You already know you cannot claim a tax loss when a principal residence is sold for less than tax basis. The privilege of claiming tax losses is reserved for sales of property used for business or investment purposes. In most cases, basis equals the original purchase price plus the cost of any improvements (not counting normal repairs and maintenance) minus any depreciation deductions (say from a deductible office in the home).

But if your client converts the principal residence into a rental and eventually sells for less than tax basis, he or she can deduct the entire loss as an IRC Section 1231 loss (assuming the property has been owned for more than one year). However, a special basis rule prevents that taxpayer-friendly outcome. The special rule says when you convert a former principal residence into a rental, the initial tax basis for calculating any later loss on sale equals the lesser of (1) the property's basis on the conversion date under the normal rule, or (2) the property's FMV on the conversion date. [See Regulation 1.165-9(b)(2).]

In effect, the special basis rule disallows the loss from a decline in value that occurs before the conversion date.

But a *post-conversion* decline will result in an allowable IRC Section 1231 loss (assuming the property has been owned for more than one year) to the extent it is not offset by depreciation write-offs. (Because depreciation lowers the property's tax basis for loss purposes, it makes it that much harder to have a loss.)

Your client must use the same unfavorable special basis rule to figure his initial tax basis for calculating depreciation deductions on the converted property. [See Regulation 1.168(i)-4(b).] (The client can depreciate basis allocable to the building—not the land—over 27.5 years.)

Tax basis for gain purposes is different

Say the value of the converted property recovers, and your client sells for a profit down the road. The property's tax basis for gain purposes is determined under the normal basis rule which, as mentioned earlier, usually equals the purchase price plus the cost of improvements minus depreciation deductions (including depreciation after the property is converted into a rental).

Key point: If a former principal residence is sold within three years after it is converted into a rental, the IRC Section 121 home sale gain exclusion break explained earlier in this chapter will usually be available. However, gains attributable to depreciation cannot be sheltered by the IRC Section 121 exclusion. [See IRC Section 121(d)(6).]

Different basis numbers can create weird results when property is sold

Because the special basis rule that is used for tax loss purposes is different than the normal basis rule that is used for tax gain purposes, your client can potentially wind up in never-never land where he or she has neither a tax gain nor a tax loss. This will happen if the sale price falls between the two basis numbers. Needless to say, this is all very confusing. To clarify things, here are some examples illustrating tax results with differing conversion date FMVs and sale prices.

Example 3-23 Tax loss on sale

1.	Basis on conversion date under normal rule	$300,000
2.	FMV on conversion date	235,000
3.	Post-conversion depreciation deductions	13,000
4.	Basis for tax loss (line 2–line 3)	222,000
5.	Basis for tax gain (line 1–line 3)	287,000
6.	Net sale price (after selling expenses)	205,000
7.	Tax loss (excess of line 4 over line 6)	17,000
8.	Tax gain (excess of line 6 over line 5)	N/A

Explanation: In this example, there is an allowable tax loss because the property continued to decline in value after the conversion date.

Example 3-24 Tax gain on sale

1.	Basis on conversion date under normal rule	$300,000
2.	FMV on conversion date	285,000
3.	Post-conversion depreciation deductions	16,000
4.	Basis for tax loss (line 2–line 3)	269,000
5.	Basis for tax gain (line 1–line 3)	284,000
6.	Net sale price	295,000
7.	Tax loss (excess of line 4 over line 6)	N/A
8.	Tax gain (excess of line 6 over line 5)	11,000

Explanation: In this example, the tax gain is caused by the post-conversion depreciation deductions plus a recovery in value after the conversion date.

Example 3-25 No tax gain or loss

1. Basis on conversion date under normal rule	$300,000
2. FMV on conversion date	235,000
3. Post-conversion depreciation deductions	13,000
4. Basis for tax loss (line 2−line 3)	222,000
5. Basis for tax gain (line 1−line 3)	287,000
6. Net sale price	260,000
7. Tax loss (excess of line 4 over line 6)	N/A
8. Tax gain (excess of line 6 over line 5)	N/A

Explanation: In this example, there is no tax gain or loss because the sale price falls between the two basis numbers.

Keep records to establish FMV on conversion date

An important thing to remember is that the property's FMV on the conversion date is often the most important factor in determining the tax results from a later sale. So make sure your client has some evidence for that, for example, a market evaluation from a local realtor. This information should be kept with the client's tax records.

Schedule E deductions are allowed when converted residence is held out for rent even when there is no rental income

IRC Section 212 allows individual owners of rental properties to claim Schedule E deductions for expenditures associated with the production of rental income (subject to the PAL rules). As a 2011 Tax Court Summary Opinion reminds us, deductions are allowed when a property is held out for rent even during periods when there is no rental income.

In *Hattie M. Bonds*, the taxpayer moved from Kansas City to Minnesota in 1988. From the time of the move through 2004 or 2005, she was able to rent out her former Kansas City principal residence. However, in 2006 and 2007, there was no rental income even though the property was available for rent. The failure to rent the property was apparently due to several factors including a lousy local economy and the property's suboptimal location. The taxpayer continued to own the property because a realtor told her she could still sell it for a profit. After her move to Minnesota, the taxpayer did not use the property for personal purposes, and it was never actually put up for sale.

On her 2006 and 2007 returns, the taxpayer claimed Schedule E rental losses from the Kansas City property of about $13,000 and $12,700, respectively. Claimed expenses including mortgage interest, property taxes, utilities, cleaning and maintenance, insurance, advertising, depreciation, and the cost of traveling by car to visit the property. As we said earlier, there was no rental income in either 2006 or 2007.

The lack of rental income apparently triggered an IRS audit of the taxpayer's 2006 and 2007 returns, and the government completely disallowed the Schedule E losses claimed on those returns. The IRS used the following three different arguments:

1. The IRS argued that the taxpayer continued to own the Kansas City property for personal reasons, because family and friends lived in the area and because she wanted to retire there, without any intention to rent it out for income. Claiming expenses on Schedule E was not allowed because using Schedule E requires an intention to produce rental income.
2. The IRS argued that even if the taxpayer was entitled to claim rental expenses on Schedule E, she could not currently deduct the net Schedule E losses from 2006 and 2007 because the losses were suspended by the PAL rules due to a lack of passive income.
3. The IRS argued that the taxpayer had no substantiation for some of her claimed expenses.

The IRS did allow Schedule A itemized deductions for mortgage interest and property taxes.

The disgruntled taxpayer went to the Tax Court seeking justice. She represented herself under the IRC Section 7463 "small case" Tax Court rules.

In its Summary Opinion, the Tax Court declared that the taxpayer was indeed entitled to deduct Schedule E net rental losses for 2006 and 2007, even though there was no rental income for those years. The Tax Court pointed out that the government's own rules say that holding property for the production of income can include income expected in future years, including an anticipated gain on sale in a future year [Regulation 1.212-1(b)]. In 2006 and 2007, the taxpayer had good reason to believe she could sell the property for a gain because a realtor told her that.

The Tax Court then rejected the IRS argument that the taxpayer's net rental losses were suspended by the PAL rules. Because she met the active participation requirement, she was eligible for the IRC Section 469(i) exception that allows individuals to currently deduct up to $25,000 of annual passive losses from rental real estate activities (the $25,000 allowance is phased-out at higher income levels).

However, the Tax Court agreed that some of the taxpayer's claimed deductions were unsubstantiated and should be disallowed or only partially allowed for that reason.

When all was said and done, the taxpayer was allowed to deduct about half of her claimed Schedule E net losses. The other half was disallowed due to lack of substantiation. (See *Hattie M. Bonds*, TC Summary Opinion 2011-122.)

Key point: The main message of the *Bonds* decision is that an individual's net rental losses from a property held out for rent can be deducted on Schedule E even when there is no rental income. The secondary message is that claimed expenses must be substantiated with decent records.

How the TCJA affects homeowners

The TCJA trimmed two important tax breaks for homeowners.

New limit on deductions for state and local taxes, including real property taxes

Under prior law (before the TCJA), you could claim an itemized deduction for an unlimited amount of personal (non-business) state and local income and property taxes on Schedule A of Form 1040. Therefore, if you had a big property tax bill, you could deduct the entire amount if you itemized. Individuals with big personal state and local income tax bills could fully deduct those, too, on Schedule A, if they itemized. Finally, you had the option of deducting personal state and local general sales taxes on Schedule A instead of state and local income taxes (beneficial if you owe little or nothing for state and local income taxes).

For 2018–2025, the TCJA changes the deal by limiting itemized deductions for personal state and local property taxes and personal state and local income taxes (or sales taxes if you choose that option) to a combined total of only $10,000 ($5,000 if you use married filing separate status). Personal foreign real property taxes cannot be deducted for 2018–2025, so no more deductions for property taxes on that place in Cabo.

These TCJA changes unfavorably affect individuals who pay high property taxes because they live in a high-property-tax jurisdiction, own an expensive home (resulting in a high property tax bill), or own both a primary residence and one or more vacation homes (resulting in a bigger property tax bill due to owning several properties). Individuals in these categories can now deduct a maximum $10,000 of personal state and local property taxes—even if they deduct nothing for personal state and local income taxes or general sales taxes.

Tax planning considerations

First, none of the preceding factors matter unless you have enough itemized deductions to exceed your allowable standard deduction. That will be the case for fewer folks than under prior law, because the TCJA almost doubled the standard deductions. Specifically, the 2018 standard deduction for married joint-filing couples is $24,000 (compared to $12,700 for 2017). The 2018 standard deduction for heads of households is $18,000 (versus $9,350 for 2017). The 2018 standard deduction for singles and those who use married filing separate status is $12,000 (versus $6,350 for 2017). For 2019, the standard deduction amounts are $24,400, $18,350, and $12,200 respectively.

Second, there is not much opportunity for gamesmanship with deductions for real property taxes. The only way you could potentially deduct more than $10,000 (or $5,000 if you use married filing separate status) is if you own a home that is used partially for business (for example, because you have a deductible office in the home) or partially rented out (for example the basement of your main residence or a vacation home during part of the year). In those situations, you could deduct property taxes allocable to those business or rental uses on top of the $10,000 limit—subject to the rules that apply to deductions allocable to those uses. (For example, home office deductions cannot exceed the income from the related business activity, and deductions for the rental use of a property that is also used as a personal residence generally cannot exceed the rental income. Source: IRC Sec. 280A.)

If you pay both state and local property taxes and state and local income taxes (or sales taxes if you choose that option), trying to maximize your property tax deduction may reduce what you can deduct for state and local income taxes. For example, if you have $8,000 of state and local property taxes and $10,000 of state and local income taxes, you can deduct the full $8,000 of property taxes but only $2,000 of income taxes. If you want to deduct more income tax, your property tax deduction goes down dollar-for-dollar.

Warning: If you are in the alternative minimum tax (AMT) mode, itemized deductions for personal state and local property taxes are completely disallowed under the AMT rules. The same is true for personal state and local income taxes (or sales taxes if you choose that option). This AMT disallowance rule was in effect before the TCJA, and it still applies in the post-TCJA world.

New limits on home mortgage interest deductions

For 2018–2025, the TCJA generally allows you to deduct interest on only up to $750,000 of mortgage debt incurred to buy or improve a first or second residence (home acquisition indebtedness). For those who use married filing separate status, the home acquisition indebtedness limit is $375,000.

For 2018–2025, the TCJA also generally eliminates the prior-law provision that allowed interest deductions on up to $100,000 of home equity indebtedness, or $50,000 for those who use married filing separate status.

Before the TCJA, you could deduct interest on up to $1m of home acquisition indebtedness or $500,000 for those who use married filing separate status. Before the TCJA, you could also treat another $100,000 of mortgage debt as home acquisition indebtedness if the loan proceeds were used to buy or improve a first or second residence, or $50,000 for those who use married filing separate status. The additional $100,000/$50,000 of debt could be in the form of a bigger first mortgage or a home equity loan. So the limit on home acquisition indebtedness under prior law was really $1.1m, or $550,000 for those who use married filing separate status.

Exceptions for grandfathered debts

Under a grandfather rule, the TCJA changes do not affect home acquisition indebtedness of up to $1m/$500,000 that was taken out: (1) before December 15, 2017, or (2) under a binding contract that was in effect before December 15, 2017, as long as the home purchase closed before April 1, 2018.

Under another grandfather rule, the $1m/$500,000 home acquisition indebtedness limits continue to apply to home acquisition indebtedness that was taken out before the TCJA and then refinanced in 2018–2025—to the extent the initial principal balance of the new loan does not exceed the principal balance of the old loan at the time of the refinancing.

Non-itemizers can ignore all of this

None of this information about property taxes or mortgage interest deductions matter unless you have enough itemized deductions to exceed your allowable standard deduction. That will be the case for fewer individuals than under prior law, because the TCJA almost doubled the standard deductions for 2018–2025.

Examples

Assuming this mortgage interest information does matter to you, the following are some examples of how the TCJA mortgage interest deduction limits work.

Example 3-26

Bill and Betty are a married joint-filing couple with a $1.5m mortgage that was taken out to buy their principal residence in 2016. In 2017, the couple paid $60,000 of mortgage interest, and they could deduct $44,000 [($1.1m ÷ $1.5m) × $60,000 = $44,000].

For 2018–2025, they can treat no more than $1m as acquisition indebtedness; so if they pay $55,000 of mortgage interest in 2019, they can deduct only $36,667 [($1m ÷ $1.5m) × $55,000 = $36,667].

Example 3-27

Same basic facts as in example 3-26, except this time assume that Bill and Betty refinance their mortgage on July 1, 2018, when it has a balance of $1.35m, by taking out a new mortgage for the same amount.

Under the grandfather rule for up to $1m of refinanced home acquisition indebtedness, the couple can continue to deduct the interest on up to $1m of the new mortgage for 2018–2025.

Example 3-28

Carlos is an unmarried individual with an $800,000 first mortgage that he took out to buy his principal residence in 2012. In 2016, he opened up a home equity line of credit (HELOC), and borrowed $80,000 to pay off his car loan, credit card balances, and various other personal debts.

On his 2017 return, Carlos can deduct all the interest on the first mortgage under the rules for home acquisition indebtedness. For regular tax purposes, he can also deduct all the HELOC interest under the rules for home equity debt (but the interest is disallowed under the AMT rules because the HELOC proceeds were not used to buy or improve a first or second residence).

For 2018–2025, Carlos can continue to deduct all the interest on the first mortgage under the grandfather rule for up to $1m of home acquisition indebtedness, but he cannot treat any of the HELOC interest as deductible home mortgage interest.

Example 3-29

Same basic facts as in example 3-28, except this time assume that Carlos used the $80,000 from the HELOC to remodel his principal residence.

On his 2017 return, Carlos can deduct the interest on the first mortgage and the HELOC, because he can treat the combined balance of the loans as home acquisition indebtedness that does not exceed $1.1m.

For 2018–2025, Carlos can continue to deduct the interest on both loans under the grandfather rule for up to $1m of home acquisition indebtedness.

Example 3-30

Paula is an unmarried individual with an $800,000 first mortgage that was taken out on December 1, 2017, to buy her principal residence. In 2018, she opens up a HELOC and borrows $80,000 to remodel her kitchen and bathrooms.

For 2018–2025, Paula can deduct all the interest on the first mortgage under the grandfather rule for up to $1m of home acquisition indebtedness. However, because the $80,000 HELOC was taken out in 2018, the TCJA's $750,000 limit on home acquisition indebtedness precludes any deductions for the HELOC interest. The entire $750,000 post-TCJA limit on home acquisition indebtedness was absorbed (and then some) by the grandfathered $800,000 first mortgage—so the HELOC balance cannot be treated as home acquisition debt, even though all of the loan proceeds were used to improve Paula's principal residence. Instead, the HELOC balance must be treated as home equity debt, and interest on home equity debt is disallowed for 2018–2025.

Example 3-31

Same basic facts as in example 3-30, except this time assume that the first mortgage taken out by Paula was only $650,000.

For 2018–2025, she can deduct all the interest on the first mortgage under the grandfather rule for up to $1m of home acquisition indebtedness. The $80,000 HELOC balance can be treated as home acquisition indebtedness, because the combined balance of the first mortgage and the HELOC is only $730,000, which is under the post-TCJA limit of $750,000 for home acquisition indebtedness. Therefore, Paula can deduct all the interest on both loans under the rules for home acquisition indebtedness.

Tax planning considerations

Interest-only mortgages look more attractive in the post-TCJA world, if all the interest can be deducted under the grandfather rules for home acquisition indebtedness. For example, if you refinance $1m of pre-TCJA home acquisition indebtedness with a new $1m interest-only loan, you can continue to deduct all the interest under the grandfather rule for refinanced home acquisition indebtedness of up to $1m. In contrast, if your $1m of home acquisition indebtedness is gradually reduced by making principal payments in 2018–2015, you will not be able to treat any part of an additional home loan as home acquisition indebtedness—because your existing loan will absorb the entire $750,000 TCJA limit.

The same concept discourages making bigger-than-required principal payments in 2018–2025 on grandfathered home acquisition indebtedness that exceeds $750,000.

Conclusion

The new TCJA limits on deducting home mortgage interest may not affect as many homeowners as the new limit on deducting state and local taxes, but homeowners with larger mortgages and home equity loans must take heed.

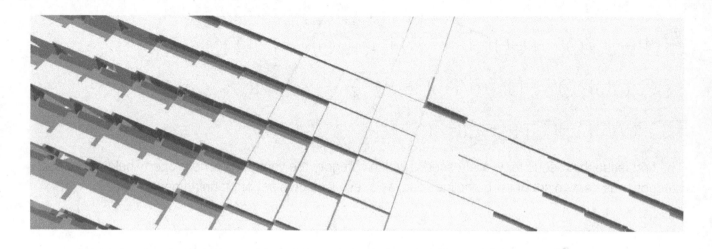

Chapter 4

Tax Planning Opportunities with Vacation Homes, Timeshares, and Co-Ownership Arrangements

Learning objectives

- Determine ways to help clients obtain maximum tax savings from vacation home and timeshare properties.

- Differentiate between the rules for "regular" vacation homes, timeshares, and co-ownership deals.

Introduction

Many clients own vacation homes and timeshares. This chapter provides a brush-up on the tax rules and planning opportunities in this confusing area of the tax law.

Rules for "regular" vacation homes (as opposed to timeshares and co-ownership deals)

The first issue that needs to be addressed is which category the vacation home property belongs in. Each category has its own set of tax guidelines and, as a result, its own set of planning opportunities.

Category 1: Rented more than 14 days—and personal use exceeds greater of 14 days or 10% of rental days

Here we are talking about vacation properties that are rented a fair amount of time with substantial personal use as well (personal use includes use by the taxpayer, family members, and anyone else who pays less than fair market rental rates).

For instance, a property that is rented for 30 days and used by family members for a month during the year falls into Category 1. Vacation homes fitting this description are considered personal residences, and they are covered by the special IRC Section 280A vacation home tax rules.

For grandfathered home acquisition debt that still falls under the rules in effect before the Tax Cuts and Jobs Act (TCJA), clients can claim an itemized deduction for the interest on up to $1m of home mortgage debt on up to two personal residences under the IRC Section 163(h) rules for qualified residence interest ($500,000 for those who use married filing separate status). For home loans taken out after December 15, 2017, the limit on home acquisition indebtedness for 2018–2025 is reduced to $750,000 ($375,000 for those who use married filing separate status). Under a grandfather rule, the TCJA change does not affect home acquisition indebtedness of up to $1m/$500,000 that was taken out: (1) before December 15, 2017, or (2) under a binding contract that was in effect before December 15, 2017, as long as the home purchase closes before April 1, 2018. Under another grandfather rule, the $1m/$500,000 home acquisition indebtedness limits continue to apply to home acquisition indebtedness that was taken out before December 15, 2017, and was then refinanced after the new TCJA limitation was in effect—to the extent the initial principal balance of the new loan does not exceed the principal balance of the old loan at the time of the refinancing.

Property taxes are potentially deductible, no matter how many homes are owned. However, for 2018–2025, clients cannot claim itemized deductions for more than a combined total of $10,000 of state and local taxes, including real property taxes on personal residences ($5,000 for those who use married filing separate status).

Rental income and expenses for Category 1 homes are handled in the following manner:

- The first step is to allocate interest and property taxes between rental and personal usage. For this, count all the time the property was not actually rented as personal. For example: Say the home is rented three months, used by family two months, and vacant seven months. Under these facts, 25% (3/12) of the interest and taxes is allocable to the rental period and 75% (9/12, which includes unoccupied time) to personal use. The personal part of the interest and taxes (75%) shows up on Schedule A as itemized deductions.
- The second step is to reduce the rental income by allocable interest and taxes (25% in our example). If there is any rental income left, allocable operating expenses—depreciation, maintenance, utilities, association fees, insurance, and so forth—can be deducted, but only to the point where the remaining income is zeroed out. In allocating these operating expenses, consider only the actual rental and personal use days.

So, in our example, 60% (3/5) of the depreciation, maintenance, utilities, and so forth is allocated to the rental period and 40% (2/5) is allocated to personal use. That 40% evaporates as a totally non-deductible item. On the client's tax return, use Schedule E to report 100% of the rental income, 25% of the interest and taxes, and the 40% of allowable operating expenses. In most cases, the bottom line on Schedule E will be zero because the allowable expenses will zero out the rental income.

When all is said and done, this procedure usually allows the client to fully deduct interest and deduct some real estate taxes (perhaps part on Schedule A and part on Schedule E) and usually enough operating expenses to wipe out any rental income. Not a bad deal.

Any disallowed expenses are carried over to future years where they can be deducted against rental profits or the rental portion of gain from selling the property.

Key point: The IRS wants taxpayers to allocate both interest and taxes and operating expenses using actual days of occupancy. This results in a greater allocation of interest and taxes to rental usage, which then diminishes the taxpayer's ability to deduct operating expenses. It also reduces the allocation of interest and taxes to Schedule A, where under tax law in effect before the TCJA, the interest and taxes could usually be fully deducted. So, under pre-TCJA law, the IRS-approved method was usually detrimental to the taxpayer. However, two court decisions say it is permissible to use 365 days and count unused days as personal days for the allocation of interest and taxes while using actual days to allocate operating expenses. [See *Dorance Bolton*, 51 AFTR 2d 83-305 (9th Cir. 1982) and *Edith McKinney*, 52 AFTR 2d 83-6281 (10th Cir. 1983).]

TCJA impact: Because the TCJA places new limits on itemized deductions for home mortgage interest and state and local taxes (including real property taxes) for 2018–2025, it may now be more beneficial to use the IRS-approved method to allocate mortgage interest and property taxes for 2018–2025. That way, more of these expenses are allocated to Schedule E where they can at least be deducted to the extent of rental income. Due to the rental income limitation, that may result in reduced current write-offs for operating expenses allocable to Schedule E (such as maintenance, utilities, and depreciation), but at least those disallowed expenses can eventually be written off when the property generates positive taxable income or is sold for a gain (if that ever happens).

Category 2: Rented more than 14 days—and personal use does not exceed greater of 14 days or 10% of rental days

Category 2 vacation homes fall under the tax rules for rental properties rather than those covering personal residences.

For instance, if the client rents for 210 days and vacations for 21 days during the year, you have a Category 2 rental property on your hands (22 days of vacation would put the property back into Category 1).

Interest, property taxes, and operating expenses should all be allocated based on actual usage (21/231 to personal use and 210/231 to rental).

For a Category 2 home, taxpayers are allowed to generate a taxable loss on Schedule E when allocable rental expenses exceed income. However, that loss will typically be covered by the IRC Section 469 passive loss rules for rental real estate and perhaps by the TCJA's new rule that limit current deductions for excess business losses for 2018–2025. In general, taxpayers can deduct passive losses only to the extent of passive income from other sources (such as rental properties that produce gains) of when the property that produced the losses is sold.

$25,000 exception to passive loss rules

A favorable exception allows write-offs of up to $25,000 of passive rental real estate losses for taxpayers who actively participate and have adjusted gross income (AGI) under $100,000. Making the property management decisions will get the client over the active participation hurdle. Unfortunately, the $25,000 exception is phased out between AGI of $100,000 and $150,000.

When average rental period is seven days or less

Unfortunately, the $25,000 exception does not apply when the average rental period is seven days or less, because the rental is considered a business rather than a rental real estate activity [see PLR 9505002; *Walter Barniskis*, TC Memo 1999-258; *B. Theodore Chapin*, TC Memo 1996-56; *Steven Rapp*, TC Memo 1999-249; and Temp. Reg. 1.469-1T(e)(3)(ii)(A)].

Because of this seven-day rule, many owners in Category 2 find their hoped-for tax losses deferred by the passive loss rules. However, there are two potential solutions to the seven-day rule dilemma.

1. The taxpayer can try to make sure the vacation property is rented for longer periods. That way, the average rental will exceed seven days, and the IRS will agree the taxpayer has a rental real estate activity rather than a business. Eligibility for the $25,000 rental real estate exception will be saved.
2. If the taxpayer cannot avoid running afoul of the seven-day rule, he or she should attempt to materially participate in the business of renting the vacation home. Material participation means there is not a passive activity in the first place, so the client can usually deduct the vacation home rental losses against all other taxable income. The easiest ways to prove material participation (see Temp. Reg. 1.469-5T) are to show that

a. the taxpayer does substantially all the work related to the property (negotiating rentals, collecting the money, performing maintenance, and so on), or

b. the taxpayer spends more than 100 hours handling the property and no other person spends more time than the taxpayer.

In meeting these rules, the client's time and his or her spouse's time can be combined. However, clients typically will not be able to meet either of the material participation standards if they use a management company to handle all the details.

Example 4-1

Leona is ineligible for the $25,000 passive loss exception because her AGI is too high. The result has been suspended passive losses from the vacation home rental activity because there has not been passive income from other sources. Leona may be able to transform the vacation home rental activity into a business by reducing the average rental period to seven days or less. Then, as long as she materially participates, the passive loss rules can be completely avoided, and the vacation home losses can be deducted in full against her other income.

Treatment of mortgage interest expense

Another problem is that the interest allocable to personal use (21/231 in our example) is non-deductible, because Category 2 homes do not qualify as personal residences. The rule allowing an itemized deduction for qualified residence interest applies only to mortgage interest on a home meeting the IRC Section 280A(d)(1) definition of a personal residence. This requires personal use that exceeds the greater of 14 days or 10% of rental days, other words Category 1 homes [IRC Section 163(h)(4)(A)(i)(II)]. Category 2 homes treated as rental properties fail this test by definition. Therefore, the mortgage interest allocable to personal use is non-deductible personal interest under IRC Section 163(h). (The personal-use portion of property taxes is still deductible on Schedule A.)

Tax planning implications

From a planning standpoint, this means clients may actually benefit from slipping in some extra vacation days during the year, which can cause the property to drop back into Category 1, where all the interest and some taxes can usually be deducted and where any remaining rental income can usually be offset by allocable operating expenses.

On the other hand, the client may have plenty of passive income from other sources. Or the client may have AGI below $100,000 and no problem with the seven-day rule. These circumstances should allow the client to fully deduct the passive loss from the vacation home rental. If the amount of non-deductible personal interest expense will be nominal, the planning suggestion is that the client should minimize vacation days to maximize the rental loss.

Category 3: Rented less than 15 days—and personal use exceeds 14 days

Category 3 vacation homes are also considered personal residences. If there are no rental days, interest and property taxes are deducted on Schedule A (subject to applicable TCJA limitations for 2018–2025)—the same as for the primary residence.

If there are some rental days but they number less than 15, a unique tax break is available under IRC Section 280A(g). The client need not declare a penny of the rental income. Interest and taxes are still deducted on Schedule A (subject to applicable TCJA limitations for 2018–2025), with no allocation nonsense to worry about. The only negative is that there are no write-offs allowed for operating expenses (depreciation, and so on) attributable to the rental period. Note that this tax law quirk also applies to primary residences and is often put to good use during major events such as the Masters Golf tournament.

Knowledge check

1. It is generally correct that the client can deduct

    a. Property taxes on only one personal residence up to $10,000.
    b. Interest on mortgages on three or more personal residences as qualified residence interest.
    c. Property taxes on only two personal residences.
    d. Mortgage interest on up to two personal residences, subject to the limitations on qualified residence interest.

2. When the client rents out a vacation home for three months during the year and has absolutely no personal use during the year,

    a. Any rental loss can always be currently and fully deducted for federal income tax purposes.
    b. Any rental loss is deemed to be a non-deductible personal expense.
    c. The home will be treated as a rental property rather than a vacation home for federal income tax purposes.
    d. The home will be treated as a personal residence for tax purposes.

3. When the client's vacation home is rented out for less than 15 days during the year and personal use of the home exceeds 14 days, the rental income is

    a. Fully taxable for federal income tax purposes.
    b. Completely tax-free for federal income tax purposes.
    c. 50% taxable and 50% tax-free for federal income tax purposes.
    d. Treated as fully taxable passive income that is also subject to the 3.8% NIIT.

Rules for timeshares and vacation home co-ownership arrangements

Inevitably, some of your clients will buy timeshares or enter into co-ownership arrangements with others to buy a resort condo or cabin. Then the tax questions arise. Here is what you need to know to supply the answers.

Key point: The rules explained in this analysis apply equally to timeshares and vacation home co-ownership arrangements where several individuals jointly own percentage interests in a vacation home.

No rental days

If the client does not rent any of his or her time, the property taxes are deductible on Schedule A, subject to the TCJA limitation on deducting state and local taxes for 2018–2025. [IRC Section 164(a)(1)]. The property tax amount is usually buried in the annual maintenance fee number. The other expenses included in the maintenance fee (for example, insurance, utilities, the homeowner's association fee, and actual maintenance expenditures) are non-deductible.

If the timeshare is mortgaged, the interest expense can be deducted as qualified residence interest as long as the other qualified residence interest rules are met [IRC Section 163(h)(4)(A)(iii)]. This is because the timeshare qualifies as a second personal residence for mortgage interest deduction purposes as long as it is not rented by the owner of that time during the year.

Therefore, the timeshare mortgage interest is deductible, provided the other requirements of IRC Section 163(h) are satisfied (loan secured by the timeshare, no more than $1m of total home acquisition debt or $750,000 if the new TCJA limitation applies, debt not in excess of fair market value and so on).

The results are the same for co-ownership situations if the co-owner does not rent any of the time allocated to him or her during the year.

Some rental days

If the unit is rented for some or all of the timeshare owner's allotted time, the property is virtually certain to be subject to the IRC Section 280A vacation home rules (the Category 1 rules for regular vacation homes explained earlier). Why? Because the 14-day/10% test is applied to the unit as a whole by counting the personal-use days of all of the unit's owners during the year [IRC Section 280A(d)(2)(A) and Prop. Reg. 1.280A-3(f)(3)].

The total number of personal-use days will generally be high enough to cause the unit to fall into Category 1. The same will likely be true for most vacation home co-ownership arrangements.

Prop. Reg. 1.280A-3(f)(5) then requires allocating each timeshare owner's expenses between personal and rental use based on usage by all of the unit's owners during the year. Under this concept, the personal-use and rental percentages will turn out to be the same for all owners of a particular unit.

Unfortunately, it is usually difficult, if not impossible, to obtain usage information from all the owners (there will often be 10 or more different owners). Unless some decent information is available regarding other owners' usage patterns, making the rental or personal allocation based on the individual owner's actual usage meets the spirit if not the letter of the government's rule.

Using some reasonable allocation percentages, the timeshare owner reduces his or her rental income by allocable rental expenses (including allocable interest and property taxes) until rental income is zeroed out on his or her Schedule E [Prop. Reg. 1.280A-3(f)(6)]. The personal portion of property taxes is then deducted on Schedule A, subject to the TCJA limitation on deducting state and local taxes for 2018–2025.

Apparently, the personal portion of any mortgage interest expense on the timeshare can be deducted as qualified residence interest only if the individual owner's personal use exceeds the greater of 14 days or 10% of his or her rental days, which would qualify the timeshare as a second residence under the definition found in IRC Section 280A(d)(1). Only the individual owner's personal and rental days (and not those of the other owners) are to be considered for this specific purpose [Temp. Reg. 1.163-10T(p)(6) and (p)(3)(iii)].

When the timeshare owner has the right to only one or two weeks a year, the more-than-14-days-or-10% test is impossible to meet by definition. Therefore, a deduction for the personal portion of timeshare mortgage interest will rarely be available under the qualified residence interest rules.

Co-owners of a vacation property are much more likely to meet the more-than-14-days-or-10-percent test because they are more likely to own at least three weeks. If the test is met, they can treat their co-ownership share as a second personal residence and thereby deduct the personal portion of their mortgage interest, as long as the other IRC Section 163(h) rules are met.

Example 4-2

Butch owns weeks 29 and 30 in unit 310 at the Sunny Mountain Timeshare Resort. He rents week 29 and uses week 30 personally. His two weeks cost a total of $40,000, partly financed by a $20,000 mortgage loan arranged through the developer.

For the current year, the interest expense is $2,400 and the maintenance fees for the two weeks total $2,800 ($900 of which is for property taxes and $1,900 of which is for maintenance fees). The current-year rental income from week 29 is $1,500. Based on his conversations with other timeshare owners at the gala annual owners' banquet, Butch estimates unit 310 is rented approximately half the year and personally used by the owners for the other half.

Using this information, the Category 1 vacation home rules apply to Butch (and to any other unit 310 owners who rent some of their time as well). His Form 1040 for the current year should show $1,500 of rental income on Schedule E. Allocable rental expenses of up to $1,500 can also be deducted on Schedule E (using 50% as the allocation percentage).

Example 4-2 (continued)

Before considering depreciation, allocable rental expenses for the current year add up to $2,600 ($1,200 mortgage interest, $450 property taxes, and $950 maintenance fees). On Schedule E, Butch can completely offset his rental income with these expenses, limited to $1,500. The $1,100 of disallowed cash expenses ($2,600 – $1,500) plus the disallowed depreciation expense carryover to the next year.

On his Schedule A for the current year, Butch deducts the other $450 of property taxes (the 50% attributable to personal use) subject to the TCJA limitation on deducting state and local taxes for 2018–2025, but the $1,200 of personal-use mortgage interest is non-deductible, because Butch does not own enough personal days to pass the more-than-14-days-or-10% test. The $950 of personal-use maintenance fees is also a non-deductible personal expense.

Tax-free rent rule

As mentioned in the earlier explanation of Category 3 regular vacation homes, IRC Section 280A(g) allows the tax-free rental of personal residences for up to 14 days. Unfortunately, few timeshare owners are likely to qualify, because Prop. Reg. 1.280A-3(f)(4) says the total rental days during the year for all of the unit's owners must be fewer than 15 for any owner to be able to claim tax-free status for his or her rental income.

Even when total rental days are fewer than 15, the individual timeshare owner's personal use must also exceed 14 days or 10% of his or her rental days for the unit to qualify as a personal residence under the IRC Section 280A(d)(1) definition. (Only personal residences are eligible for the tax-free rent rule.)

In vacation property co-ownership situations, it is somewhat more likely that a co-owner will qualify for the tax-free rent rule, because he or she may have enough personal days to exceed 14 days or 10% of his or her rental days. Remember, however, the total rental days of all owners must still be less than 15 for any owner to take advantage of the tax-free rent rule (which is not terribly likely).

Playing the gain exclusion game with multiple residences

The basic IRC Section 121 gain exclusion qualification rule is simple. The taxpayer must have owned and used the home as his or her main residence for at least two years out of the five-year period ending on the date of sale.

For married couples, the larger $500,000 exclusion is available as long as one or both spouses satisfy the ownership test and both spouses satisfy the use test.

For taxpayers affluent enough to have one or more vacation residences, there are some tax-saving games to be played here.

Example 4-3

Biff and Buffy are married and own three homes. First, there is their primary home in Connecticut, which qualifies for the $500,000 exclusion and could be sold for a $400,000 gain. The couple sells that property tax-free and moves into what was formerly a vacation home in Key West, Florida. Biff and Buffy plan to live there for two years, sell the property for an expected $300,000 gain, and exclude that gain, as well. Then they will move into their remaining vacation home in Beaver Creek, Colorado, and live there for two years, before selling and excluding the expected gain. Meanwhile, each time they sell a home, they will replace it with another property in the same or different location. Then they can start the occupy-and-sell cycle all over again with the second batch of homes.

Warning: Biff and Buffy need to be aware of the rule, explained in the following section, which can potentially negate some of the gain exclusion benefit in this scenario. In addition, they should be sure they understand the state income tax implications before committing to the multiple residence gain exclusion strategy.

Unfavorable rule for properties converted into principal residences

Before 2009, individuals could convert a former rental property or vacation home into a principal residence, occupy it for at least two years, sell it, and take full advantage of the IRC Section 121 home sale gain exclusion privilege ($250,000 maximum exclusion for unmarried individuals; $500,000 maximum exclusion for married joint-filing couples).

Unfortunately, legislation enacted in 2008 added an unfavorable provision for sales that occur after 2008. [See IRC Section 121(b)(4).] The provision makes a portion of the gain from selling an affected residence ineligible for the gain exclusion privilege. We will call the amount of gain that is made ineligible the non-excludable gain. It is calculated as follows.

Step 1: Take the total gain and subtract any un-recaptured IRC Section 1250 gain from depreciation deductions claimed against the property for periods after May 6, 1997. [This amount of gain cannot be excluded under the IRC Section 121 rules, which has always been the case pursuant to IRC Section 121(d)(6). Instead, this amount of gain must be reported on Schedule D of Form 1040.]

Step 2: Calculate the non-excludable gain fraction. The numerator of the fraction is the amount of time after 2008 during which the property is not used as the taxpayer's principal residence. These times are called periods of nonqualified use. However, periods of nonqualified use do not include temporary absences that aggregate to two years or less due to changes of employment, health conditions, or other circumstances to be specified in IRS guidance. Periods of nonqualified use also do not include times when the property is not used as the taxpayer's principal residence if those times are (1) after the last day of use as a principal residence, and (2) within the five-year period ending on the sale date. The denominator of the fraction is the taxpayer's total ownership period for the property.

Step 3: Calculate the non-excludable gain by multiplying the gain from Step 1 by the non-excludable gain fraction from Step 2.

The taxpayer must report on Schedule D the non-excludable gain calculated in Step 3. As mentioned earlier, the taxpayer must also report on Schedule D any un-recaptured IRC Section 1250 gain from depreciation for periods after May 6, 1997. The remaining gain is eligible for the IRC Section 121 gain exclusion privilege, assuming the IRC Section 121 eligibility rules are met.

Example 4-4

Your client Fern (a married joint filer) bought a vacation home on January 1, 2011. On January 1, 2015, she converts the property into a principal residence, and she lives there with her husband for 2015 through 2018. On January 1, 2019, Fern sells the property for a $480,000 gain. Her total ownership period is eight years (2011–2018). The four years of post-2008 use as a vacation home (2011–2014) result in a non-excludable gain of $240,000 (4/8 × $480,000). Fern must report the $240,000 as long-term capital gain on her 2019 Schedule D and pay the resulting tax hit. She can shelter the remaining $240,000 of gain ($480,000 − $240,000) with her $500,000 IRC Section 121 gain exclusion.

Example 4-5

Assume the same basic facts as in the previous example, except now assume that Fern has $10,000 of un-recaptured IRC Section 1250 gain from renting out the property before converting it into a principal residence. Therefore, the total gain on sale is now $490,000. Fern must report the $10,000 of un-recaptured IRC Section 1250 gain on her 2019 Schedule D. She must also report the non-excludable gain amount of $240,000 [4/8 × ($490,000 − $10,000)] on her 2019 Schedule D. She can shelter the remaining $240,000 of gain ($490,000 − $10,000 − $240,000) with her $500,000 IRC Section 121 gain exclusion.

Example 4-6

Your client Guido (an unmarried person) bought a vacation home on January 1, 2009. On January 1, 2014, he converts the property into a principal residence and lives there for 2014 through 2020. On January 1, 2021, he sells the property for a $700,000 gain. Guido's total ownership period is 12 years (2009–2020). The five years of post-2008 use as a vacation home (2009–2013) result in a non-excludable gain of $291,167 (5/12 × $700,000).

Guido can claim the $250,000 IRC Section 121 gain exclusion. Ignoring the non-excludable gain rule, he must report a $450,000 gain on his 2021 Schedule D ($700,000 − $250,000). Because the $450,000 gain that he must report anyway exceeds the $291,167 non-excludable gain, the non-excludable gain rule has no impact under the facts in this particular example.

Example 4-7

Assume the same basic facts as in the previous example, except now assume that Guido has only a $200,000 gain when he sells the property on January 1, 2021. Therefore, he now has a non-excludable gain of $83,333 (5/12 × $200,000) which he must report on his 2021 Schedule D. He can use his $250,000 IRC Section 121 gain exclusion to shelter the remaining $166,667 of gain ($200,000 − $83,333).

Key point: Comparing the results in examples 4-6 and 4-7 reveals the interesting truth that the non-excludable gain rule can hurt sellers with smaller gains (as in example 4-7) while having absolutely no impact on those with larger gains (as in example 4-6).

Example 4-8

Your client Hermione (a married joint filer) bought a vacation home on January 1, 2009. On January 1, 2012, she converts the property into a principal residence and lives there with her husband for 2012 through 2015. She then converts the home back into a vacation property and uses it as such for 2016 through 2018. Hermione then sells the property on January 1, 2019, for a $520,000 gain. Her total ownership period is 10 years (2009–2018). The first three years of post-2008 use as a vacation home (2009–2011) result in a non-excludable gain of $156,000 (3/10 × $520,000). Hermione must report the $156,000 as long-term capital gain on her 2019 Schedule D. Because she is eligible for the $500,000 IRC Section 121 gain exclusion, she can completely exclude the remaining $364,000 of gain ($520,000 − $156,000) with her exclusion.

Key point: The last three years of use as a vacation home (2016–2018) do not count as periods of nonqualified use because they occur (1) after the last day of use as a principal residence (December 31, 2015), and (2) within the five-year period ending on the sale date (January 1, 2019). Therefore, using the property as a vacation home in 2016–2018 does not make the non-excludable gain any bigger.

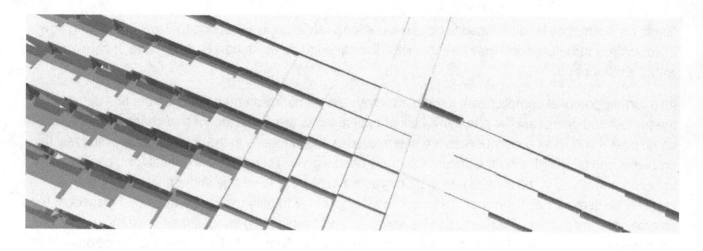

Chapter 5

Tax Planning for Marital Splits and Married Same-Sex Couples

Learning objectives

- Determine appropriate federal income tax advice for clients who are separated, divorcing, or divorced, considering one big change included in the Tax Cuts and Jobs Act (TCJA).

- Recall developments affecting married same-sex couples.

Introduction

In the United States, often-quoted statistics indicate that 40% to 50% of all first marriages end in divorce, and the risk of divorce is even higher for second marriages. The obvious emotional and financial toll on divorcing clients can be heavy. Unfortunately, without thoughtful tax planning, it is quite likely that unexpected tax liabilities will add to client woes.

Tax advisers can render valuable service by helping divorcing clients understand and plan for the federal tax implications associated with marital dissolutions.

Experience shows that this can be a challenging situation for advisers. Although some divorcing clients are able to maintain decent relations with the other party and behave reasonably in resolving financial and tax issues, this is the situation in only a limited percentage of cases. Often it will be found that the client is overwrought, hostile toward the soon-to-be ex-spouse, and generally somewhat irrational. As a result, the client may be disinclined to consider the long-range tax implications that will result from how the divorce is structured and may be especially disinclined to do anything that even hints of cooperation with the other party.

As a further potential complication, divorce attorneys are sometimes unfamiliar with the fine details of the tax law and do not always admit this lack of expertise. As the remainder of this chapter will show, some post-divorce tax consequences are determined by the language in the divorce papers, and few tax problems can be "fixed" after the documents have been signed. Therefore, it is critical for the tax adviser to become involved in the divorce negotiation process *before* the language in the final decree and property settlement has been cast in stone. It is also essential to gain the cooperation and respect of the divorce attorney so that documents can be reviewed, and tax planning suggestions implemented before the divorce is a "done deal." (The effects of divorce on the IRC Section 121 principal residence gain exclusion rules are covered in another chapter.)

This chapter also covers tax developments for married same-sex couples.

Separate versus joint returns for pre-divorce years

For federal income tax purposes, individuals are generally considered married until they are legally separated under a decree of divorce or separate maintenance [IRC Section 7703(a)]. Couples who are simply *separated* in the sense of physically living apart are still married.

Marital status for a tax year depends on whether the client is married or divorced as of December 31. In other words, a couple cannot file as married for the portion of the year they are still married and as single for the period after the divorce through the end of the year. They are treated as either married or single for the entire year.

This rule often means the client is divorced or about to be divorced now but was still married as of the end of *last year*. Therefore, the filing status for the preceding year may still be unresolved. Of course, if the divorce will not occur until *next year*, this year's filing status is the issue.

A couple that is still married at the end of the year in question (whether *this year* or *last year*) generally has the option of filing jointly or using married filing separate (MFS) status for federal income tax returns. Most married couples form the habit of filing jointly to save the time and expense of filing two returns and maintaining two sets of records. Filing jointly also saves taxes when one spouse has relatively high income and the other has little or none, because the joint rate brackets are more favorable than those for single filers.

Key points

- Depending on state domestic relations law, it may be possible to obtain a decree of separate maintenance in advance of the actual final divorce decree.
- If a decree of separate maintenance is obtained before year-end, the couple is considered legally separated (same as divorced for tax purposes) for that year [IRC Section 7703(a)].
- Then, the individuals must file as single taxpayers. However, favorable head of household filing status may be available to one or both.
- Obtaining a decree of separate maintenance before year-end will have the same *year-end tax planning effect* as getting *officially* divorced before year-end.

Marriage penalty relief

Thanks to the TCJA, all the rate brackets for *joint filers* are exactly twice as wide as those for singles for 2018–2025. The exception is the 37% bracket, which starts at taxable income of $600,000 for joint filers and $500,000 for singles for 2018 and $612,350 and $510,300, respectively for 2019. Therefore, the *marriage penalty* (a higher tax bill for a married couple than the combined tax bills that would have applied to the couple before marriage) will rarely apply in 2018–2025 unless both spouses earn about the same amount and both earn quite a bit. Instead, the *marriage bonus* (a lower tax bill for a married couple than the combined tax bills that would have applied to the couple before marriage) will more often come into play when one spouse earns more than the other and the couple files jointly.

For 2018–2025, the standard deduction for *joint filers* is exactly double the amount for singles, so the 2018 joint-filer standard deduction is $24,000 versus $12,000 for single filers. For 2019, the amounts are $24,400 and $12,200, respectively.

For 2018–2025, the tax rate brackets for *MFS* status are the same as for singles, except for the 37% bracket for singles that, for 2018, starts at taxable income of $500,000 versus $300,000 for those who use MFS status. For 2019, the 37% thresholds are $510,300 and $306,175, respectively.

For 2018–2025, the standard deduction for *MFS* status is the same as for singles. The 2018 MFS standard deduction is $12,000. For 2019, it is $12,200.

Bottom line: For 2018–2025, the TCJA's rate brackets and standard deduction amounts come close to eliminating the marriage penalty, and for most folks it is eliminated.

Filing separately to avoid liability for ex-spouse's tax miscues

For the year (or years) preceding a divorce, it is often inadvisable for clients to file a joint return because of the issue of legal liability for federal income taxes. Instead, MFS may be best.

When a joint return is filed, both spouses are jointly and severally liable for any unpaid or understated federal income taxes relating to that year [IRC Section 6013(d)(3)]. In other words, the IRS can determine that there is a tax deficiency for a joint return year and attempt to collect 100% of the amount due from either spouse, regardless of which individual actually caused the problem by understating income or overstating deductions.

In contrast, when MFS status is used, each spouse is liable only for the income tax that is shown (or should have been shown) on that spouse's separate return. Therefore, MFS is advisable when a taxpayer has any suspicions that the spouse might fail to report income or pay in the required taxes.

The joint-and-several-liability rule can be avoided to the extent the client qualifies for innocent spouse relief under IRC Section 6015, as explained later in this section. However, the innocent spouse rules, when they apply, only repair damage that has already been done. It is usually better to avoid the problem in the first place by filing separate returns.

Key points

- In pre-divorce situations, one spouse is often tempted to hide income from the other, and financial resources are generally strained because the couple is living apart and incurring higher expenses.
- Therefore, the stage is set for tax problems due to under reported income, failure to pay in taxes, or both.
- This can happen even when both spouses have previously demonstrated financial responsibility and compliance with the income tax rules.

Tax impact of filing separate returns

The division of a married couple's income and deductions when they file separate returns is a matter of state law. The most important factor is whether they live in a community property state. (The nine community property states are California, Texas, Washington, Arizona, Wisconsin, Nevada, Louisiana, New Mexico, and Idaho.)

Generally, in non-community property states, each spouse reports the income he or she earns and claims deductions for amounts he or she pays. Federal income taxes withheld from a spouse's earnings are allocated to that spouse (Regulation 1.31-1). Presumably the same is true for estimated tax payments that are made separately with respect to income earned by a spouse. Joint estimated tax payments can be allocated in any manner agreed to by the spouses. If they cannot agree, joint estimated payments will be allocated in proportion to each spouse's separate-return tax liability (Rev. Rules. 80-7, 1980-1 CB 296, and 85-70, 1985-1 CB 361).

If the spouses (1) are separated under a written separation agreement, or (2) live apart at all times during the last six months of the year, the custodial spouse is entitled to the child dependent exemption deduction (which is still deemed to exist for 2018–2025 but is equal to zero), regardless of who actually pays for the child's living expenses. The custodial spouse is the one who has custody of the child for the greater portion of the calendar year. However, by releasing the exemption on Form 8332, the custodial spouse can instead agree to let the other spouse take the deduction. [See IRC Section 152(e)(1) and (2).]

In non-community-property states, the higher-earning spouse will often pressure the lower-earning spouse to file jointly, because that would lower the required tax payments for the higher-earning spouse.

As opposed to using joint filing status (or head of household filing status, which is discussed later in this section), there are some definite disadvantages to using MFS status. For example, a taxpayer who uses MFS status

- cannot make a Roth IRA contribution if his or her AGI exceeds $10,000 [IRC Section 408A(c)(3)(A)];
- cannot claim the child and dependent care credit [IRC Section 21(e)(2)];
- cannot claim either of the higher education tax credits [IRC Section 25A(g)(6)];
- cannot claim the college loan interest write-off IRC Section 221(e)(2)];
- cannot claim the deduction for college tuition and related expenses [IRC Section 222(d)(4)];
- cannot deduct more than $1,500 of net capital losses [IRC Section 1211(b)(1)]; and
- must itemize deductions if the other spouse itemizes, even if using the standard deduction would be better for one [IRC Section 63(c)(6)(A)].

In many cases, the "liability protection" benefits of using MFS status must be balanced against the loss of some current-year tax breaks that would be available if a joint return is filed.

Filing separately in community property states

The preceding discussion of MFS tax consequences assumes the spouses do not reside in one of the nine community property states (California, Texas, Washington, Arizona, Wisconsin, Nevada, Louisiana, New Mexico, and Idaho).

In community property states, married couples are generally required to split most income, deductions, and credit for tax payments 50/50 for federal income tax purposes.

Therefore, there may not be meaningful tax savings from filing jointly versus MFS for residents of community property states. (See IRS Publication 555, *Community Property*.) That being said, it is always a good practice to "run the numbers" just to make sure particularly if either spouse has a significant amount of property that generates income.

Favorable community property rule may apply

When a couple lives apart for the entire year but is still married at year-end, a favorable special rule provided by IRC Section 66 can come into play. When applicable, the IRC Section 66 rule overrides the usual rule that most items are shared 50/50 for federal income tax purposes when separate returns are filed by spouses residing in community property states. The IRC Section 66 rule is basically intended to ensure that the spouse who gets the money from taxable community income owes the tax when community income is *not* actually shared 50/50.

Section 66 rule

The IRC Section 66 rule prevents the obviously undesirable situation of one spouse having to report and pay tax on income that he or she never sees. If such a situation were allowed to exist, an estranged spouse could effectively be forced to file a joint return (with resulting possible exposure to tax "sins" of the other spouse) in order to avoid a large separate return tax liability. For the IRC Section 66 rule to apply, all four of the following conditions must be met for the tax year in question:

- The individuals are married at year-end but lived apart for the entire year.
- A joint return is not filed for the year.
- One or both of the individuals had earned income for the year that is community income (that is, income that would be shared 50/50 under the general rule).
- There were no transfers of such earned community income between the individuals. However, per IRS Publication 555 (*Community Property*), small transfers can be disregarded. Also transfers or payments to or for a dependent child (such as court-ordered pre-divorce temporary child support payments to the other spouse) will not violate this rule. Transfers or payments to or for a dependent child will not violate this rule even if they satisfy a support obligation of the other spouse (IRS Publication 555).

If all the preceding requirements are met, each spouse must report all community income on his or her separate tax return pursuant to the following rules as set forth in IRC Section 879(a):

- Income from performing services or carrying on a trade or business (other than a partnership) is reported by the spouse performing the services or conducting the trade or business.
- Partnership income is reported by the spouse who is the partner.
- Taxable Social Security benefits are reported by the spouse who receives the benefits (per IRS Publication 555).
- To the extent income from separate property is considered community income (it is in some states), the income is reported by the spouse who owns the property.
- All other community income (interest, dividends, and so on) is reported by the spouses as such income is considered to be shared according to state community property law.

Key point If the requirements previously listed are not met by a married couple and they file separate returns, they generally must report all taxable community income on their respective returns according to how it is considered shared under state community property law (normally 50/50).

Filing separately as head of household

Before a final decision regarding filing joint or separate returns is made, determine if the divorcing client can file as a head of household (HOH). In many cases, spouses with pre-divorce primary custody of a child will turn out to be eligible.

Assessing HOH eligibility is important because the tax rates and standard deduction for HOH status are more favorable than those for MFS. For instance, for 2018, the 22% bracket starts at taxable income of $51,801 for HOH versus $38,710 for MFS; the HOH standard deduction for 2018 is $18,000 versus $12,000 for MFS.

As is the case with MFS returns, HOH returns are considered separate returns. Therefore, they protect one spouse from tax liabilities caused by the other's actions.

There are several other benefits of HOH filing status compared to MFS filing status. For instance, an MFS filer cannot (1) make a Roth IRA contribution if his or her AGI exceeds $10,000, (2) take the child and dependent care credit, (3) claim either of the college tuition tax credits or the deduction for college tuition and related expenses, (4) claim the college loan interest write-off, or (5) deduct more than $1,500 of net capital losses. Also, the AGI-based phase-out ranges for various tax benefits are lower for MFS filers than for HOH filers. For all these reasons, HOH status is almost always preferable to MFS status.

Abandoned spouse rule

The general rule is that HOH status is available only to unmarried taxpayers. However, there is an exception—the abandoned spouse rule—for married individuals who can meet all of the following conditions [IRC Sections 2(b), 2(c), 151, 152, and 7703(b)]:

- Separate returns are filed.
- The taxpayer lived apart from the spouse during the last six months of the year.
- The taxpayer's home served for more than half the year as the principal home of the taxpayer's qualifying child.
- The taxpayer paid more than half the cost of maintaining the home for the year (rent, mortgage interest, property taxes, insurance on the home, utilities, food eaten in the home, and so on, but not counting other "living expenses" such as clothing, medical care, schooling, transportation, vacations, and so on).

If a spouse meets the preceding conditions, the spouse is treated as *unmarried* for the year and eligible for HOH status. The other spouse must then use MFS or HOH status. (HOH is available for the other spouse if that spouse also meets the four requirements previously listed, for example, when each spouse has primary custody of at least one child during the pre-divorce period and they live apart for the last six months of the year.)

Other ways to avoid tax liabilities caused by spouses

The surest way for one spouse to avoid tax liabilities caused by the other is to simply file separate returns for pre-divorce tax years. As discussed earlier in this section, both MFS and HOH returns will do the trick.

However, in the interest of being able to offer other alternatives to divorcing clients, consider these additional options for protecting an *innocent* spouse from liability for tax problems caused by a *guilty* spouse.

Decree of separate maintenance before year-end

As mentioned earlier, some state domestic relations statutes allow individuals to obtain a decree of separate maintenance in advance of the final divorce decree. If a decree of separate maintenance is obtained before year-end, the couple is considered legally separated—same as divorced for tax purposes—for that year [IRC Section 7703(a)]. Legally separated individuals cannot file joint returns. Instead, they must file as single taxpayers (unless they remarry before year-end).

Thus, legal separation before year-end allows an *innocent* spouse to avoid a joint return without having to use the relatively unfavorable MFS filing status. After legal separation, the relatively favorable single filing status is a given, and the even more favorable HOH filing status may be available.

Tax liability indemnification clause in divorce agreement

Including a tax liability indemnification clause in the divorce document means one ex-spouse is legally entitled to be reimbursed if that spouse is forced to pay a tax liability caused by the actions (or inactions) of the other. Such a clause will not avoid joint and several liability with respect to unpaid taxes for joint filing years. The IRS can still enforce collection efforts against either ex-spouse (unless the innocent spouse rules apply). The indemnification clause simply gives a spouse who wrongly gets *stuck with the bill* legal recourse against the other ex-spouse.

Unfortunately, if the IRS is having trouble collecting from the *guilty* ex-spouse, it is unlikely that an indemnification clause will do the *innocent* ex-spouse much good. Still, it cannot hurt to include one in the divorce decree, especially with respect to unknown or undisclosed tax liabilities for open joint filing years before marital discord became an issue.

Innocent spouse rules

Under former IRC Section 6013(e), *innocent spouses* could under limited circumstances avoid joint and several liability. However, this relief was often unavailable because of the statutory language and IRS insistence on an exceedingly strict interpretation of said language. The longstanding problem was finally addressed with the enactment of the current version of IRC Section 6015, which contains *new and improved* innocent spouse rules.

Warning: The current version of IRC Section 6015 does not repeal the joint-and-several-liability rule. As before, the general rule is *spouses and former spouses are jointly and severally liable for taxes from years for which joint returns are filed.* However, the current version of IRC Section 6015 greatly increases the odds of qualifying for innocent spouse relief from the joint-and-several-liability rule. Still, as under prior law, the only surefire way to avoid joint and several liability is by not filing a joint return.

New IRC Section 6015(b) provides general elective relief to all joint filers, including those still married to the individual with whom a joint return was filed. Relief is available to electing individuals when there is a tax understatement attributable to *erroneous items* caused by the spouse or former spouse (the other party to the joint return) and the electing individual establishes that

- he or she did not know of the understatement;
- he or she had no reason to know of the understatement; and
- it would be unfair to hold him or her responsible for the understatement after considering all the facts and circumstances.

If the electing individual knew there were some tax problems, but did not know about their full extent, he or she can still make the IRC Section 6015(b) election and get off the hook for the unknown part of the tax understatement [IRC Section 6015(b)(2)].

Observation: Relief under this election might be tougher to qualify for than it first appears. Basically, the electing individual must be in the dark about the tax problem or at least the full extent of the problem in order to pass the did-not-know part of the test. And the electing individual generally *cannot* simply plead ignorance of the problem without failing the did-not-have-any-reason-to-know part of the test. Thus, to qualify for this election, the individual must be innocent and not be ignorant. In real-life circumstances, this will rarely be the case.

The IRC Section 6015(b) election has no impact on the liability of either spouse for any understatement caused by his or her own actions or omissions. The effect of the election is simply that the electing individual is protected from liabilities caused by the other party's actions or omissions.

"Ignorant spouse" relief

IRC Section 6015(c) provides another form of elective relief for joint filers who, at the time the election is filed, (1) are divorced or legally separated from the other party, or (2) have lived apart for the preceding 12 months from the other party.

Under this second election, the liability of the electing individual for a joint-return year cannot exceed the *separate liability* of that person. The separate liability of each joint filer is determined by allocating income and deduction amounts as if separate returns were filed [IRC Section 6015(d)].

However, the election is unavailable with respect to tax understatements, or portions thereof, caused by the other party about which the electing individual had *actual knowledge* at the time the joint return was signed. In other words, if the electing individual had actual knowledge of an understatement, that amount remains subject to the joint-and-several-liability rule.

The actual-knowledge standard is intended to be much looser than the did-not-know-and-had-no-reason-to-know standard that must be met to qualify for the IRC Section 6015(b) election previously explained. In other words, *ignorance* of tax problems is enough to qualify for the IRC Section 6015(c) election, under the did-not-have-actual-knowledge test.

Warning: The IRC Section 6015(c) election has no impact on the liability of either spouse for any understatement caused by his or her own actions or omissions. The effect of the election is simply that the electing individual is protected from liabilities caused by the other party's actions or omissions.

Equitable relief

In the 1998 IRS Restructuring and Reform Act, Congress directed Treasury to develop rules granting administrative relief to joint filers who fail to qualify for relief under the preceding rules; when all facts and circumstances indicate it's unfair to enforce joint and several liability [IRC Section 6015(f)]. Revenue Procedure 2003-61 supplies the procedures to request equitable relief.

Procedures

Form 8857 (Request for Innocent Spouse Relief) is used to take advantage of all three forms of relief previously explained.

Both the IRC Section 6015(b) election (*Innocent Spouse Relief*) and the IRC Section 6015(c) election (*Ignorant Spouse Relief*) must be made (using Form 8857) within two years after IRS collection activity against the electing individual has commenced for amounts related to a joint-return year.

Knowledge check

1. A major reason for a person who is having marital difficulties to use MFS status rather than filing jointly is to

    a. Lower the combined federal income tax bill of the two spouses.
    b. Claim various tax breaks that are not allowed to married joint-filing couples.
    c. Avoid the passive loss rules.
    d. Avoid joint and several liability for the other spouse's tax misdeeds.

Avoiding pre-divorce tax fiascos with IRA and qualified retirement plan assets

Clients contemplating divorce are generally aware that their IRA and qualified retirement plan (QRP) assets will likely be divided up as part of the divorce. IRAs and QRP accounts can be split in a tax-effective manner if this is done as part of the divorce decree or property settlement agreement.

Sometimes when the client is getting along well with the soon-to-be-ex-spouse, the client may be tempted to transact a *pre-divorce* split of IRAs and QRP accounts. This is especially likely in a community property state where the client clearly understands the spouse will wind up with half of the account balances anyway, when all is said and done.

The client may think that, before the divorce, funds can simply be withdrawn from the client's accounts and transferred tax-free into the spouse's IRA or QRP account. The client may also think that such pre-divorce *do-it-yourself* transactions will save legal and accounting fees. Although these ideas seem to make sense, nothing could be further from the truth. The danger level intensifies when the client functions as the trustee of his or her QRP and therefore has the power to unilaterally act without the benefit of professional advice.

The truth is, amounts withdrawn by the client before the divorce will generally be treated as fully *taxable* distributions to the client. They will not be taxed to the other spouse who actually receives the funds; nor will they qualify for a tax-free rollover into the spouse's IRA or QRP account. Instead, the client's spouse will own the funds tax-free, because the tax is imposed on the client.

If the client is under age 59½ at the time of the withdrawal, the 10% premature withdrawal penalty tax will generally apply *on top* of the regular income tax liability [IRC Section 72(t)]. Finally, amounts cannot be withdrawn from QRP accounts except for reasons specified in plan documents. Satisfying the client's desire to accomplish a pre-divorce split of marital assets is not one of those reasons, and a withdrawal could have the effect of disqualifying the client's retirement plan.

The message in this section is simple. Proper planning is critical to achieve acceptable tax results when dividing up IRA and QRP assets in a divorce case. In this area, irreparable damage can result when tax advisers do not find out about transactions until after they have occurred. See the following discussion for planning steps and horror stories when these steps are not followed.

Planning to achieve tax-effective splits of IRA and QRP assets

When clients divorce, IRA and QRP assets will often be divided up as part of the property settlement. The expectation of the parties is generally that the individual receiving the retirement account funds will be the one who pays the related income taxes. However, pre-divorce planning is necessary to achieve this *common-sense* tax outcome.

Splitting up IRA assets

Pursuant to a *divorce or separation instrument*, an individual can make a tax-free transfer of his or her interest in an IRA to the IRA of a spouse or former spouse. The other party then treats the receiving IRA as his or her own account and follows the usual rules regarding taxability of subsequent distributions. In other words, the other party can then withdraw the IRA funds as he or she chooses and pay the resulting taxes. The preceding treatment is under a special rule provided by IRC Section 408(d)(6).

Note that the exact same rule applies to simplified employee pension (SEP) accounts, because they are considered IRAs for this purpose.

For purposes of this rule, a divorce or separation instrument is defined as a divorce decree, a decree of separate maintenance, or a written instrument incident to such a decree (such as a divorce property settlement agreement).

Any other action that has the effect of transferring IRA funds to a spouse or ex-spouse, *before or after* a divorce, will cause the account owner to owe the income taxes, even though the other party winds up with the funds. Such transactions are simply treated as fully taxable distributions to the account owner, who is then deemed to turn the funds over to the other party. [See Ltr. Rul. 9422060; *Richard C. Czepiel*, TC Memo 1999-289; the same thing would have happened in Ltr. Rul. 199937055 if the couple had gone through with the transaction. See also *Michael G. Bunney*, 114 TC No. 17 (Tax Court, 2000). In the latter case, the fact that the wife held a community property interest in husband's IRA did not change the tax results. The husband still owed the federal income tax, plus the 10% premature withdrawal penalty, when he withdrew cash from his IRA and gave it to his ex-wife as called for by the divorce settlement.] If the account owner is under age 59½ at the time such a transfer is made, the 10% penalty tax on premature withdrawals will generally apply *on top* of the "regular" income tax liability [IRC Section 72(t)]. The funds received by the spouse or ex-spouse will not be eligible for tax-free rollover into an IRA set up for that person.

One clearly permissible method for effecting an IRC Section 408(d)(6) tax-free transfer of IRA funds is to make a *trustee-to-trustee* transfer directly from the account owner's IRA to a new IRA set up for the spouse or ex-spouse. (Such transfers do not actually pass through the hands of either the account owner or the other party.) It is less clear that a distribution check made payable to the other party followed by a rollover within 60 days into that person's IRA would also qualify.

Note: The same considerations apply to simplified employee pension (SEP) accounts, because SEP accounts are treated as IRAs for purposes of the tax rules applicable to distributions.

Example 5-1 Misguided attempt to split IRA funds before divorce

- In Private Letter Ruling 9422060, the IRS explained the tax impact of a husband's pre-divorce transfer of funds from his IRA into an IRA held by his wife.
  - Because the transfer was not an IRC Section 408(d)(6) transfer pursuant to a divorce or separation instrument, the transaction was treated as a fully taxable constructive distribution to the husband. Thus, he got the income tax bill and his wife got the money. This was certainly not what the couple expected; however, the wife presumably had no complaints after finding out she had received a tax-free windfall. (Actually, the wife's IRA trustee should not have permitted the transfer of funds into her IRA because the money did not qualify as a distribution eligible for rollover treatment.)

Note:

- PLR 8820086 reaches the same conclusion regarding attempted pre-divorce transfers from one spouse's IRA to an IRA held by the other.
- Finally, the Tax Court confirms that the same tax outcome applies when an individual attempts to make a post-divorce transfer of funds from an IRA to an ex-spouse to satisfy financial terms of the divorce decree (*Paul D. Harris*, TC Memo 1991-375).

Strategy

- Tell your clients that they should not make pre-divorce or post-divorce transfers of IRA funds except as specifically required under the terms of a divorce document.
- To ensure a tax-free transfer, the divorce document should specify that the transfer of IRA funds is intended to be tax-free under an IRC Section 408(d)(6) of the Internal Revenue Code.
- The transfer should be made via a *trustee-to-trustee* transfer of funds directly from the account owner's IRA to a new IRA set up for the spouse or ex-spouse.

Splitting up QRP account assets

A more complicated maneuver is required to effect a tax-free transfer to a spouse or ex-spouse of assets held in QRP accounts. For this purpose, QRP accounts include those under an employer's pension, profit-sharing, or Section 401(k) plan; a self-employed Keogh plan; or an IRC Section 403(b) tax-sheltered annuity plan.

The general rule is that transfers of assets in QRP accounts to anyone other than the plan participant (the individual for whom the account is set up) are not permitted [IRC Section 401(a)(13)(A)].

Transfers to other parties, including the participant's spouse or ex-spouse, are treated as fully taxable constructive distributions to the participant, who is then deemed to transfer the funds to the other party. In other words, the participant's spouse or ex-spouse could end up with the QRP funds and the participant simply ends up with the income tax bill.

Beyond this extremely adverse tax outcome, such distributions may also cause disqualification of the retirement plan, because plan terms allow distributions to participants only under specified circumstances (such as reaching retirement age, separation from service, and so on).

Qualified domestic relations orders to the rescue

Fortunately, the preceding bad news can be avoided by transferring QRP account assets to a spouse or ex-spouse via a qualified domestic relations order (QDRO).

A QDRO is a legal judgment, decree, or order (including one approving a divorce property settlement agreement) that meets certain Tax Code guidelines. It can be a separate document or simply language included as part of another divorce-related document, such as the property settlement. The QDRO establishes that one spouse or ex-spouse has the legal right to receive all or part of the other party's QRP benefits without violating the plan's benefit distribution rules.

The QDRO also has the important and desirable side-effect of ensuring that the spouse or ex-spouse receiving the benefits—and not the participant—owes the related income taxes. In other words, the person who gets the money owes the taxes, which is exactly what the parties should expect to happen.

What is needed to establish a QDRO?

For a QDRO to exist, there must be language in a divorce document that meets all of the following requirements, as set forth in IRC Section 414(p):

- It must provide for child support, alimony payments, or marital property rights for a spouse, former spouse, child, or other dependent of a qualified plan participant and it must be made pursuant to a state domestic relations law (including a community property law).
- It must create or recognize the existence of the right of the individual named, who is termed the *alternate payee*, to receive all or a portion of a participant's benefits under a QRP.
- It must specify the following:
  - Name and last known mailing address of the participant and each alternate payee covered by the order (in divorce situations there is usually only one alternate payee—the ex-spouse);
  - Amount or percentage of the participant's benefits to be paid by the plan to each alternate payee or the manner in which the amount or percentage is to be determined (when possible, the simplest way to conform with this rule is to arrange for a lump sum payment of a set amount to the alternate payee);
  - Number of payments or periods to which the order relates (again, the simplest way to comply with this requirement is by calling for a lump sum payment when possible); and
  - Each QRP to which the order applies (the simplest procedure is to call for the alternate payee to receive payment(s) from only one plan when there are several).

- To constitute a QDRO, an order must not
  - require the plan to pay increased benefits beyond what the participant is normally entitled to;
  - require the plan to pay benefits to an alternate payee when those benefits must be paid to a different alternate payee pursuant to another QDRO (such as one arising from an earlier divorce); or
  - require the plan to provide a type or form of benefit (such as a lump sum) or any option that is not otherwise provided for by the terms of the plan.
- **Key point:** Although the preceding requirements are generally not difficult to meet, failure can be disastrous, as illustrated by the real-life story in example 5-2.
- If a QRP distribution is made pursuant to divorce document language not meeting the definition of a QDRO, the plan participant can end up being taxed on funds received by the other party.
- This is truly a "one person gets the mine and the other gets the shaft" scenario.
- A tax professional does not want to be the one advising an individual on the wrong end of such a transaction.

Example 5-2 Tax results without proper QDRO language

- The tax effects of attempting to split up QRP benefits without using a QDRO are best illustrated using a real-life example. Arthur Hawkins was an orthodontist in New Mexico who functioned as the plan administrator and sole trustee of his own retirement plan. Under a 1987 divorce decree, Arthur's former wife Glenda was awarded a property settlement of $1m to be paid from Arthur's QRP account. Unfortunately, the divorce decree language did not specifically identify Glenda as an alternate payee, nor did it include her last known address.
  - The Tax Court concluded that Glenda's $1m plan payout should be treated as a taxable distribution to *Arthur* because the IRC Section 414(p) QDRO requirements were not explicitly met in writing. (If this happened today, Arthur would probably owe $350,000 in federal income tax plus the 10% penalty tax on premature withdrawals if the distribution occurred before he was age 59½.)
- Arthur appealed to the 10th Circuit and finally won at that level.
  - The Appeals Court decided Glenda's legal right to qualified plan benefits was defined in the divorce decree. Thus, she was an alternate payee even though not described as such in the document. The amount she was entitled to was clearly $1m, and the payment terms were clear. The Court waived the requirement that Glenda's last known address be included in the divorce decree, because Arthur was the plan administrator and Glenda admitted he knew her address.
  - Based on the circumstances, the Court concluded the language in the divorce decree could be construed as constituting a QDRO. Therefore Glenda, rather than Arthur, owed the taxes on the $1m. [See *Hawkins, Arthur C.*, 96-1 USTC 50,316 (10th Cir. 1996).]
- Key point
  - Although the taxpayer ultimately dodged the bullet in this case, the litigation costs were undoubtedly heavy. The entire issue could have been easily avoided by simply including proper QDRO language in the divorce decree.

Another horror story is provided by a Florida bankruptcy court decision. In this case, the taxpayer received a distribution from his QRP account and used the money to pay an amount owed to his ex-wife pursuant to the divorce decree. The language in the decree did not meet the IRC Section 414(p) QDRO requirements. Therefore, the participant, rather than the ex-wife, was taxed on the distribution even though she got the money. [See *Michael D. Boudreau*, 95-1 USTC ¶50,115 (BC-Fla. 1995).] In another case, a California taxpayer deposited his QRP distribution in his estranged wife's IRA before their subsequent divorce. The husband was taxed on the distribution. [See *Mario Rodoni v. Commissioner*, 105 TC 29 (1995).]

Key points

- When retirement plans are professionally administered (as is the case with most large-employer plans), it is less likely that a distribution pursuant to a divorce decree will be made without a proper QDRO being in place.
- However, when the divorcing client is a small-business owner who also acts as the administrator for the retirement plan in question, the odds of misbegotten distributions rise astronomically.
- Such clients have the power to make distributions unilaterally and often do so without obtaining proper professional advice.

Tax results with QDRO in place

The tax outcome from using a QDRO is what the divorcing couple would commonly tend to expect. Generally, the alternate payee (ex-spouse) *steps into the tax shoes* of the plan participant. Thus, the alternate payee is taxed when funds are withdrawn from the QRP account.

However, the 10% premature withdrawal penalty tax that generally applies to QRP distributions received before age 59½ does not apply to any distribution made pursuant to a QDRO [IRC Section 72(t)(2)(C)]. Thus, an ex-spouse need not have attained that age to avoid the 10% penalty tax.

Funds distributed to the alternate payee can also be rolled over tax-free into an IRA set up for that person [IRC Section 402(e)(1)(B)]. The rollover must be done within 60 days of the alternate payee's receipt of the distribution. Such rollovers should be accomplished via trustee-to-trustee direct transfers from the participant's QRP account to the ex-spouse's IRA. This avoids the mandatory 20% federal income tax withholding that will otherwise be taken out of the QRP distribution.

Warnings

- Attorneys specializing in domestic relations cases are usually aware of the benefits of QDROs, but they may not understand the need to comply with the specific Section 414(p) requirements.
- As a tax adviser, you should *not* assume that a divorce document will meet these requirements without intervention on your part.
- Failure to review divorce documents before they are executed can lead to client tax fiascos, as described earlier in this section.
- If that happens, there will be plenty of blame to spread around among all professionals involved with the divorce.

IRS-provided sample QDRO language

In Notice 97-11, the IRS complied. Employing the sample language should reduce the risk of the adverse tax results discussed earlier in this section.

Knowledge check

2. When QRP balances or benefits are split up in divorce, what are the federal income tax results?

   a. Without proper planning, one ex-spouse can wind up owing taxes on retirement plan balances or benefits that are actually received by the other ex-spouse.
   b. The ex-spouse who receives the retirement plan balances or benefits will always be the one who owes the related taxes when funds are withdrawn or benefits are received.
   c. The ex-spouse who is the plan participant will always be the one who owes the related taxes when funds are withdrawn by the other ex-spouse or benefits are received by the other ex-spouse.
   d. Such splits are always free of any current or future federal income tax consequences.

3. What is the preferred method to affect a tax-free transfer of the account owner's IRA money to his or her ex-spouse's IRA pursuant to a divorce or separation instrument?

   a. Via a trustee-to-trustee transfer between the account owner's IRA and the ex-spouse's IRA.
   b. Via a declaration that the account owner's intent is to make a tax-free rollover on his or her tax return.
   c. Via a distribution check written from the account owner's IRA to the other spouse's personal checking or savings account.
   d. Via a distribution to the account owner followed by a transfer to the ex-spouse followed by a tax-free rollover contribution into the ex-spouse's IRA.

4. What does setting up a QDRO ensure?

   a. That the participant of a QRP is entitled to all of the plan account balance or plan benefits to the exclusion of the participant's ex-spouse.
   b. That a couple is considered to be divorced for federal income tax purposes.
   c. That the ex-spouse of a QRP participant is entitled to all or a portion of the plan account balance or benefits and that the ex-spouse is responsible for the related taxes when amounts are withdrawn or benefits are paid.
   d. That the ex-spouse who files the QDRO cannot be contacted by the other ex-spouse regarding outstanding tax issues related to the time they were married.

Planning to achieve equitable after-tax property divisions

Property splits between divorcing couples should be structured to be fair to both parties on an after-tax basis. IRC Section 1041(a) provides the general rule that property transfers between divorcing spouses are treated as tax-free gifts, with the transferee taking over the transferor's basis and holding period. As a result, when one party ends up holding appreciated assets (such as real estate, securities, zero basis receivables, deferred compensation benefits, and so on), that person will generally owe tax when the assets are sold or converted into cash.

Key points

- An equitable property settlement will account for the reduced value of appreciated assets caused by the *built-in* tax liabilities that come along for the ride.
- After-tax values can be illustrated using a balance sheet approach.
- The couple should then decide on an equitable property division based on these after-tax amounts.

Tax-free treatment under IRC Section 1041(a) is mandatory rather than elective and applies to any property transfers that are deemed incident to a divorce. There is no gain or loss even if cash is paid by one party for property held by the other or if liabilities exceed basis. Tax-free treatment applies whether the property was originally jointly owned or separately owned [however, IRC Section 1041(a) does not apply to transfers to nonresident aliens].

A transfer is incident to a divorce if

- the transfer occurs within one year after the date on which the marriage ceases (with the date this occurs to be determined under state law), or
- the transfer is related to the cessation of the marriage—any transfer pursuant to a divorce or separation instrument within six years after the date the marriage ceases is presumed to be related to the cessation of the marriage.

Transfers between former spouses that fall outside the time limits are treated as taxable sales or as gifts, depending on the circumstances. Transfers falling within these limits are presumed to be incident to the divorce and are therefore tax-free under IRC Section 1041.

For instance, one ex-spouse can acquire property after the divorce and transfer it tax-free to the other ex-spouse as long as this occurs within one year of the date of divorce. [See IRC Section 1041(c) and Temp. Reg. Section 1.1041-1T(b), Q&As 6 and 7.]

Taking advantage of the tax-free transfer rule

The ability to transfer property tax-free (within the listed limits) can help the parties deal with cash flow problems, as the following examples illustrate.

Example 5-3 Post-divorce transfer of property for cash

- Bill and Karen are divorced on July 1. Shortly thereafter, Karen realizes that she is facing a major cash crunch. Bill is willing to help her solve the problem by giving Karen $36,000 cash in exchange for her rare stamp collection, which is worth $50,000 and has a tax basis of $200.
- The deal is done on August 15. Because this is within one year of the divorce date, the transaction is tax-free under IRC Section 1041(a).
    - Bill takes over Karen's $200 tax basis in the collection. He will eventually owe tax on the difference between FMV and $200, which is why he was willing to pay only $36,000. (If Bill does not understand the carryover basis rule, he may unwittingly pay the full FMV of $50,000, which would be a windfall for Karen.)

Note

- If Bill bought the card collection more than one year after the divorce, it would be treated as a taxable purchase or sale transaction, unless it was called for in the divorce decree and occurred within six years of the divorce date.
- If taxable purchase or sale treatment applies, Karen should insist on receiving the full $50,000 FMV, because Bill would obtain a stepped-up tax basis in the collection and she would owe tax on the gain.

When the divorcing individuals face significantly different marginal tax rates after the split, it can be beneficial to take advantage of the IRC Section 1041(a) tax-free transfer rule by transferring appreciated property from the higher-income spouse to the lower-income spouse in order to save taxes when the property is sold.

Example 5-4 Post-divorce transfer saves taxes

- Chuck (a starving artist) and Donna (a successful attorney) will become divorced on February 1. Prior to finalizing the decree, the couple has tentatively agreed that Donna will be obligated to pay Chuck $100,000 as soon as possible after the divorce as part of the property settlement. However, Donna's marginal tax rate (federal and state combined) is 45%, and her only significant liquid asset is short-term capital gain property worth $100,000 with tax basis of $20,000. Chuck's marginal tax rate is only 18%.
    - If Donna sells the property and pays the taxes, she will net only $64,000 and will still be $36,000 short of what she needs to pay Chuck. However, if she transfers the property to Chuck and he sells it, he will net $85,600. Chuck will agree to this if Donna agrees to pay him an additional $20,000 to cover his taxes. Donna agrees.
    - Under this arrangement Donna is out of pocket for $20,000 of cash, but this is much better than the $36,000 of taxes that she would have to pay otherwise. Chuck will collect a total of $120,000 and owe taxes of $18,000 [$18\% \times (\$80,000 + 20,000)$]. The transfer of appreciated property allows both parties to come out ahead on an after-tax basis.

Transfers of ordinary-income assets

For years, the IRS appeared to say that the IRC Section 1041 tax-free transfer rule applied only to capital gain assets. (See, for example, Revenue Ruling 87-12, Private Letter Ruling 8813023, and Field Service Advice 200005006.)

For instance, if you transferred business receivables, inventory, or vested nonqualified stock options to your spouse in divorce, the IRS wanted you to report the date-of-transfer difference between fair market value and basis as ordinary income on your Form 1040. In other words, you paid the tax, even though your ex got the assets.

Now, it appears the IRS has reversed its field and concluded that most ordinary-income assets can be transferred tax-free under the IRC Section 1041(a) rule. If so, the spouse who winds up with the asset must recognize the income when the asset is sold, converted to cash, or exercised in the case of stock options. Fair enough.

Key point: In support of the preceding conclusion, see Revenue Ruling 2002-22 which deals specifically with vested nonqualified employer stock options and nonqualified deferred compensation rights but which appears to have wider applicability.

Knowledge check

5. For post-divorce asset transfers between two ex-spouses who are both U.S. citizens, it is generally true that transfers occurring within how many years of the date of divorce are automatically tax-free?

    a. 10.
    b. 8.
    c. 7.
    d. 1.

Treating payments as deductible alimony

One of the most commonly encountered client situations is the ex-spouse who expects the payments made to the other to be deductible as alimony. However, there are a number of requirements that must be met for alimony treatment to apply. Unfortunately, attorneys often draft divorce papers in such a way that alimony treatment is not available.

When payments fail to meet the federal income tax definition of alimony, they are generally treated as either child support payments or as payments to divide the marital property (that is, part of the divorce property settlement). In either case, the payments are non-deductible personal expenses for the payer and tax-free income to the payee.

On the other hand, payments that meet the federal Tax Code's definition of alimony are treated as such for federal income tax purposes, regardless of how the payments are described in the divorce agreement or under state law. (For example, see *Thomas H. Nelson, et ux. v. Commissioner*, TC Memo 1998-268.)

TCJA eliminates alimony deductions, but not only for payments under post-2018 divorce agreements

In divorce situations, one spouse or ex-spouse may be legally obligated to make payments to the other party. Because payments are often substantial, locking in tax deductions for the payer has often been a substantial issue. Under prior law (pre-TCJA), payments that meet the tax law definition of alimony could always be deducted by the payer for federal income tax purposes, and they always had to be reported as taxable income by the recipient.

This prior-law treatment continues for alimony payments made under pre-2019 divorce agreements. But for payments made under post-2018 agreements, things have changed dramatically.

For payments required under divorce or separation instruments executed after December 31, 2018, the deduction for alimony payments is eliminated. Recipients of such alimony payments will no longer include them in taxable income. [See IRC Sec. 215 as repealed by the TCJA and IRC Secs. 62(a)(10) and 61(a)(8).] For high-income individuals who pay alimony, this can be an expensive change because the tax savings from being able to deduct alimony payments can be big.

Effective date: The new treatment of alimony payments applies to payments required under divorce or separation instruments that are (1) executed after December 31, 2018, or (2) modified after that date if the modification specifically states that the new TCJA treatment of alimony payments (i.e. not deductible by the payer and not taxable income for the recipient) now applies. Unlike many of the TCJA changes that affect individual taxpayers, the new law's treatment of alimony payments is a permanent change.

For payments required by pre-2019 divorce agreements, it's still business as usual

For payments required by pre-2019 divorce agreements to qualify as deductible alimony, payers must still satisfy a list of specific requirements. If those requirements are met, alimony payments can be deducted above-the-line on the payer's federal income tax return. This means the payer does not have to itemize to benefit. The following discussion of what it takes for payments to be deductible alimony payments still pertains to payments required by pre-2019 divorce agreements.

Requirements for payments to constitute alimony

Payments that qualify as alimony represent above-the-line deductions for the payer and taxable income to the payee [IRC Sections 71(a) and 215(a)]. As mentioned, whether or not payments qualify is determined strictly by the Tax Code and not by the divorce decree, court order, or intentions of the divorcing couple. This essential fact is misunderstood by many otherwise competent divorce attorneys.

In other words, a payment may be referred to as *alimony* in the divorce papers and be intended by the parties to be alimony but still fail to qualify as such under the Tax Code. Non-qualifying payments will be considered non-deductible child support or divisions of marital property for federal income tax purposes. On the other hand, it is also possible (although relatively unlikely) for payments not referred to as, or intended to be, alimony to meet the Tax Code's definition. In such case, they will be deductible by the payer and taxable income to the payee.

In order for a payment to be treated as alimony for federal income tax purposes, all of the following requirements (explained in more detail later in this section) must be met:

- It must be made under a written divorce or separation instrument and the instrument cannot state the payment is not alimony (qualifying payments can occur both before and after the couple is divorced or legally separated).
- After divorce or legal separation (meaning the couple is considered divorced for federal income tax purposes), the ex-spouses cannot live in the same household or file a joint return.
- The payment must be made to a spouse or ex-spouse and be in cash or a cash equivalent.
- The payment must not be fixed or deemed child support (child support payments are non-deductible to the payer and tax-free to the payee).
- The obligation to make payments (other than payment of delinquent amounts) must cease when the payee dies.

Key points

- The last two requirements cause the most trouble.
- If payment obligations continue after the payee ex-spouse dies, the payments are not alimony. Period. For example, an ex-husband's monthly payments intended to cover his ex-wife's mortgage payments will not qualify as alimony if the husband's payments are required to continue after the ex-wife's death. Such payments would be a non-deductible expense for the ex-husband and tax-free money to the ex-wife. (See *Elizabeth S. Pettet* v. U.S., E.D.N.C., November 10, 1997.)

- On the other hand, the payer ex-spouse's estate can be required to continue to make payments after the payer dies without running afoul of the federal income tax definition of alimony.

Payment obligations deemed to be child support payments are discussed later in this section.

Divorce instruments will often call for one or both parties to make a variety of payments to each other. Each payment or stream of payments is tested independently to determine if it qualifies as alimony. The fact that one payment or stream fails does not affect the ability of other payments or streams of payments to meet the definition.

Knowledge check

6. When a payment to an ex-spouse is not alimony under the federal income tax rules, how is it generally treated?

    a. As taxable income to the recipient ex-spouse.
    b. Either as child support or as part of the divorce property settlement.
    c. As gifts from the payor to the payee.
    d. As an itemized deduction for spousal support.

7. For federal income tax purposes, payments under pre-2019 divorce agreements that qualify as alimony are

    a. Deducted by the payor "above-the-line."
    b. Received tax-free by the payee.
    c. Free of any federal income tax consequences for both the payor and the payee.
    d. Deducted by the payor as a miscellaneous itemized deduction item.

8. For federal income tax purposes, payments that qualify as alimony are

    a. Deducted by the payor "above-the-line" if the payments are required under a pre-2019 divorce agreement.
    b. Received tax-free by the payee.
    c. Free of any federal income tax consequences for both the payor and the payee.
    d. Deducted by the payor as a miscellaneous itemized deduction item.

Example 5-5 Testing different payment streams

- Bob and Carol divorced on December 1, 2018. Pursuant to the divorce decree, Bob is required to make the following post-divorce payments to Carol:
    - $1,500 per month designated as child support until such time as the couple's child is age 21 or no longer living.
    - $1,000 per month for 10 years (designated in the decree as alimony).

Example 5-5 Testing different payment streams (continued)

- If Bob dies, his estate is obligated to make the preceding payments.
  - Under the rules listed earlier in this section, none of these payments will qualify as alimony. The monthly amounts stated to be child support are disqualified for that reason. The monthly amounts stated to be alimony are disqualified because they do not cease upon Carol's death.
  - If the divorce decree instead stated that the $1,000-per-month payments would cease upon Carol's death, they would qualify as deductible alimony.
- Mick and Annie divorced on July 15, 2018. Under the terms of the decree, Mick is obligated to make payments to Annie of $2,000 per month, starting on August 1, for 10 years or until she dies, whichever comes first. If Mick dies, his estate must continue to meet his obligation to Annie. If Annie dies, Mick must continue to pay $900 per month until Jarvis, their child, reaches age 18 (these post-death payments would be to a trust set up for the child's benefit).
  - In this example, there are actually two payment streams—one that ceases upon Annie's death, and one that continues. The one that continues ($900 per month) does not qualify as alimony. Therefore, Mick can deduct only $1,100 per month as alimony, under these facts.
  - If the decree states that Mick owes a lump sum upon Annie's death equal to the difference between $240,000 (10 years' worth of payments) and the payments already made, none of the payments will qualify as alimony. This is because the decree includes an *acceleration clause* which effectively causes the full amount to be paid, whether or not Annie actually lives for 10 years [Temp. Reg. Section 1.71-1T(b)].

Written instrument rule

A written divorce or separation instrument includes a divorce decree, a separate maintenance decree, or a separation instrument [IRC Section 71(b)(2)]. The difference between these documents is that a divorce decree is issued when the marriage is dissolved. A separate maintenance decree means the couple is legally separated and living apart, but the marriage is not yet legally dissolved. However, the couple is considered legally separated and thus no longer married for federal income tax purposes.

A separation instrument settles the terms of the couple's marital rights and can be issued in advance of a divorce or separate maintenance decree.

Other written court orders and decrees such as temporary support orders (which cover the time after a divorce or separate maintenance petition is filed but before the divorce or legal separation is granted) also qualify as divorce or separation instruments. *Temporary alimony* payments under temporary support orders can qualify as alimony as long as the other requirements listed earlier are met [Reg. Section 1.71-1(b)].

Pre-divorce payments under both separation agreements and temporary support orders can qualify even when the couple continues to live in the same household. After a divorce or separate maintenance decree is granted, the couple must live apart in order for payments to qualify.

Key points

- Payments made prior to executing a written divorce or separation instrument or prior to the effective date of a court order or decree cannot be considered alimony.
  - Such payments are considered voluntary because they are made before there is any legal requirement to do so.
- The same is true for any payments in excess of what is required under a written divorce or separation instrument or court order or decree. Clients should be advised of this before they make voluntary payments.

Cash or cash equivalent rule

Checks and money orders count as cash equivalents. Marketable securities, bonds, promissory notes, and so on, do not, nor do transfers of services or property rights, such as free rent for use of the payer's residence or free maintenance work done by the payer [Temp. Reg. Section 1.71-1T(b), Q&A 5].

Payment to third parties

Alimony can be paid directly to or indirectly on behalf of the payee spouse or ex-spouse. However, for indirect payments to qualify, they must be made under the terms of the divorce or separation instrument or at the written request of (or with the written consent of) the payee. Any written request or consent must state the payments are intended to be alimony and the payer spouse must have the document before the tax return is filed for the year the payments were made [Temp. Reg. Section 1.71-1T(b), Q&As 6 and 7].

For instance, the payer may be required to make the payee's mortgage payments under terms of the divorce decree, or the payee may request that his or her rent or medical bills be paid in lieu of part of that month's alimony payment.

However, the payer cannot deduct payments to maintain property still owned by the payer.

For example, an individual cannot deduct as alimony mortgage payments on a house he or she owns but that is used by the spouse or ex-spouse.

Ceases on death of payee rule

Payment obligations that do not cease upon the death of the payee cannot be considered alimony. Regardless of what they may be called in the divorce papers, such payments are considered either child support or divisions of marital property, for federal income tax purposes.

Each payment stream is tested separately to determine if it ceases upon death of the payee. Amounts that continue are disqualified, but this does not affect the ability of other payments to qualify.

Payments may be required to continue after the death of the payer as obligations of his or her estate. Such a requirement does not disqualify the payments as alimony. Only payments that continue after the death of the *payee* are disqualified.

If the divorce papers do not indicate whether or not payments must continue in the event of the payee's death, state law controls. In other words, if under state law the payer must continue to make the payments, they are not alimony. If under state law the payments cease, they qualify as alimony as long as the other requirements listed earlier are satisfied.

Taxable alimony received is earned income for IRA contribution purposes

Contributions to traditional or Roth IRAs cannot exceed the contributor's earned income amount for the year. For purposes of this rule, taxable alimony received is considered earned income [IRC Section 219(f)(1)]. Thus, an individual whose only other sources of income are "unearned" (say from investments or trust fund distributions) is still able to make IRA contributions based on the earned income from taxable alimony payments received.

Payments treated as child support

The seemingly simple rule that deductible alimony does not include amounts considered to be child support causes many problems in real life. Payments are for child support if they are

- fixed child support, or
- deemed child support.

Fixed child support

Fixed child support means amounts designated as such in the divorce or separation instrument (for example, when the document explicitly requires a father to pay $1,000 per month for child support until the children reach certain ages).

Deemed child support

Deemed child support is a much trickier concept and creates a trap for unwary taxpayers. Deemed child support payments are amounts that are not identified as such in the divorce or separation agreement, but that are considered to be child support under the federal income tax rules. Specifically, amounts are considered deemed child support to the extent of payment *reductions* triggered by certain contingencies relating to a child (such as the child reaching age 18). This is the case even if the divorce or separation instrument unambiguously states the full payment is to be considered alimony for federal income tax purposes [Temp. Reg. Section 1.71-1T(c)]. Contingencies relating to a child include the following:

- Attaining age 18, 21, or the local age of majority (adulthood)
- Death
- Marriage
- Completion of schooling
- Leaving the household
- Attaining a specified income level
- Employment

"Clearly associated" rules

In addition to the preceding *triggering events*, payment reductions that occur *within six months* before or after a child reaches age 18, 21, or the local age of majority are considered *clearly associated* with (and thus triggered by) a contingency related to a child.

Also, when there are two or more children and payments are to be reduced on two or more occasions, and any of the reductions occurs *within one year* before or after the date each child reaches any age between 18 and 24 inclusive (with the same age being used for each child), the reductions are considered *clearly associated* with a contingency related to a child.

> ### Example 5-7 Fixed child support
>
> - Buck and Jewel divorced on July 1, 2018. Under terms of the decree, Buck must pay Jewel $4,000 per month for 120 months (10 years), starting on July 15. The requirement to make payments ceases if Jewel dies. The payments meet all of the other requirements for alimony explained earlier, except the document states that $1,800 per month is for the support of the couple's two children (ages 3 and 5) who will live with Jewel.
> - Any amount designated as child support is not alimony (even though the child support payments would stop if Jewel dies). Therefore, Buck can deduct as alimony only $2,200 per month.

Avoiding alimony recapture

Congress realized that taxpayers would attempt to disguise what were actually divisions of marital property as deductible alimony payments. Accordingly, the IRC Section 71(f) alimony recapture rules were enacted to prevent this.

These rules impose a mechanical test to measure whether purported alimony payments are excessively "front-loaded" during the first three calendar years that alimony payments are made. When payments are excessively front-loaded, the presumption is that part of the payments are actually in the nature of a property settlement. Therefore, part of the alimony deductions taken in the first *two* years is recaptured. The payer must take the recaptured amount back into gross income in the third year, and the payee gets an alimony deduction for the same amount in that year.

Failure to recognize and *plan around* the recapture rules can result in unexpected loss of alimony deductions and the inevitable client dissatisfaction.

Affected payments

The alimony recapture rules do not affect payments occurring after the first two years, and they do not apply at all when payments in the first two years are $15,000 or less. Recapture does not apply to the second-year amount when it exceeds the third-year amount by $15,000 or less, nor to the first-year amount when it exceeds the average of the second- and third-year amounts by $15,000 or less.

For example: A payment stream of $22,500 in the first year, $15,000 in the second year, and zero in the third year does not result in any recapture.

See the worksheet in IRS Publication 504 to calculate alimony recapture amounts, if any.

Exceptions to recapture rules

The recapture calculation is based on a three-year period starting with the first-year alimony payments that are made under a divorce decree, separate maintenance decree, or separation agreement. Thus, alimony recapture does not apply to payments made pursuant to other decrees or court orders such as temporary support orders because such payments are before the commencement of the three-year period [IRC Section 71(f)(5)(B)].

Alimony recapture also does not apply when the reason for the excessive front-loading is the death of either spouse within the three-year period or the remarriage of the payee spouse within the three-year period [IRC Section 71(f)(5)(A)].

Finally, alimony recapture does not apply to payment obligations that over the three-year period are based on a fixed portion of the payer's income from a business, property, or compensation from employment or self-employment [IRC Section 71(f)(5)(C)]. This is because payments based on these items can fluctuate for reasons beyond the payer's control.

Key point: There are no exceptions for payment fluctuations caused by other factors such as illness, loss of job, cash flow problems, or amendments to the divorce decree.

Tax developments affecting married same-sex couples

In its *Windsor* decision, the Supreme Court opined that the federal Defense of Marriage Act (DOMA), which became law in 1996, is unconstitutional (*Edith Windsor*, 111 AFTR2d 2013-2385, Sup. Ct. 2013).

In Revenue Ruling 2013-17, the IRS followed up with some initial guidance on the federal tax implications of same-sex marriages for both individuals and their employers. In a related move, the IRS supplied additional guidance by posting FAQ on its website at www.irs.gov.

In its 2015 *Obergefell v. Hodges* decision, the Supreme Court ruled that same-sex marriages must be respected in all the states.

This analysis summarizes these developments and offers some tax planning suggestions.

Guidance in Revenue Ruling 2013-17

Edie Windsor and Thea Spyer were New York State residents. In 2007, they were married in Canada. The marriage was recognized under New York state law. In 2009, Spyer died and left her substantial estate to Windsor. Because DOMA said Windsor and Spyer were not married to each other for federal tax purposes, the IRS said the federal unlimited marital deduction privilege was not allowed for Windsor's inheritance. As a result, Spyer's estate was charged with a $363,000 federal estate tax bill. In her capacity as executor, Windsor paid the tax bill and then sued for a refund on the grounds that the unlimited marital deduction privilege should have been available to the estate, because DOMA was unconstitutional. Windsor prevailed in District Court and in the Second Circuit Court of Appeals, but the case had to go to the Supreme Court for final resolution. (See *Edith Windsor*, 111 AFTR2d 2013-2385, Sup. Ct. 2013.)

Shortly after the *Windsor* decision, the IRS issued Revenue Ruling 2013-17. It serves as the primary guidance on the federal tax implications of *Windsor* and can be briefly summarized as follows.

1. Meaning of terms

For federal tax purposes, the terms *spouse*, *husband*, *wife*, and *husband and wife* include persons of the same sex if they are lawfully married under state law. The term *marriage* also includes a state law marriage between two individuals of the same sex. For federal tax purposes, the term *state* means any domestic or foreign jurisdiction that has the legal authority to sanction marriages. Therefore, same-sex individuals who are married under the laws of foreign jurisdictions are now considered married for federal tax purposes.

Key point: In contrast to Rev. Rul. 2013-17, *Obergefell v. Hodges* apparently does not require states to recognize same-sex marriages performed in foreign jurisdictions. The decision refers only to *states* without any reference to foreign jurisdictions.

2. General rule: Same-sex marriages are recognized for federal tax purposes

For federal tax purposes, the IRS adopts a general rule of recognizing any same-sex marriage that was validly entered into under a state law that authorizes marriages of two individuals of the same sex. This new general rule applies even if the same-sex couple now resides in a state that does not recognize same-sex marriages.

3. Domestic partnerships and civil unions are not marriages

For federal tax purposes, the terms *spouse*, *husband*, *wife*, and *husband and wife* do not include individuals (whether same-sex or opposite-sex) who have entered into a registered domestic partnership, civil union, or a similar formal relationship that is recognized under state law but that is not designated as a marriage under the laws of that state. Similarly, the term *marriage* does not include such relationships. Therefore, individuals in these relationships are treated as unmarried taxpayers for federal tax purposes.

Taxpayers can rely *retroactively* on the guidance in Rev. Rul. 2013-17 with respect to any employee benefit plan or arrangement, or any benefit provided under such plan or arrangement, for purposes of filing original returns, amended returns, adjusted returns, and claims for credit or refund for overpayment of federal income or employment taxes with respect to employer-provided health coverage or fringe benefits that are potentially excludable from income under IRC Sections. 106 (health coverage, 117(d) (tuition reduction), 119 (meals or lodging provided for the convenience of the employer), 129 (dependent care assistance), or 132 (work-related fringe benefits) based on the employee's marital status.

If an employee made a before-tax salary reduction election for health coverage under the employer's Section 125 cafeteria benefit plan and also elected to provide health coverage for a same-sex spouse on an after-tax basis under the employer's group health plan, the employee can now treat amounts that were paid by the employee for such after-tax coverage of the same-sex spouse as before-tax salary reduction amounts. In this situation, the employer can also act to recover overpaid Social Security and Medicare taxes, including the portion withheld from employee wages via the FICA tax.

Key point: In Notice 2013-61, the IRS provided details about how to obtain refunds and adjustments for overpaid Social Security and Medicare taxes.

Impact on cafeteria benefit plans, flexible spending accounts, and health savings accounts

In Notice 2014-1, the IRS provided specific guidance on the how the IRC Section 125 rules for cafeteria benefit plans and healthcare and dependent care flexible spending account plans should be applied to participants who are legally married to same-sex spouses.

Notice 2014-1 also covers how the IRC Section 223 health savings account rules should be applied to legally married same-sex spouses. The guidance was effective as of December 16, 2013.

Impact on retirement plans

IRS Notice 2014-19 stated that if an employer-sponsored retirement plan defined a marital relationship in a way that was inconsistent with *Windsor* and Revenue Ruling 2013-17, the plan had to be amended by December 31, 2014 to remove the inconsistency. Although a plan was not treated as failing to meet the requirements of IRC Sec. 401(a) merely because it did not recognize a participant's same-sex spouse as a spouse before June 26, 2013, it had to comply with *Windsor* and Revenue Ruling 2013-17 as of that date.

Impact on federal estate and gift taxes

Now that same-sex marriages are considered legal for both federal and state purposes, federal estate and gift tax benefits are available to all married same-sex couples. Terms that previously applied only to married persons of the opposite-sex or same-sex spouses legally married in jurisdictions that recognized such marriages now apply to all married persons, regardless of the couple's domicile or sexual orientation.

The estate and gift tax benefits now available to all married couples include the following:

Unlimited marital deduction privilege

If all requirements are met, married same-sex couples are entitled to take advantage of the unlimited marital deduction privilege for lifetime gifts or transfers at death.

Key point: Most states that impose estate or inheritance taxes allow exemptions for bequests to spouses, which now include same-sex spouses.

Qualified Terminable Interest Property (election

Same-sex spouses can now use Qualified Terminable Interest Property (QTIP) trust elections to take advantage of the unlimited marital deduction privilege. A QTIP election ensures that the deceased spouse's assets are available after his or her death to care for the surviving spouse yet allows the decedent to determine who receives the property when the surviving spouse dies.

Qualified domestic trust privilege

Same-sex spouses can create qualified domestic trusts, which are trusts that can qualify for the unlimited marital deduction privilege when the surviving spouse is not a U.S. citizen.

Portability election

Surviving spouses (including surviving same-sex spouses) can use their deceased spouse's unused unified federal estate and gift tax exemption amount under the so-called estate tax portability rules. Gift-splitting privilege

Same-sex spouses, if both spouses consent, can elect to treat gifts made by one spouse as if they were made one-half by each spouse. This gift-splitting privilege effectively doubles the annual federal gift tax exclusion amount ($15,000 per donee for 2019 and $14,000 for 2018).

Amended returns

Members of married same-sex couples may wish to amend previously filed federal and state estate and gift tax returns (assuming the statute of limitations has not expired) to claim benefits for which they were previously not eligible. For example, if the deceased spouse made gifts during his or her lifetime or at death to a same-sex surviving spouse, there may be an opportunity to file an amended gift or estate tax return to claim the unlimited marital deduction. This could potentially reduce the amount of applicable exclusion that was used and may result in a refund of any gift or estate tax paid. Or, if one spouse made a large gift (one that exceeded the annual exclusion amount) to someone other than his or her spouse, the married same-sex couple can choose to amend prior gift tax returns to take advantage of the gift-splitting privilege.

Planning implications

Now that the standard federal estate and gift tax benefits are available to members of married same-sex couples, planning steps may be necessary to take advantage, and some previously-done planning may no longer be necessary. For example, estate planning documents may need to be modified to take advantage of the unlimited marital deduction privilege. Certain trusts that were created by married same-sex couples may no longer be necessary. For example, irrevocable life insurance trusts that were set up to avoid federal estate tax on life insurance death benefits may no longer be necessary now that married same-sex couples can take advantage of the unlimited marital deduction privilege and the portability election.

Supreme court legalizes same-sex marriages in all states

The Supreme Court's *Obergefell v. Hodges* decision (issued in late June 2015) requires all states to license and recognize marriages between same-sex couples. Specifically, the decision states that same-sex couples can exercise the fundamental right to marry in all states and that there is no lawful basis for a state to refuse to recognize a lawful same-sex marriage performed in another state. [See *Obergefell v. Hodges,* 115 AFTR 2d 2015-2309 (Sup. Ct. 2015).]

Therefore, same-sex couples who are legally married in any state are now allowed to file joint state income tax returns wherever they reside. Also married same-sex couples should now be able to amend previously filed state returns for open years to reflect joint-filer status and claim refunds.

State tax implications

Since the Supreme Court's 2013 *Windsor* decision and follow-up IRS guidance, members of same-sex married couples generally can and must file federal tax returns as married individuals (starting with the 2013 tax year, and for earlier years if the original return was filed on or after September 16, 2013).

However, members of married same-sex couples who live in states that did previously not recognize same-sex marriages had to file state income tax returns as unmarried individuals. This caused added complexity and expense in filing state returns. For example, some states that did not recognize same-sex

---

marriages required affected individuals to prepare "dummy" federal returns showing unmarried status in order to reconcile the numbers reported on their state returns.

Obergefell v. Hodges essentially makes the *Windsor* decision applicable for state tax purposes as well as for federal tax purposes. In other words, members of same-sex couples who are legally married under the laws of any state are now considered married for both state and federal tax purposes, regardless of where they live. Therefore, members of married same-sex couples who were previously not allowed to file state returns as married individuals should evaluate whether it is advantageous to file amended state returns for open years. (As you know, filing joint returns is not always beneficial.) Going forward, members of married same-sex couples will file state returns in the same fashion as any other married individuals.

Other state tax implications of being married can include the following:

- The decision to itemize deductions or claim the standard deduction for state income tax purposes
- Eligibility for various state income tax deductions and credits that were not previously available due to stricter income phase-out rules for unmarried individuals
- Exposure to state death taxes (For example, some states have beneficial rules similar to the federal unlimited marital deduction privilege and the federal gift-splitting privilege.)

Non-tax implications

In *Obergefell v. Hodges*, the Supreme Court noted that other implications of an individual's marital status include inheritance and property rights; rules of intestate succession; spousal privilege in the law of evidence; hospital access; medical decision making authority; adoption rights; the rights and benefits of survivors; birth and death certificates; professional ethics rules; campaign finance restrictions; workers' compensation benefits; health insurance; and child custody, support, and visitation rights.

Social Security benefits are also impacted because members of same-sex married couples can now receive spousal and survivor benefits in all states. Previously, that was not true if an affected individual was married in one state but was currently domiciled in another state that did not recognize same-sex marriages.

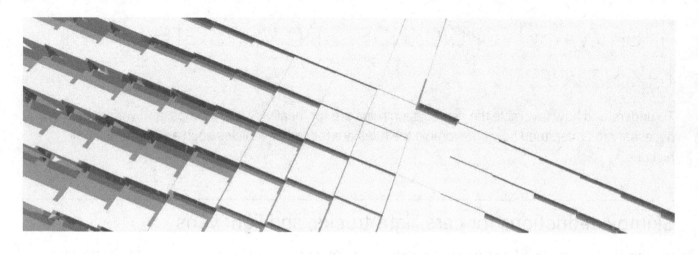

Chapter 6

Tax-Saving Tips for Self-Employed Clients

Learning objectives

- Apply available vehicle depreciation and expensing rules for sole proprietors and small business owners to enable them to minimize self-employment (SE) income, and Social Security and Medicare taxes.

- Identify strategies that will reduce Social Security and Medicare taxes for husband-wife businesses and new strategies opened up by the Tax Cuts and Jobs Act (TCJA).

Introduction

The tax advantages of self-employment are often overstated. When clients initially enter the self-employment arena, they may have visions of deducting enormous retirement plan contributions, deducting 100% of their auto expenses, deducting the cost of entertaining themselves and their friends, and so on. It is highly recommended that you educate your current and prospective clients and address their expectations in these regards.

In reality, self-employed individuals are eligible for some decent tax breaks, but they must manage their expectations. Self-employed individuals also face some tax disadvantages, and one of the most highly targeted issues by tax practitioners and their clients is self-employment tax.

This chapter presents some planning ideas to maximize the advantages of self-employed status, while minimizing the disadvantages.

"Heavy" SUVs, pickups, and vans are still big tax-savers

To understand how favorable the depreciation rules are for "heavy" SUVs, pickups, and vans, it is necessary to understand how unfavorable the rules are for lighter vehicles such as cars and small pickups.

Skimpy deductions for cars, light trucks, and light vans

Per the IRC Section 280F(a) luxury auto depreciation limitations, lower federal income tax depreciation allowances apply to cars, light trucks, and light vans used for business. For such vehicles placed in service during 2018, the maximum depreciation deductions (assuming 100% business use) follow (more generous thanks to the TCJA.

For *new or used* passenger vehicles that are placed in service after December 31, 2017, and used over 50% for business, the maximum annual depreciation deductions allowed under the TCJA are as follows:

- $10,000 for Year 1
- $16,000 for Year 2
- $9,600 for Year 3
- $5,760 for Year 4 and thereafter until the vehicle is fully depreciated

Key point: For 2017, the prior-law limits for passenger cars were $11,160 for Year 1 for a new car or $3,160 for a used car, $5,100 for Year 2, $3,050 for Year 3, and $1,875 for Year 4 and thereafter. Slightly higher limits apply to light trucks and light vans.

Key point: When the vehicle is used less than 100% of the time for business, the numbers shown previously must be proportionately reduced to account for non-business usage. If business use is 50% or less, depreciation must be further reduced by using the straight-line method to calculate deductions.

Knowledge check

1. What is the maximum first-year depreciation allowance for an auto (new or used) that is subject to the luxury auto depreciation limitations and that is placed in service in 2019?

    a. $25,500.
    b. $11,160.
    c. $10,000.
    d. $17,500.

Bigger deductions for heavy vehicles used more than 50% for business

The tax-saving strategy is to buy something outside the passenger auto classification. Specifically, a passenger vehicle is not considered to be a passenger auto if it has a gross vehicle weight rating —the manufacturer's maximum weight rating when loaded to capacity—greater than 6,000 pounds. [See IRC Section 280F(d)(5)(A); Proposed Section Regulation 48.4001-1(b)(2)(ii) and (iii) via Regulation Section 145.4051-1(e)(3); and Ltr. Rul. 9520034.]

Passenger vehicles that meet the preceding "heavy" definition are considered trucks for depreciation purposes, that is, five-year MACRS property, which is also eligible for the IRC Section 179 deduction.

New (not used) heavy vehicles are also eligible for first-year bonus depreciation.

However, to be eligible for the IRC Section 179 deduction, first-year bonus depreciation, and accelerated MACRS depreciation, the heavy vehicle must be used more than 50% for business purposes.

$25,000 IRC Section 179 deduction limitation for heavy SUVs

Congress placed a reduced $25,000 limit on IRC Section 179 deductions for heavy SUVs with gross vehicle weight ratings (GVWRs) between 6,001 and 14,000 pounds [IRC Section 179(b)(6)]. This limitation is adjusted periodically for inflation. For tax years beginning in 2019, the limitation is $25,500.

That is the bad news. The good news is that the $25,500 limitation has no impact on vehicles that are not considered to be SUVs. Per IRC Section 179(b)(6), "non-SUVs" include vehicles that meet the following descriptions:

- Vehicles designed to seat more than nine passengers behind the driver's seat. For example, many shuttle vans and minibuses will qualify for this exception.
- Vehicles equipped with a cargo area that is not readily accessible directly from the passenger compartment and that is at least six feet in interior length. The cargo area can be open or designed to be open but enclosed by a cap. For example, many pickups with full-size cargo beds will qualify for this exception. Some "quad cabs" and "extended cabs" with shorter cargo beds may not.
- Vehicles with
    - an integral enclosure that fully encloses the driver's compartment and load carrying device,
    - no seating behind the driver's seat, and
    - no body section protruding more than 30 inches ahead of the leading edge of the windshield. (For example, many delivery vans will qualify for this exception.)

Key point: Vehicles with GVWRs greater than 6,000 pounds that meet the preceding descriptions are still eligible for the full IRC Section 179 deduction ($1m for tax years beginning in 2018; $1.02m for tax years beginning in 2019).

It is important to understand that heavy SUVs still have a huge depreciation advantage over vehicles classified as passenger autos. This is because heavy SUVs used more than 50% for business still qualify for: (1) 100% first-year bonus depreciation for both new and used vehicles placed in service between

September 28, 2017, and December 31, 2022, (2) the $25,500 IRC Section 179 deduction for both new and used vehicles placed in service in tax years beginning in 2019, and (3) % accelerated MACRS depreciation over five years for the balance of a new or used vehicle's depreciable basis, after subtracting any first-year bonus depreciation and any IRC Section 179 deduction. In contrast, passenger autos fall under the relatively skimpy, luxury auto depreciation limits listed earlier.

Example 6-1

Phil buys a $40,000 used heavy SUV in 2019 and uses it 100% in his Schedule C business. The maximum first-year depreciation deduction is the full $40,000, thanks to 100% first-year bonus depreciation.

In contrast, the maximum first-year depreciation deduction for a $40,000 used passenger auto placed in service during the year and used 100% for business is only $10,000. That is a big difference in favor of the SUV. (See the following section for more on the impact of bonus depreciation for vehicles used for business.)

Bonus depreciation means bigger first-year write-offs for heavy SUVs

As mentioned earlier, the maximum IRC Section 179 deduction for one of those heavy SUVs is $25,500 for tax years beginning in 2019. Congress keeps making noises about completely eliminating the IRC Section 179 deduction for heavy SUVs, but it has not happened yet. In fact, the 100% first-year bonus depreciation allowance established by the TCJA makes heavy SUV's placed in service between now and the end of 2022 into really great tax-saving machines.

To qualify for 100% first-year bonus depreciation under the TCJA, an SUV that is placed in service between September 28, 2017, and December 31, 2022, can be new or used, but it must be used more than 50% for business, and it must have a GVWR of more than 6,000 pounds. You can usually find the GVWR on an imprinted label on the inside of the driver's door where the hinges meet the frame.

Example 6-2

Reilly buys a new $65,000 Cadillac Escalade and uses it 80% in her single-member LLC software services business during 2019. The depreciable cost of the vehicle is $52,000 (.8 × $65,000). On her Form 4562, she can claim a $52,000, 100%, first-year bonus depreciation deduction. Therefore, the entire business-use portion of the cost can be written off in Year 1.

No income limitation or phase-out rule for bonus depreciation

Unlike the IRC Section 179 deduction, there is no income limitation on first-year bonus depreciation deductions. Therefore, they can create or increase a net operating loss (NOL) that can be carried forward to future years (for NOLs arising in tax years beginning in 2018 and beyond, the TCJA allows only the NOLs to be carried forward, but they can be carried forward indefinitely).

IRS confirms that heavy SUVs escape luxury auto depreciation limits whether built on truck or car chassis

As explained earlier, the luxury auto depreciation limitations apply only to passenger autos [IRC Section 280F(a)(1)(A)]. When a vehicle used more than 50% for business is not classified as a passenger auto, it can be depreciated under the more generous MACRS rules for transportation equipment, which is considered to be five-year property. In addition, new and used vehicles that fall outside the passenger auto classification are eligible for first-year bonus depreciation in years when it is available, subject to the bonus depreciation rules for those years [IRC Section 168(k)]. Finally, new and used vehicles that fall outside the passenger auto classification are also eligible for the IRC Section 179 deduction. However, heavy SUVs are subject to a reduced IRC Section 179 allowance of only $25,500 (for tax years beginning in 2019), as explained earlier.

The tax-smart strategy is to buy vehicles that fall outside the passenger auto classification. A passenger vehicle with an enclosed body that is built on a truck or unibody chassis is not considered to be a passenger auto if it has a gross vehicle weight rating--the manufacturer's maximum weight rating when loaded to capacity—greater than 6,000 pounds. See Rev. Proc. 2008-22 (which does not define trucks and vans as having to be built on a truck chassis, which was apparently intended to leave the tax-smart door open for heavy crossover SUVs with unibody construction such as the Porsche Cayenne); IRC Section 280F(d)(5)(A); Proposed Regulation 48.4001-1(b)(2)(ii) and (iii) via Regulation 145.4051-1(e)(3); and PLR 9520034.

IRS Chief Counsel Advice (CCA) 201138048 further clarifies that heavy SUVs are exempt from the passenger auto classification whether they are built on a truck chassis or an auto chassis. With this additional guidance, there is apparently no doubt that heavy SUVs built on any kind of chassis (truck, unibody, car, whatever) are eligible for the aforementioned favorable depreciation treatment.

Do not forget IRC Section 179 taxable income limitation

A taxpayer's annual IRC Section 179 deduction cannot exceed that year's aggregate net business taxable income from all sources (calculated before the IRC Section 179 write-off). This rule prevents taxpayers from claiming big IRC Section 179 deductions in order to create tax losses that could then be carried back to earlier years.

If the client conducts his or her business as a sole proprietorship, or as a single-member LLC treated as such for federal tax purposes, he or she can count any salary, wages, and tips that the client may earn as an employee as additional net business taxable income. If the client is married and files jointly, the client can also count his or her spouse's earnings from employment as well as any net SE income he or she may earn from business activities in which he or she actively participates. These taxpayer-friendly loopholes reduce the odds that the client's business will be adversely affected by the taxable income limitation. Still, watch out for this rule.

Warning: Be careful if the client runs his or her business as an S corporation, partnership, or multi-member LLC. Why? Because the maximum IRC Section 179 deduction limitation ($1m for tax years beginning in 2018; $1.02m for tax years beginning in 2019) and the net business income limitation apply at both the entity level and at the client's personal level. The rules are complicated, and planning may be required to get the most tax-saving mileage out of the IRC Section 179 deduction.

Do not forget IRC Section 179 deduction phase-out rule

This next limitation will not affect most small businesses, but tax advisers still need to know about it. The taxpayer's maximum IRC Section 179 deduction is reduced dollar for dollar (but not less than zero) by the amount of *excess IRC Section 179 property* (assets that would otherwise qualify for the deduction) placed in service during the tax year. The threshold for this unfavorable phase-out rule is $2.5m for tax years beginning in 2018 and $2.55m for tax years beginning in 2019. For post-2019 years, the threshold will be adjusted for inflation.

Example 6-3

A calendar-year client places $2.6m of IRC Section 179 property in service during 2019. The maximum IRC Section 179 deduction for the year is $970,000 ($1.02m "normal" maximum for tax years beginning in 2019 minus the $50,000 excess over the $2.55m phase-out threshold for tax years beginning in 2019).

Do not forget over-50% business use requirement

Because heavy vehicles are classified as listed property, they must be used more than 50% of the time for business for favorable depreciation rules to apply. Otherwise, the business-use percentage of the vehicle's cost must be depreciated using the ADS straight-line method, which takes six tax years to fully depreciate that cost. [See IRC Section 280F(d)(4)(A)(ii), (b)(1), and (d)(1); and IRC Section 168(g).]

Mind stricter rules for corporate-owned vehicles

When a heavy SUV, pickup, or van is owned by the client's C or S corporation, the vehicle must be used more than 50% for actual corporate business activities in order to qualify for the IRC Section 179 deduction. Any personal use by an employee who is also a more-than-5% shareholder (like the client) does not count as business use for this purpose, even when the personal-use value is reported as additional taxable compensation on the shareholder-employee's Form W-2. This is also true for corporate employees who are related to more-than-5% shareholders (like the client's spouse and kids). When the over-50% business use test is failed, the corporation must depreciate the vehicle using the straight-line method, which means it will take six years to fully depreciate it. And the corporation can say goodbye to any IRC Section 179 deduction. [See Regulation Section 1.179-1(d); IRC Sections 280F(b), 280F(d)(4)(A)(ii), and 280F(d)(6)(C)(i)(II).]

Combine "heavy" vehicle with deductible home office for major tax savings

In the previous tip, we covered the tax depreciation advantages of "heavy" SUVs, pickups, and vans. We also mentioned that these advantages are available only when business use of the vehicle exceeds 50%.

The home office angle

Many self-employed individuals have the flexibility to set up deductible offices in their homes. Clients who do so can gain a big head start in passing the over-50% business use test for a vehicle, which is a prerequisite to claiming the IRC Section 179 deduction, first-year bonus depreciation, and accelerated MACRS depreciation for a heavy vehicle.

Specifically, if the client has a home office that qualifies as a principal place of business, all the client's commuting from home to various temporary work locations (customer sites, office supply store, FedEx shipping office, and the like) counts as business mileage. Ditto for commuting mileage from home to any regular place of business, such as the client's "official" office in town (if there is one). Finally, the client can treat all the mileage between the "official" office in town (if there is one) and various temporary work locations (customer sites and so forth) as business mileage. These taxpayer-friendly rules are found in Rev. Rul. 99-7.

The point is, when self-employed taxpayers' home offices qualify as a principal place of business, it's usually pretty easy to accumulate lots of business mileage, which makes it much easier to clear the over-50%-business-use hurdle and thereby qualify for favorable vehicle depreciation rules. Of course, a higher business-use percentage also means bigger (perhaps much bigger) vehicle depreciation deductions. The home office deduction itself is a bonus.

How to make a home office a principal place of business

The IRC gives a self-employed client two easy ways to make a home office a principal place of business. [See IRC Sec. 280A(c)(1) and Rev. Rul. 94-24.]

First way

The client conducts most of his or her income-earning activities in the home office.

Second way

The client performs administrative and management functions in the home office. However, to take advantage of this second way, the client cannot make substantial use of any other fixed location for administrative and management chores. (It's okay if the client has another fixed location where he or she could perform administrative and management work, as long as the client actually does substantially all such work in the home office.)

Key point: To have a deductible office in the home, the client generally must use the office space regularly and exclusively for business purposes during the year in question, as explained in the following tip [IRC Section 280A(c)(1)]. This requirement may prevent the client from setting up a home office that qualifies as a principal place of business this year. If so, the purchase of a heavy SUV, pickup, or van can be postponed until early next year, and the client can take pains to have a home office that qualifies as a principal place of business next year.

Home office deduction options

For 2013 and beyond, eligible self-employed individuals have been able to use a simplified safe-harbor method for calculating home office deductions. Worksheets for making the calculation are provided in the Schedule C instructions and in Publication 587. The safe-harbor method, which is optional, was established by Rev. Proc. 2013-13 and is intended to reduce the administrative, recordkeeping, and compliance burdens of determining allowable home office deductions. In other words, the safe-harbor method represents an alternative to the familiar and more complicated actual-expense method.

Home office deduction basics

The general rule for home offices states that no deductions are allowed for the business use of a dwelling unit that's also used by the taxpayer as a residence during the tax year in question [IRC Section 280A(a)]. An exception to the general rule allows deductions if certain requirements are met. Properly calculated and substantiated home office deductions are generally allowed only if part of the home is used regularly and exclusively as a principal place of business or as a place to meet or deal with customers or clients in the ordinary course of business. In the case of a detached separate structure (such as a converted barn, detached garage, or pool house), deductions are allowed if the structure is used regularly and exclusively in connection with the taxpayer's business. Employees must pass an additional test to claim unreimbursed business expense deductions (subject to the 2%-of-adjusted gross income (AGI) threshold) for home office usage: the use of the home office must be for the convenience of the employer. [See IRC Section 280A(c)].

TCJA change: For 2018–2025, miscellaneous deductions that were formerly subject to the 2%-of-AGI deduction threshold are completely disallowed. Therefore, unreimbursed employee business expenses are non-deductible for those years.

A home office qualifies as the principal place of business if most of the income-earning activities occur there. However, a home office can also be a principal place of business if the taxpayer's administrative or management activities are conducted there, and there is no other fixed location where the taxpayer conducts substantial administrative or management activities. [See IRC Section 280A(c)(1).]

Rented home office deductions are allowed

The dwelling unit need not be owned for deductions to be claimed. Allowable expenses from a rented dwelling unit can be deducted if the basic requirements for home office deductions are met. [See IRC Section 280A(c)(3).]

Special rule for inventory storage space

Expenses allocable to space in a dwelling unit that's used on a regular basis for storing inventory or product samples kept for use in the taxpayer's business of retail or wholesale selling of products are deductible if the dwelling unit is the sole fixed location of the business [IRC Section 280A(c)(2)]. Exclusive use of the space for such purpose is not required (regular use is required).

Special rule for daycare business

Expenses allocable to the part of a dwelling unit that's used on a regular basis in the taxpayer's business of providing day care for children, for individuals who have attained age 65 or older, or for individuals who are physically or mentally incapable of caring for themselves are deductible [IRC Section 280A(c)(4)]. Exclusive use of the space for such purposes is not required (regular use is required).

Business income limitation

Home office deductions are limited to the gross income from the applicable business activity reduced by (1) other expenses for which deductions are allowed in the absence of business use (such as qualified residence interest, real estate taxes, and casualty losses); and (2) business deductions that are not allocable to the use of the home (such as advertising, and supplies). Deductions that are disallowed under this business income limitation are carried forward to the following year, subject to the same business income limitation in that following year. [See IRC Section 280A(c)(5).]

Direct and indirect expenses are allowed

Expenses that are directly allocable to the home office space, such as repair and maintenance costs, are deductible subject to the aforementioned limitations. Indirect expenses—such as utilities, property taxes, casualty insurance premiums, homeowner association fees, security monitoring, depreciation, and so forth—can be allocated to the home office space based on square footage or the number of rooms in the residence (assuming all the rooms are of similar size) and deducted subject to the aforementioned limitations.

Safe-harbor deduction is simple, but it cannot exceed $1,500

The safe-harbor method allows an eligible taxpayer to claim a home office deduction of $5 per square foot of space used for *qualified business use*, limited to 300 square feet, with no questions asked about actual expenses and no required documentation of expenses. Therefore, the maximum annual safe-harbor allowance is limited to $1,500 ($5 × 300).

The $5-per-square-foot allowance can be updated from time to time by the IRS.

Qualified business use means uses for which home office deductions would be allowed under the "regular" IRC Section 280A rules summarized earlier. Put another way, taxpayers who use the safe-harbor method must still satisfy all the basic requirements for home office deduction eligibility that were explained earlier (regular use and so forth).

Warning: The safe-harbor method is not available to an employee with a home office if he or she receives advances, allowances, or reimbursements for expenses related to the qualified business use of the employee's home under a reimbursement or other expense allowance arrangement with the employer [Rev. Proc. 2013-13, Section 4.01(4)].

Impact of using safe-harbor method

The safe-harbor method is an alternative to deducting actual home office expenses. So, if the safe-harbor method is used, actual expenses cannot be deducted, subject to the exceptions explained in the two paragraphs immediately following. The additional implications of using the safe-harbor method are explained in the other paragraphs that follow.

Home-related itemized deductions

Taxpayers who itemize deductions and use the safe-harbor method to calculate their home office deduction for the tax year in question can deduct on Schedule A any allowable expenses related to the home that are deductible without regard to business use of the home. For instance, choosing to use the safe-harbor method has no impact on the taxpayer's ability to deduct qualified residence interest, property taxes, or casualty losses. (The same is true for taxpayers who use the longstanding actual-expense method to calculate home office deductions.) For taxpayers who use the safe-harbor method, however, no part of these itemized deduction amounts can be subtracted from business gross income in determining business net income, nor are these itemized deduction amounts considered in determining the home office deduction business income limitation. [See Rev. Proc. 2013-13, Sections 4.04 and 4.08(2).]

Example 6-4

For all of 2019, Audrey uses over 300 square feet of her residence as a qualified home office [meaning it meets the IRC Section 280A(c)(1) requirements for home office deductions]. She elects to use the safe-harbor method to claim a $1,500 home office deduction (300 square feet × $5). In 2019, Audrey paid $10,000 of qualified residence interest and $5,000 of real property taxes for the property. Her use of the safe-harbor home office deduction method has no impact on her ability to claim itemized deductions for the qualified residence interest and real property taxes.

Business deductions unrelated to home office usage

Taxpayers who use the safe-harbor method for the tax year in question can still deduct any allowable business expenses that are unrelated to the qualified business use of the home office space. Examples of such expenses include advertising, wages, and supplies. (See Rev. Proc. 2013-13, Section 4.05.)

Business income limitation

When the taxpayer uses the safe-harbor method, the business income limitation still applies. In other words, the safe-harbor deduction cannot exceed the gross income from the business reduced by allocable business expenses (not including itemized deduction amounts, as explained previously). Any safe-harbor amount that is disallowed by the business income limitation cannot be carried over to a later year. [See Rev. Proc. 2013-13, Section 4.08(2).]

Example 6-5

For all of 2019, Jack used more than 300 square feet of his residence as a qualified home office. His net business income was only $1,200 before considering any allowable home office deduction. Jack's safe-harbor deduction cannot exceed $1,200 (even though the tentative safe-harbor deduction is the maximum $1,500 amount). The $300 difference between the tentative deduction and the allowable deduction is disallowed and cannot be carried forward to future years.

Disallowed expenses from earlier year

Taxpayers who use the safe-harbor method for the tax year in question cannot deduct any amount that was disallowed by the business income limitation in an earlier year for which the taxpayer used the actual-expense method to calculate the home office deduction. Instead, the taxpayer can deduct carried-over amounts in a later year for which the actual-expense method is used (to the extent there is sufficient business income). [See Rev. Proc. 2013-13, Section 4.08(3).]

Depreciation

Taxpayers who use the safe-harbor method for the tax year in question cannot deduct any depreciation (including otherwise allowable first-year bonus depreciation or IRC Section 179 deductions) for the part of the home that is used as a home office for that year. The allowable depreciation deduction for that part of the home for that year is deemed to be $0. The taxpayer can switch back to the actual-expense method for a later year and resume deducting depreciation. In such case, the optional depreciation table [most easily found in IRS Publication 946 (How to Depreciate Property)] must be used to calculate the property's remaining depreciation deductions (even if the table wasn't used in the year the property was placed in service). The applicable year for purposes of using the table is based on the year the property was placed in service. (See Rev. Proc. 2013-13, Sections 4.06, 4.07, and 4.09.)

Example 6-6

For all of 2018, Ace uses more than 300 square feet of his residence as a qualified home office. The room has a cost basis for depreciation purposes of $10,000. It was placed in service on January 1, 2015. For 2015–2017, Ace depreciated the room as nonresidential real property using the optional depreciation table (based on straight-line depreciation over 39 years using the mid-month convention). His annual depreciation deductions from the table were $256, for a total of $758 for 2015–2017. As of January 1, 2018, the adjusted basis of the room was $9,242 ($10,000 − $758).

For 2018, Ace elects to use the safe-harbor method to calculate his home office deduction. As explained previously, his allowable depreciation for 2018 is deemed to be $0.

Example 6-6 (continued)

For 2019, Ace resumes using the actual-expense method to calculate his home office deduction. Accordingly, he resumes using the table to calculate his depreciation deduction, using the percentage for Year 5 (because the property was placed in service in 2015, and 2019 is the fifth year of business usage). The depreciation percentage from the table is 2.564%, so Ace's 2019 depreciation deduction is $256 (2.564% × $10,000 original cost basis). As of December 31, 2019, the room's adjusted basis is $8,986 ($10,000 minus $758 depreciation for 2015-2017 minus $256 depreciation for 2019).

Business use during only part of the year

Taxpayers who use the safe-harbor method for only part of the tax year in question (for example in a newly started business or seasonal business) or a taxpayer whose square footage of business use changes during the year must calculate the average monthly square footage amount based on no more than 300 square feet for any month of business use. Calculate the average monthly square footage by adding the amount of allowable square feet used in each month (subject to the 300-square-foot limit) and dividing the sum by 12. No square footage is counted for a month during which qualified business use is less than 15 days. [See Rev. Proc. 2013-13, Section 4.08(4).]

Example 6-7

On July 20, 2018, Erin began using more than 300 square feet of her home as a qualified home office, and she continued using the space exclusively for business for the remainder of the year. Erin's average monthly allowable square footage is 125 square feet: 300 square feet for August through December—which adds up to 1,500—divided by 12 = 125). No square footage is counted for July because there were less than 15 days of business use in that month. Erin's allowable safe-harbor deduction for the year is $625 ($5 per square foot × 125 = $625), assuming no problem with the business income limitation.

More than one home office

There can be more than one office in a home. For example, two married or unmarried individuals may share a home and each use separate areas for their respective home offices. Each individual is entitled to use the safe-harbor method for up to 300 square feet of separate home office space. [See Rev. Proc. 2013-13, Section 4.08(5).]

- In the case of an electing qualified husband-wife joint venture, the spouses report their respective shares of income and deductions from the joint venture on separate Schedules C filed with their joint Form 1040 (as opposed to having to file a partnership return for the joint venture on Form 1065 and issue Schedules K-1 to both spouses). If the couple uses the safe-harbor home office deduction method for the joint venture's business use of their home, Publication 587 states that they should split the home office square footage in the same manner as they split other tax items from the joint venture. Then, each spouse should separately calculate his or her allowable safe-harbor deduction. It appears that each spouse is entitled to a separate 300-square foot limitation for purposes of calculating his or her allowable deduction.

- If a taxpayer with two or more businesses and two or more separate offices in the same home elects to use the safe-harbor method, it must be used for all the offices; and the 300-square-foot limit applies to the combined space of all the offices. [See Rev. Proc. 2013-13, Section 4.08(6).]
- If the taxpayer has offices in two or more homes, the safe-harbor method can only be used for one home. The actual-expense method can be used for the other(s). [See Rev. Proc. 2013-13, Section 4.08(7).]

Calculating and claiming the safe-harbor deduction allowance (Form 8829 not required)

Schedule C filers are supposed to use Form 8829 (Expenses for Business Use of Your Home) to calculate and report their allowable home office deductions under the actual-expense method. However, Form 8829 is not required for Schedule C filers who use the safe-harbor deduction method. Instead, the allowable safe-harbor deduction is claimed by simply entering it on line 30 of Schedule C. In the spaces to the left of line 30, enter the total square footage of the home and the square footage used as a qualified home office. The instructions for line 30 of Schedule C include a worksheet to calculate the safe-harbor deduction amount.

For taxpayers who do not file Schedule C (such as employees, partners, and farmers), use the worksheets found in Publication 587 to calculate safe-harbor deduction amounts.

Electing in and out of the safe-harbor method

Taxpayers can elect from year to year whether to use the new safe-harbor method or the actual-expense method to determine home office deductions.

A taxpayer elects the safe-harbor method simply by using the method to calculate the allowable home office deduction and then claiming it on a timely filed original federal income tax return for the year in question.

Once made, the election is irrevocable for that particular year. However, the taxpayer can change from the safe-harbor method to the actual-expense method, or vice versa, for any later year. Such changes are not considered accounting method changes, and no tax return statements are required to make such changes. (See Rev. Proc. 2013-13, Section 4.03.)

Conclusion

The safe-harbor home office deduction method is allowed, but it's not for everyone. Some clients will have substantial home office deductions that far exceed the safe-harbor allowance. However, for clients who can claim only modest home office deductions under the actual-expense method, the safe-harbor method has the attraction of eliminating the need to keep records of actual expenses. Consider using the safe-harbor method for clients who are not so good at recordkeeping and who would be entitled to only modest deductions even with perfect recordkeeping.

Knowledge check

2. The safe-harbor home office deduction allowance for individual taxpayers is

    a. Just a proposed rule until further notice.
    b. Allowed only for 2019 and beyond.
    c. Allowed for 2013 and beyond.
    d. Only allowed for married taxpayers who file jointly.

Additional 0.9% Medicare tax on high earners

Before 2013, the Medicare tax on salary or SE income was 2.9%. An employee had 1.45% withheld from his or her paychecks, and the other 1.45% was paid by the employer. If self-employed, the employee pays the whole 2.9% on his or her own.

For 2013 and beyond, an extra 0.9% Medicare tax is charged on (1) salary or net SE income greater than $200,000 for an unmarried individual, (2) combined salary or net SE income greater than $250,000 for a married joint-filing couple, and (3) salary or net SE income greater than $125,000 for those who use married filing separate status. These thresholds are not adjusted for inflation, so as time goes on more and more folks will probably be affected. [See IRC Sections 1401(b)(2) and 3101(b)(2).]

In 2013, the IRS issued final regulations (TD 9645), implementing the additional 0.9% Medicare tax.

Knowledge check

3. At what rate is the *additional* Medicare tax on wages or net SE income earned by higher income individuals imposed?

    a. 2.9%.
    b. 0.9%.
    c. 6.2%.
    d. 3.8%.

Impact on self-employed individuals

For self-employed individuals, the effect of the additional 0.9% Medicare tax comes in the form of a bigger SE tax bill. For 2013 and beyond, the maximum rate for the Medicare tax component of the SE tax is 3.8% (2.9% + 0.9%).

Key point: The additional SE tax impact from the additional 0.9% Medicare tax does not qualify for the above-the-line deduction for 50% of SE tax [IRC Section 164(f)(1)].

Calculating the additional 0.9% Medicare tax for self-employed individuals who also have wage income

Some individuals have both net SE income to the SE tax and wage income subject to the FICA tax. These folks must take the following three steps to determine their liability for the additional 0.9% Medicare tax.

Step 1: Calculate the additional 0.9% Medicare tax on any wages in excess of the applicable threshold ($200,000 or $250,000 or $125,000, whichever applies).

Step 2: Reduce the applicable threshold (but not less than zero) by the total amount of wages subject to the "regular" Medicare tax.

Step 3: Calculate the additional 0.9% Medicare tax on SE income in excess of the reduced applicable threshold calculated in Step 2.

The following examples illustrate the three-step drill.

Example 6-8

Kyle is an unmarried individual. In the current year, he has $150,000 of wages subject to the "regular" Medicare tax. Because his wages are less than the $200,000 withholding threshold for the 0.9% Medicare tax, Kyle's employer does not withhold anything for the additional 0.9% Medicare tax.

Kyle also has net SE income of $175,000 in the current year from a profitable side business. To calculate the additional 0.9% Medicare tax on his SE income, the $200,000 applicable threshold for unmarried individuals is reduced by his $150,000 of wages, resulting in a reduced threshold of $50,000 ($200,000 − $150,000). Kyle owes the additional 0.9% Medicare tax on $125,000 of SE income ($175,000 − $50,000 reduced threshold), which amounts to a $1,125 extra tax hit.

Example 6-9

Mindy and Mike are married joint-filers. In the current year, Mindy has wages subject to the "regular" Medicare tax of $195,000. Because her wages are less than the $200,000 withholding threshold for the additional 0.9% Medicare tax, her employer does not withhold anything for the additional 0.9% Medicare tax.

Mike has net SE income of $155,000. To calculate the additional 0.9% Medicare tax on his SE income, the $250,000 applicable threshold for joint-filing couples is reduced by Mindy's $195,000 of wages, resulting in a reduced threshold of $55,000 ($250,000 − $195,000). Mindy and Mike owe the additional 0.9% Medicare tax on $100,000 of SE income ($155,000 − $55,000 reduced threshold), which amounts to a $900 extra tax hit.

Example 6-10

Newt is an unmarried individual. In the current year, he has $225,000 of wages subject to the "regular" Medicare tax. His employer withholds the additional 0.9% Medicare tax on $25,000 of wages ($225,000 – $200,000 withholding threshold), which results in an additional tax hit of $225.

Newt also has net SE income of $80,000 in the current year. To calculate the additional 0.9% Medicare tax on his SE income, the $200,000 applicable threshold for unmarried individuals is reduced, but not less than zero, by his $225,000 of wages, resulting in a reduced threshold of $0 ($200,000 – $225,000 + $25,000 to stay greater than zero).
Newt owes the additional 0.9% Medicare tax on the entire $80,000 of SE income ($80,000 – $0 reduced threshold), which amounts to a $720 extra tax hit.

Bottom line: Newt owes the additional 0.9% Medicare tax on $105,000 ($25,000 of wages plus $80,000 of SE income), which amounts to a $945 extra tax hit. Newt will receive a federal income tax withholding credit on his current-year Form 1040 for the $225 withheld from his wages.

Employing owner's children in the business

There are some powerful tax incentives for clients operating sole proprietorships and husband-wife partnerships to hire their under-age-18 children as employees (in most cases, this will be on a part-time basis).

The child's wages are exempt from Social Security and Medicare taxes, so there is no employer share of these taxes to pay and no withholding for the employee's share of these taxes.

Similarly, there is no FUTA tax (actually the FUTA exemption extends to under-age-21 children). [See IRC Sections 3121(b)(3)(A), 3306(c)(5), and Circular E.]

The wages paid to the child are a business expense and accordingly reduce both the income tax and SE tax bills of the parent(s). The AGI of the parent(s) is reduced, which generally can have only beneficial side effects. Finally, paying the child wages provides a way to transfer funds to the child in a tax-favored manner. In many cases, this is money that would have otherwise simply been given to the child or paid to someone outside the family to do the necessary work.

On the child's side of the equation, up to $12,200 of 2019 wage income can be sheltered by his or her standard deduction. An additional $6,000 of wage income can be sheltered by contributing to a deductible IRA. Alternatively, the child could contribute up to $6,000 to a Roth IRA (no deduction).

Bottom line: The parental employer saves Social Security and Medicare taxes and gets an income tax and SE tax deduction, and the child is generally able to shelter most or all of the wage income from any form of federal tax.

Example 6-11

- Bailey operates a very profitable sole proprietorship marketing business. Her marginal federal income tax rate is 35% and her marginal SE tax rate is 3.8%. Over the summer, Bailey pays her two children (ages 15 and 17) $2,000 each ($10 per hour) to select and install new computer hardware and software, teach her how to use it, update all her computerized records, assist in redoing some marketing materials, and so on.
  - The $4,000 wage deduction reduces Bailey's federal income tax liability by $1,400 and her SE tax bill by $152 (ignoring the effects of the reduced deduction for 50% of her SE tax and the reduction in her AGI).
- There are no Social Security, Medicare, or FUTA taxes on the wages, and the children owe no federal income tax because their wage income is completely sheltered by their standard deductions.
  - Bailey has succeeded in funneling $4,000 to her kids for the summer in a tax-effective manner, accomplishing a necessary technology upgrade for her business, and providing a good work experience for her offspring. She has also succeeded in putting off the tax impact for her children, because they will not yet realize that federal payroll and income taxes ordinarily take a big amount out of one's wages.
- Remember that wages paid to kids must be reasonable in relation to the work performed. So this idea works best with teenagers who can be assigned meaningful duties, as in this example.

Example 6-12

- Assume the same basic facts as in the previous example, except this time Bailey operates her business as an S or C corporation.
  - In this case, the wages paid to the children are subject to Social Security, Medicare, and FUTA taxes under the same rules that apply to regular employees. This diminishes the appeal of the hiring-the-kids idea, but Bailey still comes out ahead by doing so.
  - In the case of an S corporation, the wage expense, the company's share of the Social Security and Medicare taxes, and the FUTA tax reduce Bailey's pass-through income and thus reduce her AGI and federal income tax; the money is kept in the family; and the children owe no income tax.
  - In the case of a C corporation, the wage expense, the company's share of the Social Security and Medicare taxes, and the FUTA tax are all deductible and therefore reduce the corporation's income tax bill.

What to do when both spouses are active in the self-employment activity

Advantages of hiring the business owner's spouse

Hiring the spouse can be a good idea when the spouse is already involved in the business, but his or her status has not been formalized. In such case, the IRS can mount an argument that the intended sole proprietorship (single-member LLC) is actually a husband-wife partnership, even though there is no written or oral partnership agreement.

IRS Publication 334 (*Tax Guide for Small Business*) stipulates that a partnership return (Form 1065) should be filed when there is a husband-wife partnership. This can be extremely detrimental, because it results in two Schedules SE instead of just one; meaning there can potentially be two taxpayers subject to the 15.3% rate on the first $132,900 of 2019 net SE income, instead of just one.

Key point: For 2019, the 12.4% Social Security tax component of the SE tax stops at net SE income above $132,900. The 2.9% Medicare tax continues to apply up to all net SE income above that threshold. The additional 0.9% Medicare tax is applied to all income above much higher income thresholds.

Naturally, the IRS is likely to argue that the SE income should be split 50/50 between the spouses, because that will maximize the SE tax damage to the previously unsuspecting duo.

The best advice is to head this potential problem off at the pass by formalizing the arrangement between the spouses before the IRS identifies the issue.

Treating the less-involved spouse as the other spouse's employee will often yield the best tax answer. The employer-spouse can pay some of the employee-spouse's *reasonably low* compensation in the form of health benefits coverage and the rest in the form of a modest cash wage. Then 100% of the health costs can be deducted, and only the cash wage will be subject to Social Security and Medicare taxes (collectively referred to as federal employment taxes).

Federal tax status of unincorporated husband-wife businesses

Once again, assume that the client operates his or her business as a sole proprietorship or single-member LLC (SMLLC) treated as such for federal tax purposes. The client's spouse has some involvement with the business from time to time. However, his or her participation has never been given any recognition for tax purposes.

Upon audit, the IRS could attempt to reclassify the client's single-member LLC (SMLLC) as a husband-wife partnership (husband-wife LLC). The government could then argue that all business income and deductions must be split 50/50 between husband and wife (or 70/30, or whatever).

The risk of the IRS making this argument was thought to be particularly acute in community property states, where under state law, a husband and wife are generally deemed to co-own all assets (including small business operations) on a 50/50 basis. If successful, the government's argument might not change the federal income tax results in any meaningful way. (The exception would be when tax elections required to be made at the husband-wife partnership (LLC) level were missed, because the client did not believe any such partnership (LLC) existed.)

However, the government's argument could have a disastrous effect on the client's SE tax results, as the following example illustrates.

> ### Example 6-13
>
> Assume Stella's SMLLC business generates annual SE income substantially greater than the ceiling for the Social Security tax component of the SE tax ($132,900 for 2019). Stella has always treated her SMLLC as a sole proprietorship for federal tax purposes. Stella's husband, Steve, participates in the business from time to time. However, the couple's tax returns have never given any hint of Steve's involvement.
>
> Say the IRS audits Stella and Steve and argues that Stella's business is actually a husband-wife LLC that must be treated as a partnership for federal tax purposes. In this case, the IRS will reallocate a portion of the net business income from Stella to Steve. This may have no impact on the couple's federal income tax bill. However, all or part of the net SE income shifted from Stella to Steve will now be taxed at 15.3% instead of 2.9%. (This assumes Steve does not have enough wage income or unrelated SE income to hit the $132,900 Social Security tax ceiling for 2019.)

Key point: The husband-wife partnership (LLC) argument could cause a big part of SE income to be reallocated from one spouse to the other with a resulting multi-thousand dollar increase in the couple's joint SE tax liability.

Knowledge check

4. For 2019, the Social Security tax component of the SE tax cuts out at SE income greater than

    a. $128,400.
    b. $250,000.
    c. The Social Security tax component continues to hit SE income without any limit.
    d. $132,900.

5. If the IRS successfully asserts that a purported sole proprietorship is actually a husband-wife partnership,

    a. It would generally have no SE tax or federal income tax consequences.
    b. It would generally have serious federal income tax consequences.
    c. The couple would be required to file a joint federal income tax return.
    d. It would often have significant SE tax consequences but no federal income tax consequences (assuming the couple files jointly).

Rev. Proc. 2002-69 relief for husband-wife business in community property states

Rev. Proc. 2002-69 explicitly provides that the IRS will not make the husband-wife partnership (LLC) argument against qualifying residents of community property states. Instead, the IRS will respect the taxpayer's treatment of an unincorporated business entity as either (1) a sole proprietorship (which would include an SMLLC treated as a sole proprietorship); or (2) a partnership (which would include a multi-member LLC treated as a partnership).

Put another way, when husband and wife treat their unincorporated business entity as a sole proprietorship for federal tax purposes, the IRS will not object, even when both spouses are active in the business activity. Alternatively, if husband and wife treat their unincorporated business as a husband-wife partnership for federal tax purposes and file partnership returns, the IRS will not object to that either.

It is very important to note that the relief offered by Rev. Proc. 2002-69 is limited to *qualified entities*. A business entity is a qualified entity when

- it is wholly owned by husband and wife as community property under the laws of a state, foreign country, or U.S. possession;
- no person other than the husband or wife (or both) would be considered an owner for federal tax purposes; and
- the entity is not treated as a corporation under the check-the-box entity classification rules of Regulation 301.7701-2.

Rev. Proc. 2002-69 also says: "A change in reporting position will be treated for federal tax purposes as a conversion of the entity." The following two examples illustrate the significance of this rule.

Example 6-14

Pursuant to Rev. Proc. 2002-69, Dave and Linda (married residents of a community property state) want to change the federal tax treatment of a qualified entity that has up until now been treated as a husband-wife partnership (that is, a husband-wife partnership or husband-wife LLC treated as such for federal tax purposes). Dave and Linda convert the qualified entity into a sole proprietorship for federal tax purposes (or SMLLC treated as such for federal tax purposes) by filing an initial Schedule C for the conversion year. Naturally, all the other federal tax consequences of converting and operating as a sole proprietorship must be considered as well. However, those consequences are generally benign, and there are usually no adverse or unexpected federal income tax consequences from the conversion itself. [See IRC Sections 731, 732, 735(b), and 1223(1).]

> **Example 6-15**
>
> Pursuant to Rev. Proc. 2002-69, Sandy (a married resident of a community property state) wants to change the federal tax treatment of a qualified entity that has up until now been treated as a sole proprietorship (that is, a sole proprietorship or SMLLC treated as such for federal tax purposes). Sandy can *convert* the qualified entity into a husband-wife partnership for federal tax purposes (or into a husband-wife LLC treated as such for federal tax purposes) by filing an initial Form 1065 for the year of conversion. Naturally, Sandy must also consider all the other federal tax consequences of converting and operating as a partnership. However, those consequences are generally benign, and there are usually no adverse or unexpected federal income tax consequences from the conversion itself. [See IRC Sections 721(a), 722, 723, and 1223(1).]

Self-employment tax planning opportunities in community property states

According to Rev. Proc. 2002-69, the rules previously explained apply "for federal tax purposes," which means they clearly apply for federal SE tax purposes. This opens up some nice SE tax planning strategies. Before getting into the strategies, however, let us first go over the basic SE tax rules for residents of community property states.

Under state community property laws, business income (including from a partnership) is generally community income. As such, it must be split 50/50 between the spouses for federal income tax purposes. Of course, this rule makes no difference on a joint return. However, the 50/50 rule does not apply for SE tax purposes. Instead, the following does apply:

When any of the income from a *non-partnership* business is considered community income, 100% of the gross income and deductions from said business must be allocated for SE tax purposes to the spouse who carries on the business.

In the case of business income from a *partnership*, the community property SE tax rule says the spouse who is the partner must report 100% of his or her distributive share of partnership income for SE tax purposes, and the non-partner spouse reports none [IRC Section 1402(a)(5)(B)]. When both spouses are partners in the partnership (including a husband-wife partnership), however, each spouse should report his or her distributive share of partnership income on his or her separate Schedule SE.

With that background information in mind, here are some SE tax planning strategies.

Convert husband-wife partnership into sole proprietorship

Community property state residents who own qualified entities currently treated as husband-wife partnerships (or husband-wife LLCs treated as such for federal tax purposes) should consider converting them into sole proprietorships (or SMLLCs treated as such for federal tax purposes) when converting would produce meaningful SE tax savings. Consider the following example.

Example 6-16

Pursuant to Rev. Proc. 2002-69, Clark and Cindy (married residents of a community property state) decide to convert their 50/50 husband-wife partnership, which produces SE income of $230,000, into a sole proprietorship treated as belonging to Clark for federal tax purposes. Assume Clark and Cindy have no wage income and no other SE income from other sources. The conversion reduces the couple's 2019 SE tax bill by $12,040 [($115,000 × .153 × 2) = $35,190 before the conversion compared to $23,150 after the conversion ($132,900 × .153) + ($97,100 × .029)].

The conversion is accomplished by liquidating the assets (if any) of Clark and Cindy's husband-wife partnership into the "new" post-conversion sole proprietorship considered to be owned by Clark. In most cases, the only federal income tax impact of the conversion will be ceasing to file Form 1065 and instead filing Schedule C for the "new" post-conversion sole proprietorship. However, the SE tax savings from the conversion can be substantial, as this example illustrates.

Variation: Assume the same basic facts, except this time assume Clark and Cindy run the business as a 50/50 husband-wife LLC treated as a partnership for federal tax purposes. They convert the husband-wife LLC into an SMLLC treated as a sole proprietorship belonging to Clark for federal tax purposes. The tax results would be the same as previously mentioned.

Key point: The conversion of a qualified entity for federal tax purposes will not necessarily require any action under state law and will not necessarily have any significance for general state law purposes (except to the extent the entity's federal tax treatment affects its treatment under state law). Therefore, implementing the conversion may involve nothing more than filing federal tax forms to properly reflect the conversion. In the preceding example, for instance, the liquidation of the husband-wife partnership into the "new" sole proprietorship may be a "deemed" transaction for federal tax purposes only and not an actual transaction for state law purposes. However, the state income tax implications (if any) of any conversion (whether actual or deemed) should always be evaluated before any action is taken.

Convert sole proprietorship into husband-wife partnership

Community property state residents who own qualified entities currently treated as sole proprietorships (or SMLLCs treated as such for federal tax purposes) should consider converting them into husband-wife partnerships (or husband-wife LLCs treated as such for federal tax purposes) when converting would produce SE tax savings. Consider the following example.

Example 6-17

Frieda and Fritz are married residents of a community property state. Frieda's sole proprietorship generates $100,000 of SE income. Her husband Fritz earns a salary of $150,000 from an unrelated job. Pursuant to Rev. Proc. 2002-69, Frieda converts her sole proprietorship into a 50/50 husband-wife partnership for federal tax purposes. This action shifts $50,000 of SE income from Frieda to Fritz, which reduces the couple's SE tax bill by a cool $6,200 ($50,000 of SE income shifted to Fritz's Schedule SE, where it is taxed at only 2.9%; versus 15.3% if the same $50,000 is reported on Frieda's Schedule SE).

The conversion is accomplished by contributing the assets (if any) of the sole proprietorship to the "new" post-conversion husband-wife partnership. In most cases, the only federal income tax impact of the conversion will be ceasing to file Schedule C and instead filing Form 1065 for the "new" post-conversion husband-wife partnership. However, as illustrated by this example, the SE tax savings from a conversion can be substantial.

Variation: Assume the same basic facts, except this time assume Frieda runs her business as an SMLLC treated as a sole proprietorship for federal tax purposes. She converts the SMLLC into a 50/50 husband-wife LLC for federal tax purposes. The tax results would be the same as previously mentioned.

Key point: Once again, the conversion of a qualified entity for federal tax purposes will not necessarily require any action under state law and will not necessarily have any significance for general state law purposes (except to the extent the entity's federal tax treatment affects its treatment under state law). Therefore, implementing the conversion may involve nothing more than filing federal tax forms to properly reflect the conversion. In the preceding example, for instance, the contribution of assets to create the "new" husband-wife partnership may be a "deemed" transaction for federal tax purposes only and not an actual transaction for state law purposes. However, the state income tax implications (if any) of any conversion (whether actual or deemed) should always be evaluated before any action is taken.

Federal tax status of unincorporated husband-wife businesses in non-community property states

As explained earlier, the favorable guidance in Rev. Proc. 2002-69 is limited to unincorporated business entities (including sole proprietorships) owned by husband and wife as community property (with no other owners in the picture). What about unincorporated businesses in non-community property states? Several IRS publications attempt to create the *false* impression that involvement by both spouses in an unincorporated business activity *automatically* creates a partnership for federal tax purposes in non-community property states. (See, for example, IRS Publications 225 and 541.) Of course, when husband-wife partnership status applies, Form 1065 must be filed along with a separate Schedule SE for each spouse. This can result in a much higher SE tax bill for the couple. (Ditto when husband-wife LLC status applies.)

The truth is that in most cases, the IRS will have a very tough time making the husband-wife partnership (LLC) argument. For proof, consider the following direct quote from PLR 8742007. "Whether parties have formed a joint venture is a question of fact to be determined by reference to the same principles that govern the question of whether persons have formed a partnership which is to be accorded recognition for tax purposes. Therefore, although all circumstances are to be considered, the essential question is whether the parties intended to, and did, in fact, join together for the present conduct of an undertaking or enterprise. The following factors, none of which is conclusive, are evidence of this intent: (1) the agreement of the parties and their conduct in executing its terms; (2) the contributions, if any, that each party makes to the venture; (3) control over the income and capital of the venture and the right to make withdrawals; (4) whether the parties are co-proprietors who share in net profits and who have an obligation to share losses; and (5) whether the business was conducted in the joint names of the parties and was represented to be a partnership. See *Commissioner v. Tower*, 327 U.S. 280 (1946), 1946-1 C.B. 11; *Commissioner v. Culbertson*, 337 U.S. 733 (1949), 1949-2 C.B. 5; *Luna v. Commissioner*, 42 T.C. 1067 (1964); and Rev. Rul. 82-61, 1982-1 C.B. 13." Private Letter Rulings cannot be cited as authority. Nevertheless, the preceding analysis is technically correct and right on point, because it was written specifically to address the husband-wife partnership issue.

Of course, in many (if not most) client situations where both spouses have some involvement in a purported sole proprietorship (or SMLLC treated as such for federal tax purposes), only one or two of the five factors listed in the PLR are present. In such circumstances, the IRS should not be successful in making the husband-wife partnership (LLC) argument. Regardless of the presence or absence of the other factors previously listed, the author believes the husband-wife partnership argument is especially weak when (1) the spouses have no discernible partnership agreement and (2) the business has not been represented as a partnership to third parties.

Key point: Pursuant to Rev. Proc. 2002-69, the IRS has now officially abandoned the husband-wife partnership (LLC) argument in community property states (where spouses are generally 50/50 co-owners as a matter of state law), which undeniably makes the husband-wife partnership (LLC) argument just that much weaker in non-community property states (where 50/50 co-ownership by spouses is definitely not preordained by state law).

Warning: Although it will often be possible to make a convincing argument that a husband-wife partnership does not exist, please do not get carried away. In the worst-case scenario, the IRS could attempt to assess the penalty for failure to file a partnership return (Form 1065). For partnership tax returns required to be filed in 2019 (for example, returns for calendar year 2018 for partnerships that use the calendar year), the penalty amount is $200 per month for each spouse for up to 12 months, or until a partnership return is filed. (See IRC Section 6698.) For a husband-wife business, the maximum penalty for failing to file a calendar year 2018 partnership return would be $4,800 ($200 × 2 × 12). Therefore, taking a stand on this issue may not be worth the risk in some situations. That said, Rev. Proc. 84-35 provides a limited exemption from the failure-to-file penalty. The exemption is available only to domestic partnerships with 10 or fewer partners when all the partners have reported their proportionate shares of income and deductions on timely filed returns. When income or deductions are not allocated proportionately, the Rev. Proc. 84-35 exemption is unavailable.

Simplified compliance rules for unincorporated husband-wife businesses in non-community property states

The general rule is that an unincorporated husband-wife business that is properly classified as a partnership for federal income tax purposes must comply with the partnership tax provisions—which include the requirement to file an annual Form 1065 partnership return and issue each spouse an annual Schedule K-1. This general rule applies equally to a husband-wife LLC that is properly classified as a partnership for federal income tax purposes.

Unfortunately, partnership tax status can create compliance headaches. The partnership tax rules are relatively complicated, and the required Forms 1065 and Schedules K-1 are notoriously difficult to prepare.

A simplification provision that allows certain unincorporated husband-wife businesses to elect out of partnership tax status for federal income tax purposes (state income tax rules may or may not be different). To be eligible for the election out, the spouses must file jointly, and the husband-wife business must be a qualified joint venture (QJV).

After electing out of partnership tax status, the spouses must separately report their respective shares of the venture's tax items on the appropriate IRS forms. For example, income and expenses from an eligible husband-wife business activity other than farming would generally be reported on separate Schedules C filed with the couple's joint Form 1040. Income and expenses from an eligible husband-wife farming activity would be reported on separate Schedules F. Similarly, the spouses must separately report their respective shares of net SE income (if any) from the husband-wife operation on separate Schedules SE filed with the couple's joint Form 1040. Each spouse then receives credit for his or her share of the SE income for Social Security benefit eligibility purposes. [See IRC Sections 761(f) and 1402(a)(17).]

How to elect out of partnership status

The election out is accomplished by the spouses separately reporting their respective shares of tax items from the QJV and separately reporting their shares of SE income (if any) in the fashion previously explained.

Key point: Electing out of partnership tax status will not change the married couple's joint federal income tax liability or their joint SE tax liability. However, electing out has the beneficial effect of eliminating the need to (1) comply with the complicated partnership tax rules, and (2) prepare and file an annual Form 1065 and related Schedules K-1.

Definition of QJV

According to the statutory language, a QJV is an unincorporated business venture in which

1. the husband and wife are the only members of the venture,
2. both spouses materially participate in the venture's business, and
3. both spouses elect out of partnership tax status in the manner previously explained.

A husband-wife venture conducted by an entity that is classified as an S or C corporation for federal tax purposes cannot be a QJV. Corporations must always file separate federal returns on Form 1120S (for an S corporation) or Form 1120 (for a C corporation).

The IRS has issued two clarifications on when a husband-wife business can meet the definition of a QJV. One clarification is good news for taxpayers, but the other is not.

IRS admits husband-wife rental real estate business can be QJV

The IRS admits that an unincorporated husband-wife rental real estate business can meet the definition of a QJV and thus be eligible for the election out of partnership tax status. See CCA 200816030. Before 2008, it was unclear if the election out would be allowed for a rental real estate activity. If the election out is made, net income from the rental real estate operation is not subject to SE tax.

To make the election out for a rental real estate activity, the spouses should (1) report their respective shares of the QJV's income and expense items on separate Schedules E filed with the couple's joint Form 1040; and (2) check the QJV box on Line 2 of their Schedules E.

Unofficial IRS guidance says husband-wife LLC cannot be QJV

Now for the bad news. According to an IRS website article (https://www.irs.gov/businesses/small-businesses-self-employed/election-for-married-couples-unincorporated-businesses), a husband-wife joint venture that is operated as an LLC and that is currently treated as a husband-wife partnership for federal tax purposes does not meet the definition of a QJV. Therefore, according to the article, the election out of partnership tax status is not allowed. And, therefore, according to the article, a husband-wife LLC must comply with the burdensome partnership tax rules, with no relief in sight.

This IRS stand is also puzzling. Neither the statutory language, nor the legislative history, nor common sense provide any support for the notion that a husband-wife LLC that is treated as a husband-wife partnership for federal tax purposes cannot be a QJV if the requirements explained earlier are met. Here is why.

QJV status is clearly limited to unincorporated businesses, but an LLC is not an incorporated entity under applicable state law (LLCs are LLCs rather than corporations). In addition, an LLC that is classified as a partnership for federal tax purposes is obviously not an incorporated entity for those purposes either.

Last, but not least, the IRS is out of bounds in using a website article to take the controversial position that a husband-wife LLC cannot be a QJV. The IRS should only take such a position in authoritative guidance such as a regulation or revenue ruling. An article on the IRS website has no technical authority and need not be followed by taxpayers unless it is supported by statutory language, legislative history, or some other form of legitimate official guidance.

For the reasons explained, some taxpayers might choose to ignore the unofficial guidance in the IRS website article and treat husband-wife LLCs as QJVs when the requirements explained earlier are met. However, taxpayers should be warned that the IRS has taken a contrary position in unofficial guidance, for what it is worth

Warning: In the worst-case scenario, the IRS could attempt to assess the penalty for failure to file a partnership return (Form 1065). For partnership tax returns required to be filed in 2019, the penalty amount is $200 per month for each spouse, for up to 12 months or until a partnership return is filed. (See IRC Section 6698.) For a husband-wife business, the maximum penalty for failing to file a calendar year 2018 partnership return would be $4,800 ($200 × 2 × 12). Therefore, going against the IRS on this issue may not be worth the risk—even though it is quite likely the IRS is wrong. That said, Rev. Proc. 84-35 provides a limited exemption from the failure-to-file penalty. The exemption is available only to domestic partnerships with 10 or fewer partners when all the partners have reported their proportionate shares of income and deductions on timely filed returns. When income or deductions are not allocated proportionately, the Rev. Proc. 84-35 exemption is unavailable.

Update on tax-smart health savings accounts

The Affordable Care Act (ACA) makes health savings accounts (HSAs) more popular than ever.

Growing popularity

According to a recent survey conducted by Devenir (an HSA investment provider), HSA assets exceeded $51bn as of June 30, 2018. That number represented a year-over-year increase of 20.4%. The total number of HSAs grew to 23.4 million as of June 30, 2018, up 11.2% compared to a year earlier. Devenir projects that by the end of 2020, there will be about 29 million HSAs with assets approaching $75bn. Back in 2010, the Employee Benefit Research Institute reported that there were 5.7 million HSAs with account balances totaling $7.7bn.

The ACA effect

Under the ACA, health insurance plans are categorized as Bronze, Silver, Gold, or Platinum. Bronze plans have the highest deductibles and least-generous coverage and are therefore the most affordable. Platinum plans have no deductibles and cover much more, but they are also much more expensive. Some of the less generous plans can allow recipients to make tax-saving HSA contributions. Those tax savings can partially offset the cost of premiums and provide coverage otherwise unaffordable to many taxpayers.

HSA basics

The statutory language for HSAs is found in IRC Section. 223.

For the 2019 tax year, individuals can make a deductible HSA contribution of up to $3,500 if they have qualifying self-only coverage or up to $7,000 with qualifying family coverage.

For 2018, the maximum contributions were $3,450 and $6,900, respectively.

For those who are age 55 or older as of year-end, the maximum deductible contribution for both types goes up by $1,000.

Individuals must have a qualifying high-deductible health insurance policy (and no other general health coverage) to be eligible for the HSA contribution privilege.

For 2019, a high-deductible policy is defined as one with a deductible of at least $1,350 for self-only coverage or $2,700 for family coverage.

For 2018, the minimum deductibles were the same.

For 2019, qualifying high-deductible policies can have out-of-pocket maximums of up to $6,750 for self-only coverage or $13,500 for family coverage.

For 2018, the out-of-pocket maximums were $6,650 and $13,300, respectively.

HSA contributions

If an individual is eligible to make an HSA contribution for the tax year in question, the deadline is April 15 of the following year (adjusted for weekends and holidays) to open an account and make a deductible contribution for the earlier year (same deadline as for IRA contributions).

The deduction for HSA contributions is an above-the-line deduction [IRC Section 62(a)(19)]. Therefore, it can be taken whether the taxpayer itemizes or not. The HSA contribution privilege also is not lost just because the individual happens to be a high earner. If an individual covered by qualifying high-deductible health insurance, he or she can make contributions and collect the resulting tax savings. (Of course, this assumes that the individual meets all the other HSA eligibility rules explained later in this analysis.)

However, no HSA contributions are allowed for any person who can be claimed as a dependent on another person's federal income tax return for the year in question [IRC Section 223(b)(6)].

IRS Form 8889, *Health Savings Accounts (HSAs)*, is used to determine allowable HSA contribution amounts.

Key point: Sole proprietors, partners, LLC members, and S corporation shareholder-employees are generally allowed to claim separate above-the-line deductions for 100% of their health insurance premiums [IRC Section 162(l)]. This is true whether or not they have high-deductible coverage that qualifies them for the HSA contribution privilege. Unfortunately, neither the HSA deduction nor the separate deduction for health insurance premiums will reduce anyone's self-employment tax bill.

HSA distributions

HSA distributions used to pay qualified medical expenses of the HSA owner, spouse, or dependents are federal-income-tax-free. However, the HSA owner is allowed to build up a balance in the account if contributions plus earnings exceed withdrawals for medical expenses. Any income earned is federal-income-tax-free. Therefore, if the account owner is in very good health, the HSA can be used to build up a substantial medical expense reserve fund over the years while earning tax-free income all along the way.

If the account owner still has an HSA balance after reaching Medicare eligibility age, the account can be drained. The account owner will owe federal income tax on the withdrawals, but the 20% penalty tax that generally applies to withdrawals not used for medical expenses will not apply. There is no penalty on withdrawals after disability or death either. [See IRC Section 223(f)(2) and (f)(4).]

Alternatively, the account owner can use the HSA balance to pay uninsured medical expenses incurred after reaching Medicare eligibility age. If the HSA still has a balance when the account owner dies, the surviving spouse can take over the account tax-free and treat it as his or her own HSA—provided that the surviving spouse is named as the account beneficiary [IRC Section. 223(f)(8)(A)]. In other cases, the date-of-death balance of the HSA must generally be included in taxable income on that date by the person who inherits the account. A reduction is allowed for any decedent medical expenses paid by the inheritor within one year of the date of death. [See IRC Section. 223(f)(8)(B).]

To summarize thus far, an HSA can work a lot like an IRA if the account owner can maintain good health and avoid big medical bills. Even if the account owner has to drain the account every year to pay uninsured health costs, the HSA arrangement allows those expenses to be paid with pretax dollars.

Warnings: HSA funds cannot be used for tax-free reimbursements for medical expenses that were incurred before the account was opened. Also, if money is taken out of an HSA for any reason other than to cover eligible medical expenses, it will trigger a 20% penalty tax, unless the account owner has reached Medicare eligibility age [IRC Section. 223(f)(4)]. Therefore, individuals need to be sure they can afford to put money into their HSAs and possibly leave it there for a while. If they are not sure, they should not do it.

Example 6-18

Ben and Betty are a married couple. They are both self-employed, and they both have separate HSA-compatible individual health insurance policies for all of 2019. Both policies have $2,000 deductibles. For 2019, Ben and Betty can both contribute $3,500 to their respective HSAs and claim a total of $7,000 worth of tax-saving write-offs on their joint return. If they are in the 32% federal income tax bracket, this strategy cuts their 2019 tax bill by a cool $2,240 (.32 × $7,000). If Ben and Betty do this for 10 years, they will save $22,400 in taxes. If they invest that money and earn 5% after taxes, they will accumulate $28,175 in the HSA after 10 years.

Example 6-19

For all of 2019, Hannah has qualifying family health insurance coverage with a $3,000 deductible. If Hannah will be 55 or older as of December 31, 2019, she can contribute up to $8,000 to an HSA for the 2019 tax year (the "normal" $7,000 limitation + $1,000 extra due to her age). If Hannah's spouse is also 55 or older as of December 31, 2019, and is covered by the high-deductible family insurance policy, Hannah can contribute up to $9,000 to her HSA (the "normal" $7,000 limitation + $1,000 extra due to her age + another $1,000 extra due to her spouse's age). However, Hannah will lose the right to make HSA contributions after she reaches Medicare eligibility age.

Details on HSA contribution eligibility

According to the general rule, eligibility to make HSA contributions is determined on a monthly basis. So, when an individual has qualifying high-deductible health coverage for only part of the year, he or she can contribute and deduct 1/12 of the annual limitation amount for each month that qualifying coverage is in effect [IRC Section 223(b)(1) and (2)]. More specifically, an individual is eligible for any month that he or she is covered under a qualifying high-deductible health plan as of the first day of that month.

Under an exception to the aforementioned general month-by-month eligibility rule, an individual who is eligible to make HSA contributions as of the last month of the year can be treated as eligible for the entire year and can therefore contribute up to the full maximum amount for that year [IRC Section 223(b)(8)]. Although the ability to make a full HSA contribution based on end-of-year eligibility is helpful, a harsh recapture rule may apply if the individual becomes ineligible for HSA contributions during the subsequent "testing period." The recapture amount equals the amount of additional contributions deducted under the aforementioned eligibility exception compared to the pro-rated amount that would have been allowed under the general month-by-month eligibility rule. The recapture amount is also subject to a 10% penalty tax [IRC Section 223(b)(8)]. The testing period begins with the last month of the tax year and ends on the last day of the 12th month following that month. The recapture amount is included in income (and the 10% penalty is charged) for the tax year that includes the first day during the testing period that the taxpayer becomes ineligible for HSA contributions.

Example 6-20

On December 1, 2018, Bob becomes covered by a qualifying high-deductible health plan that provides self-only coverage. Bob is 45 years old. He can make a deductible HSA contribution of up to $3,450 for his 2018 tax year (the maximum allowable amount for an individual his age with self-only coverage). Assume he does that and claims the deduction on his 2018 Form 1040. Under the general month-by-month rule, Bob's contribution for 2018 would be limited to only $288 ($3,450 ÷ 12), because Bob is covered only for one month out of 12. So far, so good. However, if Bob becomes ineligible for HSA contributions anytime in 2019, he must report recapture income of $3,162 ($3,450 − $288) on his 2019 return and pay the 10% penalty tax on that amount.

Observation: As this example illustrates, the recapture rule can potentially come into play in the year after a larger HSA contribution is made. This may discourage folks from making larger contributions than would be allowed under the general month-by-month contribution limitation rule.

Impact of other health coverages

An individual is ineligible to make an HSA contribution for any month that he or she is also covered under any non-high-deductible health plan that provides coverage for any benefit that is covered under the high-deductible plan [IRC Section 223(c)(1) and (2)]. For purposes of this rule, however, the following types of health-related coverages are ignored:

- Plans that provides only preventive care benefits (see IRS Notice 2004-23 for a long list of what qualifies as preventive care)
- Workers compensation insurance
- Insurance for a specific disease or illness (such as cancer insurance)
- Insurance that pays a fixed amount per day or other period of hospitalization (hospital benefit insurance)
- Coverage (whether through insurance or otherwise) for accidents, disability, dental care, vision care, or long-term care [See IRC Section 223(c)(3).]

HSAs and healthcare FSAs don't mix

In a 2014 CCA, the IRS confirmed that HSAs and healthcare FSAs don't mix. Specifically, an individual cannot make contributions to both types of accounts in the same tax year, and carryovers of unused healthcare FSA balances count as contributions for purposes of this rule (CCA 201413005). As explained earlier, an individual is ineligible to make an HSA contribution if he or she is covered by another health plan that is not a high-deductible health plan if that other plan provides coverage for any benefit that is also covered by the high-deductible plan. Because a healthcare FSA that reimburses for qualified medical expenses without restrictions (a general-purpose healthcare FSA) counts as another health plan, coverage under such an FSA makes the covered individual ineligible to make HSA contributions for the entire healthcare FSA plan year (IRS Notice 2005-86).

Impact of healthcare FSA carryover on eligibility for HSA contributions

In CCA 201413005, the IRS said individuals are considered covered by a healthcare FSA for the entire FSA plan year if they have any carryover into that year of an unused healthcare FSA balance from a prior plan year—even if they make no healthcare FSA contribution for the current plan year. Therefore, if the individuals have a carryover into the current plan year, they are ineligible to make an HSA contribution for the entire plan year. This is the case even if they use up the FSA carryover amount early in the plan year.

Under an exception, an individual who

- participates in a general-purpose healthcare FSA;
- elects for the following year to participate in an HSA-compatible healthcare FSA; and
- elects to have any unused balance from the general-purpose healthcare FSA carried over to the new HSA-compatible healthcare FSA can contribute to an HSA during that following year.

Examples of an HSA-compatible healthcare FSA would include a healthcare FSA that has a deductible that least equals the minimum high-deductible health plan deductible ($1,350 for self-only coverage or $2,700 for family coverage for 2019) or a healthcare FSA that covers only qualified preventive care expenses.

Employer-funded HSAs

Employers are also permitted to make deductible contributions to HSAs set up for their employees—subject to the same dollar limits and eligibility rules explained earlier. Employer-funded contributions are exempt from federal income tax and from Social Security, Medicare, and FUTA taxes too. This is because employer-funded HSA contributions are considered to be for an accident or health plan. As such, they are exempt from federal income and employment taxes.

However, the employer may face a 35% excise tax if comparable contributions are not made on behalf of all employees with comparable coverage during the same period. For this purpose, "comparable contribution" means the same amount or the same percentage of the health plan deductible. The comparability rule is applied separately to part-time employees who customarily work less than 30 hours per week. (See IRC Section 4980G.)

There is an important exception to the HSA comparable contribution requirements. The exception allows employers to make larger HSA contributions for non-highly compensated employees than for highly compensated employees without incurring a penalty [IRC Section 4980G(d)]. Comparable contributions must still be made to HSAs of non-highly compensated employees (under Regulations 54.4980G-1 through -5). For this purpose, a highly compensated employee is defined under IRC Sec. 414(q) to be an employee who (1) was a more-than-5% owner at any time during the current year or the preceding year; or (2) for the preceding year, had compensation exceeding $100,000 (indexed for inflation--$120,000 for 2018) and, if elected by the employer, was in the top 20% of employees ranked by compensation.

Finally, eligible employees can choose to make salary-reduction HSA contributions under an employer-sponsored IRC Section 125 "cafeteria benefit plan." [See IRC Section 125(d)(2)(D).]

There is generally nothing to prevent clients from making HSA contributions for themselves as employees of their own C or S corporation, assuming the clients do not mind covering the other employees too (if any). Of course, if those other employees are all family members, they probably will not mind. Remember: Contributions to employee HSAs are (1) deductible by the employer and (2) exempt from federal income and employment taxes.

Establishing an HSA

An HSA is an IRA-like trust or custodial account that can be set up at a bank, insurance company, or any other entity the IRS decides is suitable (such as brokerage firms). The HSA arrangement must be exclusively for the purpose of paying the account owner's qualified medical expenses. These include uninsured costs incurred by the account owner (the person for whom the HSA is established), his spouse, and his dependents.

Otherwise, HSAs are subject to rules very similar to those that apply to IRAs. For example, HSA contributions for a particular year can be made as late as April 15 of the following year (extended for weekends and holidays). Account owners can also make tax-free rollovers from one HSA to another, limited to one rollover per 12-month period. [See IRC Section 223(d), (e), and (f)(5).]

Key point: An eligible individual has until April 15, 2020, to make a deductible HSA contribution for the 2019 tax year.

Forms 5305-B (Health Savings Trust Account) and 5305-C (Health Savings Custodial Account) are used to set up HSAs. The forms are model trust and model custodian account agreements, respectively. Each takes only a moment to complete. The completed Form 5305-B or 5305-C is not filed with the IRS. Instead, it should be kept with the account owner's permanent tax records.

HSA investment options and providers

In theory, HSAs offer the same investment options (stocks, mutual funds, bonds, CDs, and so forth) as IRAs. That said, some HSA trustees may limit investment choices to very conservative options.

HSA trustees can be found with an internet search. Some health insurance companies and brokerage firms have pre-arranged deals with HSA trustees. For example, Anthem Blue Cross Blue Shield uses JPMorgan Chase Bank to act as the trustee for their HSA-eligible policyholders.

Conclusion

HSAs are a good tax-saving deal. Best of all, they are simple and easy to establish and operate. Many clients may not be lucky enough to have generous employer-paid health coverage. If these folks are not currently doing anything to create tax-favored treatment for their health costs, buying qualifying high-deductible insurance coverage and setting up an HSA to make tax-saving contributions seems simple.

Knowledge check

6. For individual taxpayers, HSA contributions for a particular tax year must be made by

    a. December 31 of that year.
    b. The un-extended due date of the Form 1040 for that year (April 15, adjusted for weekends and holidays).
    c. The extended due date of the Form 1040 for that year (October 15, adjusted for weekends and holidays).
    d. September 30 of that year (the end of the federal government's fiscal year).

7. What date determines an individual's eligibility status to determine the maximum allowable HSA contribution for that year?

    a. March 1 of that year.
    b. September 1 of that year.
    c. October 1 of that year.
    d. December 1 of that year.

Section 199A – The qualified business income deduction

Before the TCJA, net taxable income from sole proprietorships, partnerships, LLCs treated as sole proprietorships or as partnerships for tax purposes, and S corporations was simply passed through to individual owners and taxed at the owner level at the standard rates for individual taxpayers.

For tax years beginning in 2018–2025, the TCJA establishes a new deduction for non-corporate taxpayers to be applied against their qualified business income (QBI). This break is available to individuals, estates, and trusts. IRS regulations on the QBI deduction refer to all three as "individuals," and we will follow that convention here. The deduction can be up to 20% of QBI, subject to restrictions that can apply at higher income levels and another restriction based on taxable income. (See IRC Sec. 199A.)

Key point: The QBI deduction can also be claimed for up to 20% of an individual's qualified dividends from real estate investment trusts (REITs) and up to 20% of an individual's qualified income from publicly traded partnerships (PTPs) [Reg. 1.199A-3(c)].

Pass-through QBI deduction basics

An individual's QBI deduction can be up to 20% of QBI from pass-through entities. This would include partnerships (and LLCs treated as partnerships for tax purposes), S corporations, and sole proprietorships (including single-member LLCs treated as sole proprietorships for tax purposes) plus 20% of aggregate qualified dividends from REITs, cooperatives, and qualified PTPs (special rules apply to specified agricultural and horticultural cooperatives).

The QBI deduction is a "below-the-line" deduction and as such is not subtracted in calculating the taxpayer's AGI. It is based upon the eligible taxpayer's taxable income, and other limitations may apply.

The QBI deduction also does not reduce an individual's net earnings from self-employment for self-employment tax purposes nor does it reduce net investment income for purposes of the 3.8% net investment income tax (NIIT).

Definition of QBI

QBI is the net domestic business taxable income, gain, deduction, and loss from a qualified business. Investment-related items like capital gains and losses, dividends, and interest income generally don't count as QBI. However, interest income that is properly allocable to a business does count and so do the aforementioned qualified dividends from REITs, cooperatives, and PTPs. Employee compensation paid to an S corporation shareholder-employee and guaranteed payments paid by a partnership to a partner (including an LLC member who is treated as a partner for tax purposes) don't count as QBI to the payee.

Qualified items of income, gain, deduction, and loss must be effectively connected with the conduct of a trade or business within the United States (including Puerto Rico).

Finally, QBI is calculated without considering any adjustments under the alternative minimum tax rules.

W-2 wage/UBIA of qualified property limitations

The QBI deduction generally cannot exceed the greater of the individual's share of

- 50% of W-2 wages paid to employees by the qualified business during the tax year, or
- the sum of 25% of those W-2 wages plus 2.5% of the unadjusted basis immediately after acquisition of qualified depreciable property used in the business (UBIA of qualified property).

Qualified property means depreciable tangible property (including real estate) owned by a qualified business as of the tax year-end and used by the business at any point during the tax year for the production of QBI. Also, to be qualified property, an asset must not have reached the end of its depreciable period (as defined under the QBI deduction rules) as of the end of the tax year. The *depreciable period* is defined as beginning on the date the property is first placed in service by the taxpayer and ending on the later of

- 10 years after that date or
- the last day of the last full year in the applicable recovery period under IRC Section 168 (MACRS).

For 2018, these limitations apply only when the individual has taxable income (calculated before any QBI deduction) above $157,500 or $315,000 for a married joint-filing couple. These income limits are indexed for inflation. The limits for 2019 are $160,700 and $321,400, respectively (Rev. Proc. 2018-57). The W-2 wage/ UBIA of qualified property limitations are phased in over a taxable income range of $50,000 or $100,000 for a married joint-filing couple. For example, these limitations are fully phased in for 2018 once taxable income for that year exceeds $207,500 or $415,000 for a married joint-filing couple.

Example 6-21 W-2 wage limitation applies

For 2018, you and your spouse file a joint return reporting taxable income of $355,000 (before considering any QBI deduction or any long-term capital gains (LTCGs) or qualified dividends). Your spouse has $150,000 of net income from a qualified business that is not a service business. Your tentative QBI deduction is $30,000 (20% × $150,000). Your spouse's share of W-2 wages paid by the business is $40,000. The W-2 wage limitation is $20,000 (50% × $40,000). The $10,000 difference between the $30,000 tentative QBI deduction and the $20,000 W-2 wage limitation is 40% phased in [($355,000 − $315,000) ÷ $100,000 = .40)]. Your QBI deduction is limited to $26,000 [$30,000 − (40% × $10,000)].

Variation: Your taxable income is $300,000 (before considering any QBI deduction or any LTCGs or qualified dividends). Because your taxable income is below the $315,000 threshold for the phase-in of the W-2 wage limitation, you are unaffected by the limitation. Therefore, your QBI deduction is the full $30,000.

Special QBI deduction limitation for service businesses

For specified service trades and businesses (SSTBs), the QBI deduction is phased out and then completely disallowed above stipulated income levels. For 2018, phase-out starts once taxable income exceeds $157,500 or $315,000 for a married joint-filing couple. The phase-out thresholds for 2019 are $160,725 and $321,400, respectively (Rev. Proc. 2018-57). The QBI deduction for SSTBs is phased out over a taxable income range of $50,000 or $100,000 for a married joint-filing couple. For example, phase-out is complete for 2018 once taxable income for that year exceeds $207,500 or $415,000 for a married joint-filing couple.

Overall QBI deduction limitation

In addition to the aforementioned limitations, an individual's allowable QBI deduction cannot exceed the lesser of

- 20% of QBI from qualified businesses plus 20% of qualified REIT dividends plus 20% of qualified PTP income or
- 20% of the individual's taxable income calculated before any QBI deduction and before any net capital gain amount (net LTCGs in excess of net short-term capital losses plus qualified dividends). [See IRC Sec. 199A(a) and (b).]

Example 6-22 Service business limitation applies

For 2018, you file as a single taxpayer and report taxable income of $187,500 (before considering any QBI deduction or any LTCGs or qualified dividends). You have $125,000 of net income from an SSTB. Your tentative QBI deduction is $25,000 (20% × $125,000). Assume you are unaffected by the W-2 wage/UBIA of qualified property limitation. Under the SSTB limitation, you can consider only 40% of the SSTB income, or $50,000, because the SSTB limitation is 60% phased in. [($187,500 − $157,500) ÷ $50,000 = .60 phased in; (40% × $125,000) = $50,000.] Your QBI deduction is limited to $10,000 (20% × $50,000).

Variation: Your taxable income is $150,000 (before considering any QBI deduction or any LTCGs or qualified dividends). Because your taxable income is below the $157,500 threshold for the phase-in of the SSTBs limitation, you are unaffected by the limitation. Therefore, your QBI deduction is the full $25,000.

Example 6-23 Taxable income limitation applies

For 2018, you file a joint return reporting taxable income of $175,000 (before considering any QBI deduction or any LTCGs or qualified dividends). Your tentative QBI deduction after considering any impact from the W-2 wage/UBIA of qualified property limitation or the SSTB limitation is $40,000. Due to the taxable income limitation, your QBI deduction is limited to $35,000 (20% × $175,000).

Variation: Your taxable income is $225,000 (before considering any QBI deduction or any LTCGs or qualified dividends). The QBI deduction limitation based upon taxable income is $45,000 (20% × $225,000). Because your $40,000 tentative QBI deduction is less than 20% of your taxable income, you are unaffected by the taxable income limitation. Therefore, your QBI deduction is the full $40,000.

Exception for certain specified service businesses based on taxable income below the threshold

Section 199A(d)(3) provides an exception for certain service businesses. If the taxable income of any taxpayer is less than the sum of the threshold amount plus $50,000 ($100,000 for a joint return), the business will be treated as a qualified trade or business.

To calculate the adjustment, only the applicable percentage of qualified items of income, gain, deduction or loss, W-2 wages, and the unadjusted basis immediately after acquisition of qualified property that is allocable to the business are considered in computing QBI.

Therefore, a specified service business that has income below the top of the phase-out range is still entitled to the deduction. If taxable income is within the phase-out range, the qualifying income and, therefore, the deduction are reduced ratably.

If a taxpayer in a specified service business has taxable income in excess of the top of the phase-out threshold, the income from that business will not qualify for the QBI deduction.

Qualified businesses operated as partnerships, LLCs, and S corporations

For qualified businesses that are conducted as partnerships, including LLCs that are treated as partnerships for tax purposes, or S corporations, the QBI deduction and the applicable limitations are determined at the owner level. Each owner considers his or her share of each qualified item of income, gain, deduction, and loss from the pass-through entity and his or her share of W-2 wages paid by the entity and his or her share of the UBIA of qualified property.

For example, a partner's share of partnership W-2 wages (for determining the W-2 wage limitation under the QBI deduction rules) must be the same as the partner's share of partnership wage expense. The same requirement exists for members of LLCs that are treated as partnerships for tax purposes.

Similarly, each S corporation shareholder considers his or her pro rata share (based on stock ownership) of each qualified item of S corporation income, gain, deduction, and loss. Each shareholder is treated as having W-2 wages equal to his or her pro rata share of the total W-2 wages paid by the S corporation and his or her share of the UBIA of qualified property.

IRS regulations

In January of 2019, the IRS issued final QBI deduction regulations [Regs. 1.199A-1 through -6 and 1.643(f)-1]. The 148-page Preamble to the final regulations is generally more understandable than the actual regulations and is helpful for that reason. The Preamble is broken down into eight parts. Part I provides an overview of the new regulations. Part II covers operational rules, definitions, computational rules, special rules, and reporting requirements. Part III explains how to calculate W-2 wages and the UBIA of qualified property. Part IV explains how to determine QBI, qualified REIT dividends, and qualified PTP income. Part V covers the rules that potentially allow the aggregation of businesses for purposes of calculating QBI deductions. Part VI covers the special rules for SSTBs and the business of being an employee. Part VII contains rules for pass-through entities, PTPs, beneficiaries, trusts, and estates. Part VIII has special rules for multiple trusts.

Key point: Taken together, the Preamble and the text of the final regulations are 247 pages long.

Rental real estate enterprises

The final regulations do not include any meaningful news on whether income from rental real estate ventures can qualify for the QBI deduction. However, IRS Notice 2019-7 (issued at the same time as the final regulations) provides a helpful safe-harbor rule for eligible rental real estate enterprises.

Rental to controlled business

Under a special rule, the rental or licensing of tangible or intangible property to a related business is treated as a business for QBI deduction purposes if the rental or licensing activity and the other business are commonly controlled (50% common ownership). The final regulations clarify that this special rule is limited to situations in which the rental is to another business owned by the individual or to a pass-through entity that is commonly controlled. For example, if an individual rents property to his or her 100%-owned S corporation, the rental activity would count as a business for QBI deduction purposes. On the other hand, renting property to a controlled C corporation will not count as a business for QBI deduction purposes. The final regulations also state that the related party rules under IRC Sec. 267(b) or Sec. 707(b) are used to determine whether common control exists for purposes of the special rule. [See Regs. 1.199A-1(b)(14) and 1.199A-4(b)(1)(i)).]

Net capital gains

Individuals with investment interest expense (typically from brokerage firm margin accounts) can elect to treat net LTCGs and qualified dividends as ordinary investment income to increase their allowable deductions for investment interest expense. If this election is made, Part I of the Preamble clarifies that it does not change the individual's net capital gain amount for purposes of the overall QBI deduction limitation explained earlier.

Calculating QBI

According to the final regulations [Reg. 1.199A-3(b)(1)]:

- Guaranteed payments to a partner (or LLC member treated as a partner for tax purposes) for the use of capital are not considered business income. Therefore, these payments are not counted as income in calculating a recipient partner's (LLC member's) QBI.
- Business-related losses or deductions that were suspended, disallowed, or limited in earlier tax years (for example by the passive loss rules) but that are allowed in the current year are generally considered in calculating QBI for the current year. These now-allowed losses are utilized in the current year in order from the oldest to the most recent (FIFO method). However, losses or deductions that were disallowed, suspended, or limited in tax years ending before January 1, 2018 are not considered in calculating QBI for later years.
- Generally, an NOL deduction is not considered a business loss and is not counted in calculating QBI. However, allowable current-year deductions for disallowed excess business losses from earlier years (treated as NOLs) are considered in calculating QBI for the current year.
- The final regulations state that the deductible portion of self-employment tax, the self-employed health insurance deduction, and deductions for contributions to self-employed retirement plans are considered business expenses—to the extent that the individual's gross income from the related business is considered in calculating QBI. With multiple businesses, these amounts are allocated in proportion to gross income from the businesses.

Carryover of negative QBI amounts

If the individual's total QBI amount is less than zero, the negative amount is treated as negative QBI from a separate business in the following tax year of the individual. This carryover rule does not affect the deductibility of losses under any other tax code provisions.

Key point: W-2 wages and UBIA of qualified property from a business that produces negative QBI for the current tax year are not considered for purposes of the W-2 wage and UBIA of qualified property limitations for the current year, and the W-2 wages and UBIA of qualified property are not carried over to the following tax year.

Calculating W-2 wages

The Preamble to the final regulations confirms that W-2 wages paid to S corporation shareholder-employees count as W-2 wages for purposes of the W-2 wage limitation. However, W-2 wages paid to an S corporation shareholder-employee do not count as QBI.

Concurrent with the release of the final QBI deduction regulations, the IRS issued Revenue Procedure 2019-11, which explains allowable methods for calculating W-2 wages of a business for purposes of the W-2 wage limitation. Revenue Procedure 2019-11 also supplies guidance on when employee elective deferral (salary reduction) contributions to retirement plans can be counted as W-2 wages. The guidance in Revenue Procedure 2019-11 applies to tax years beginning after December 31, 2017.

Calculating UBIA of qualified property

For a business operated by an individual or pass-through entity, qualified property means tangible depreciable property that

- is used in the business for the production of QBI at any time during the tax year,
- is held by and available for use in the business at the end of the tax year, and
- has not reached the end of its depreciable period (as defined under the QBI deduction rules) as of the end of the tax year.

Claiming first-year bonus depreciation does affect the depreciable period. The depreciable period is defined as beginning on the date the property is first placed in service by the taxpayer and ending on the *later* of

- 10 years after that date or
- the last day of the last full year in the applicable recovery period under IRC Section 168 (MACRS).

In calculating the UBIA of qualified property, the final regulations set forth the following rules. [See Reg. 1.199A-2(c).]

- Each partner's share of the UBIA of qualified partnership property follows how depreciation is allocated for book purposes under the partnership tax allocation regulations [Reg. 1.704-1(b)(2)(iv)(g)] as of the last day of the partnership's tax year. The same rule applies to members of LLCs treated as partnerships for tax purposes.
- Each shareholder's share of the UBIA of qualified S corporation property follows the shareholder's stock ownership percentage as of the last day of the S corporation's tax year.
- The UBIA of qualified property received in an IRC Section 1031 like-kind exchange (replacement property) generally equals the UBIA of the property that is relinquished in the exchange. However, if

the taxpayer receives money or non-like-kind property in the exchange or gives up money or non-like-kind exchange property in the exchange, the taxpayer's UBIA in the replacement property is adjusted accordingly.

- When qualified property that is not of like kind to the relinquished property is received in IRC Section 1031 exchange, the received qualified property (the replacement property) is treated as separate qualified property that is placed in service when placed in service by the taxpayer that receives the replacement property.
- An IRC Section 743(b) basis adjustment to a partner's (LLC member's) share of partnership (LLC) qualified property when a partnership (LLC) interest is transferred is treated as qualified property to extent the basis adjustment reflects an increase in the fair market value of the underlying partnership property. The final regulations include a procedure to implement this rule. The basis adjustment is treated as a separate item of qualified property that is placed in service when the transfer of the partnership (LLC) interest occurs.
- For qualified property acquired from a decedent and immediately placed in service, the UBIA of the property generally equals its fair market value on the date of the decedent's death.

Effective dates

For tax years ending in 2018, taxpayers can generally choose to rely on the rules in the 2019 final regulations in their entirety or the rules in the earlier proposed regulations (issued in August of 2018) in their entirety. However, anti-abuse rules in the final regulations [see Regs. 1.199A2(c)(1)(iv), 1.199A-3(c)(2)(ii), 1.199A-5(c)(2), 1.199A-5(d)(3), and 1.199A-6(d)(3)(vii)] apply to tax years ending after December 22, 2017. And rules intended to prevent abuse by trusts (see Reg. 1.643-1) apply to tax years ending after August 16, 2018.

New proposed QBI deduction regulations

In addition to the final QBI deduction regulations covered previously, the IRS also released in January of 2019 new proposed QBI deduction regulations that include rules on

- the treatment of previously suspended losses,
- regulated investment companies (mutual funds),
- charitable remainder trusts, and
- split interest trusts.

The proposed rules would apply to tax years ending after the date they are adopted in the form of final regulations. Until then, however, taxpayers can rely on the proposed rules, if they wish. (See Prop. Regs. 1.199A-3 and -6 in REG-134652-18.)

Conclusion

This analysis of IRC Section 199A provides a good foundational knowledge for CPAs and financial planners, but additional factors not covered here can come into play (for example, how to calculate the deduction when the taxpayer has multiple pass-business interests). IRC Section 199A, in essence, provides owners of pass-thru entities and sole proprietors a benefit on par with the 21% flat tax rate afforded to C corporations. Clients will continue to consider choice of entity tax implications of whether to operate as a pass-through entity, providing owners a potential 20% QBI deduction, or operate as a corporation subject to a 21% flat tax.

Should your client's business switch to C corporation status?

Thanks to the TCJA, the federal income tax rate on C corporations is now a flat 21% for tax years beginning in 2018 and beyond. This is a permanent change. So, this may mean that your client should consider running his or her business as a C corporation instead of as a sole proprietorship, partnership, LLC, or S corporation.

The 21% corporate tax rate is great compared to the 37% maximum federal rate on an individual's income from a sole proprietorship or pass-through entity. But C corporations also have certain tax disadvantages that clients need to understand.

Double taxation

Income earned by a C corporation can potentially be taxed twice—once at the corporate level and again at the shareholder level when corporate profits are paid out as taxable dividends. Under current law, dividends received by individual shareholders and trusts and estates are taxed at a maximum federal rate of 20%, but dividends have been taxed at much higher rates in the past. And there is no guarantee that the tax rate on dividends will not be higher in the future—maybe much higher. In addition, dividends can be hit with the 3.8% NIIT.

Double taxation can also arise more indirectly if you sell your C corporation shares for a profit. The corporation's income is taxed once at the corporate level, and undistributed profits can be indirectly taxed again at the shareholder level—in the form of capital gains tax when your shares are sold. Under current law, the maximum federal income tax rate on LTCGs from shares held for more than one year is 20%. However, the 3.8% NIIT may also apply.

The double taxation threat generally makes it a bad idea to use a C corporation to own appreciating assets such as real estate and patents. When the corporation sells an appreciated asset, it can trigger tax at the corporate level and tax at the shareholder level if the sales proceeds are distributed as dividends. It can trigger tax as liquidation proceeds if the company is disbanded after the asset sale or if you sell your shares for a profit.

The fundamental tax planning objective for C corporations was not changed by the TCJA. However, we still want to avoid double taxation if at all possible.

Accumulated Earnings Tax

One way to avoid double taxation is simply to keep all corporate profits and gains inside the corporation. However if you do that, your corporation runs the risk of exposure to the Accumulated Earnings Tax (AET).

The AET is a corporate-level tax assessed by the IRS (as opposed to a tax that is paid voluntarily with a corporate tax return). The IRS can assess the AET when

- a C corporation's accumulated earnings exceed $250,000 (or $150,000 for a personal service corporation) and
- the corporation cannot demonstrate economic need for the "excess" accumulated earnings.

When the AET is assessed, the rate is the same as the maximum federal rate on dividends received by individuals. Currently, that rate is 20%, but the rate has been much higher in the past. And there is no guarantee that the rate will not be raised again in the future.

The good news is you can document that your corporation does not have excess retained earnings if it really doesn't.

Remember: when owed, the AET is on top of the regular corporate federal income tax bill.

Personal Holding Company tax

The Personal Holding Company (PHC) tax is another corporate-level tax that is intended to prevent C corporations from avoiding double taxation by simply keeping all profits and gains inside the corporation. Whether a corporation is a PHC or not is determined year-by-year. Specifically, a corporation is a PHC for a particular tax year only if it passes both an income test and an ownership test. The risk is that a corporation can inadvertently fall into the PHC trap when it has not been a PHC in previous years. So, the tax planning objective is to maximize the odds that your corporation will fail either the income test, the ownership test, or both.

The income test

Failure is the goal of the income test, and most closely held C corporations will find it easier to fail. If the income test is failed, you can ignore the ownership test (explained as follows), which will probably be harder to fail.

To fail the income test, a corporation's PHC income must be less than 60% of its adjusted ordinary gross income (AOGI). [See IRC Sec. 542(a)(1).]

- PHC income equals the portion of AOGI that consists of dividends, interest income, royalties, annuities, rents, taxable distributions from estates and trusts, and income from personal service contracts.
- A corporation's ordinary gross income is gross income from operations (from Line 11 of Form 1120) minus gains from the sale or disposition of capital assets (typically investment assets) and IRC Section 1231 assets (business assets that are taxed similarly to capital assets) [See IRC Sec. 543(b)(1).] AOGI is ordinary gross income adjusted for certain rental property expenses, certain expenses allocable to revenues from oil and gas and mineral production, and certain other items [IRC Sec. 543(b)(2)].

The ownership test

Failure is the goal here too.

A corporation passes the ownership test for a particular tax year if more than 50% of its stock value is owned directly or indirectly by five or fewer individuals during any part of the second half of that tax year. [See IRC Sec. 542(a)(2).]

Because ownership by five or fewer individuals can potentially occur at any time during the second half of a year, the test cannot be based solely on year-end ownership percentages if there have been any ownership changes during the second half. However, if the ownership structure will result in the corporation passing the ownership test in the second half of the year, the shareholders may be able to adjust their ownership percentages during the first half so the test will be failed during the second half.

Consequences of passing both tests (not good)

A corporation that passes both the income and ownership tests is a PHC. As such, it is subject to the PHC tax which equals 20% (under the current tax regime) of its undistributed PHC income (UPHCI). UPHCI is calculated by adjusting the corporation's regular taxable income amount. [The adjustments are set forth in IRC Sec. 545(b) and (c).] After these adjustments are made, a deduction is taken for any dividends paid. The balance remaining is the UPHCI amount subject to the 20% PHC tax.

Remember: when owned, the PHC tax is on top of the regular corporate federal income tax bill.

Reducing or avoiding the PHC tax by paying dividends

The sole purpose of the PHC tax is to encourage corporations that are classified as PHCs to pay out earnings as taxable dividends to shareholders. So, paying dividends during the tax year can reduce or eliminate the PHC tax. But those dividends will be taxed on the shareholders' personal returns, probably at the maximum 20% rate. If so, it's basically a wash from a federal income tax perspective. The trick is to avoid exposure to the PHC tax in the first place, usually by managing to fail the income test.

Conclusion

After TCJA, should your client now be running his or her business as a C corporation? Not surprisingly, the initial answer is maybe. It could be a great idea or a terrible one depending on the circumstances. You can help the client put the pieces of the puzzle together to derive the best answer for the client's specific situation.

Final note: given the number of entities that may convert to C corporation status to take advantage of the new 21% corporate federal income tax rate, the AET and PHC tax are likely to become hot issues for IRS auditors. So, avoiding these taxes is likely to become a key planning goal for many businesses. Once again, you can help clients with that.

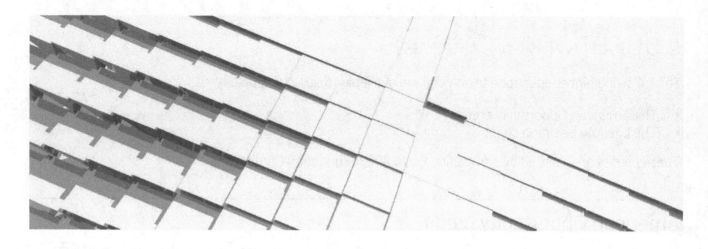

Chapter 7

Tax-Smart College Financing Strategies

Learning objectives

- Recognize ways to help middle-class clients identify college financing tax breaks.

- Identify specific requirements of the American Opportunity credit, the Lifetime Learning credit, and student loan interest deductions.

- Recognize situations that will subject children and young adults to the Kiddie Tax.

- Identify tax-saving college financing maneuvers for higher-income clients who are ineligible for the well-known education tax breaks.

- Identify strategies for how parents can employ their children through their closely held business.

Introduction

This chapter covers the key tax-savings opportunities in the college funding arena for middle-income clients, as well as planning tips for higher-income individuals.

This chapter also includes some last-minute college financing tips that may work for middle-income taxpayers.

Education tax credits

The following higher education tax credits are available to qualifying taxpayers:

- The American Opportunity credit
- The Lifetime Learning credit

These credits are claimed by completing Form 8863 (Education Credits).

American Opportunity credit

The American Opportunity tax credit, under IRC Section 25, equals 100% of the first $2,000 of eligible postsecondary education expenses, plus 25% of the next $2,000. So the maximum annual credit is $2,500 (assuming the adjusted gross income-based—or AGI-based—phase-out rule explained later does not apply).

Eligibility rules

The credit is potentially available for the taxpayer, his or her spouse, and any person for whom the taxpayer can claim a dependent exemption deduction. More than one credit can be claimed on the same return (one for each qualifying individual).

However, those who use married filing separate status are completely ineligible.

Eligible students

A student's expenses are eligible for the American Opportunity credit as long as the student has not already completed four years' worth of college work as of the beginning of the tax year in question. The credit can be claimed only for a maximum of four years for a particular student.

The American Opportunity credit rules provide that the determination of a student's year-of-study status is made as of the beginning of the tax year in question. For example, if the student had not yet achieved four years' worth of academic progress on January 1, 2019, tuition for schooling during all of 2019 can be counted as an eligible expense for purposes of the American Opportunity credit (assuming all the other rules are met for claiming the credit).

Regulation 1.25A-3(d) clarifies that a student's year-of-study status depends on his standing at the current institution. In other words, when a student has previously attended another school, only credits that are successfully transferred to the new school are counted in determining the student's year-of-study status at the new school. College academic credit that is awarded based solely on performance on proficiency exams does not count for purposes of determining if the student has completed four years' worth of academic work. So "testing out" of college classes or taking college classes before enrolling in a college degree program (for example, while in high school) will not undermine the student's eligibility for the credit. To sum up, only actual class credit earned while enrolled in a college degree program is

---

counted in determining the student's year-of-study status for American Opportunity credit purposes. [See Regulation 1.25A-3(d).]

The American Opportunity credit is allowed only for a year during which the student carries, for at least one academic period beginning in that year, at least half of a full-time course load in a program that would ultimately result in an associate's degree, bachelor's degree, or some other recognized credential. [See Regulation 1.25A-3(d)(1).] So, although one has to be a fairly serious student to claim the credit, one does not actually have to intend to complete a degree or credential program.

Key point: It is possible for one family to have several students who qualify for the American Opportunity credit in the same tax year. In such cases, a separate credit of up to $2,500 can be claimed for each student's college costs (assuming all the other American Opportunity requirements are met).

Eligible expenses

Eligible expenses for the American Opportunity credit include tuition, mandatory enrollment fees, and course materials, including books. However, optional fees for things like student activities, athletics, and health insurance do not count. Neither do room and board costs.

Eligible institutions

The student must attend an *eligible institution*. Fortunately, virtually all accredited public, nonprofit, and for-profit postsecondary schools meet this definition, and many vocational schools do, too. The two main criteria are that the school must offer programs that lead to an associate's degree, bachelor's degree, or some other recognized credential; and the school must qualify to participate in federal student aid programs. An eligible school will have a Federal School Code, which can be verified at www.fafsa.gov.

Income phase-out rule

The American Opportunity credit is phased out (reduced or completely eliminated) if modified adjusted gross income (MAGI) is too high.

- The phase-out range for unmarried individuals is between MAGI of $80,000 and $90,000.
- The phase-out range for married joint filers is between MAGI of $160,000 and $180,000.
- These ranges are set by statute, so they will apply to future years regardless of inflation.
- MAGI means "regular" AGI increased by income from outside the United States that is tax exempt under IRC Section 911, 931, or 933.

Credit is partially refundable

The American Opportunity credit can be used to offset the client's entire federal income tax bill, including any AMT. Any credit amount that is left over after reducing the client's tax bill to $0 is refundable to the extent of 40% of the allowable credit amount (the amount after any reduction under the AGI-based phase-out rule explained in the previous paragraph). The refundable amount can be either refunded to the taxpayer in cash or applied to the following year's estimated tax payments. The following example illustrates how the partial refundability concept works.

Example 7-1

Ellen's allowable American Opportunity credit is $2,500. The refundable part of the credit is $1,000 (40% × $2,500), and that amount is treated on her Form 1040 as a tax payment (same as if she had the $1,000 withheld from her wages for FIT or paid it in via estimated FIT payments). The remaining $1,500 (60% × $2,500) is a nonrefundable credit that does not do Ellen any good, unless she has a federal income tax liability.

- If Ellen does not owe any federal income tax because of deductions or other credits, the entire $1,000 refundable credit amount counts as a tax overpayment and is refunded to her in cash. In this case, the nonrefundable $1,500 part of the credit does not do Ellen any good, but the refundable credit deal gets her a $1,000 check from the government that she would not have otherwise received. Alternatively, Ellen can apply some or all of her $1,000 refundable credit toward her estimated tax payments for the following year.
- Assume that Ellen's federal income tax liability after deductions or other credits is $1,900. In this case, the nonrefundable $1,500 part of the credit is used to reduce her tax bill to $400. Then the first $400 of the refundable credit reduces her tax bill to $0. Finally, the last $600 of the refundable credit is refunded to her in cash. In this case, the credit wipes out Ellen's entire tax bill, and the refundable credit deal gets her a $600 check from the Feds that she would not have otherwise received. Alternatively, Ellen can apply some or all of her $600 refundable credit toward her estimated tax payments for the following year.
- Finally, assume that Ellen's federal income tax bill is $4,500. In this case, the $1,500 nonrefundable part of the credit reduces her tax bill to $3,000. Then the $1,000 refundable credit further reduces her tax bill to $2,000. In this case, the credit simply reduces Ellen's tax bill by $2,500, and that is the end of the story.
- The preceding results are determined by filling out Form 8863 (Education Credits) and transferring some numbers to the applicable lines on page 2 of Form 1040.

Warning: The 40% refundable credit privilege is not allowed to individuals who fall under the Kiddie Tax rules. In this case, the entire American Opportunity credit is treated as a nonrefundable credit. (The Kiddie Tax rules can potentially cause part of an under-age-24 individual's unearned income to be taxed at the rates that apply to trusts and estates.)

Year-end planning

Creditable expenses must actually be paid in the tax year in question for courses in academic periods beginning in that year, or for courses in academic periods beginning in the first three months of the following tax year [Regulation 1.25A-5(e)(1) and (2)].

Because academic years span two calendar years, it may sometimes be necessary to prepay some expenses in order to collect the maximum American Opportunity credit when expenses are relatively modest (for example, when the student attends a community college). Put another way, the client can claim a 2019 credit for eligible expenses that are paid in 2019 for courses that begin in 2019 and expenses that are paid in 2019 for courses that begin in January through March 2020. Therefore, prepaying some expenses that are due in early 2020 could lower the client's 2019 tax bill.

Lifetime Learning credit

The Lifetime Learning credit equals 20% of up to $10,000 of eligible education expenses, for a maximum annual credit of $2,000 (assuming the income phase-out rule explained later does not apply).

Unlike the American Opportunity credit, there is no limit on the number of years the Lifetime Learning credit can be claimed, nor is there any course load requirement.

Therefore, the Lifetime Learning credit can be used to help offset costs for undergraduate study that drags on for more than four years, or for undergraduate years when the student carries a light course load, or for graduate school courses, or for courses to improve job skills or maintain professional certifications, or for courses taken for just about any other reason.

Key point: A self-employed client will often be better off claiming a Schedule C deduction for work-related education expenses that would also qualify for the Lifetime Learning credit. The tax benefit from the credit is only 20%. In contrast, claiming a Schedule C deduction will often save taxes at a 22% or higher marginal rate while also reducing the SE tax hit at a marginal rate of 15.3%, 2.9%, or 3.8% if the additional 0.9% Medicare tax applies.

Eligibility rules

A client is ineligible for the Lifetime Learning credit if he or she is married and does not file a joint return with his or her spouse.

The maximum annual credit is $2,000, regardless of how many students are in the family.

Finally, a client cannot claim both the American Opportunity credit and the Lifetime Learning credit for expenses paid for the same student for the same year.

However, a client can potentially claim the American Opportunity credit for one or more students in the family while also claiming the Lifetime Learning credit for expenses paid for one or more different students in the family.

Eligible expenses for the Lifetime Learning credit include tuition and mandatory enrollment fees. Course supplies and materials (including books) are eligible expenses only if they are required to be purchased directly from the school itself. Other expenses, including optional fees and room and board, are off limits.

Finally, the school must be an *eligible institution* using the same definition as for the American Opportunity credit.

Income phase-out rule

Like the American Opportunity credit, the Lifetime Learning credit is also phased out if MAGI is too high. However, the phase-out ranges for the Lifetime Learning credit are at much lower income levels.

- For 2019, the phase-out range for unmarried individuals is between MAGI of $58,000 and $68,000.
- The phase-out range for married joint filers is between MAGI of $116,000 and $136,000.
- MAGI means "regular" AGI increased by income from outside the United States that is tax-exempt under IRC Section 911, 931, or 933.

Credit is not refundable

There is no partial refundability deal for the Lifetime Learning credit. The credit can be used to reduce the client's regular federal income tax bill, as well as any AMT liability.

Key point: The client can claim a 2019 credit for eligible expenses that are paid in 2019 for courses that begin in 2019 and expenses that are paid in 2019 for courses that begin in January–March of 2020. So, prepaying some expenses that are due early in 2020 could lower the client's 2019 tax bill.

Rules applying to both credits

If the student is claimed as a dependent of the parent, only the parent can take the American Opportunity or Lifetime Learning credit, even if the qualifying expenses are paid by the child. This is because the expenses are deemed paid by the parent [IRC Section 25A(g)(3)].

Qualifying expenses are reduced by any IRC Section 117 scholarships, veteran and military education assistance payments, and most tax-free payments for educational expenses or attributable to enrollment [IRC Section 25A(g)(2)].

Finally, the same tuition expense dollars cannot be used to qualify for one of the credits and also to qualify for the interest income exclusion for U.S. Savings Bonds redeemed to pay for college expenses. In other words, tuition expenses used to take advantage of the savings bond break must be reduced by tuition expenses considered in computing either the American Opportunity or Lifetime Learning credit [IRC Section 135(d)(2)].

If a *third party* (someone other than the taxpayer, taxpayer's spouse, or a claimed dependent) pays education costs for the taxpayer, spouse, or a claimed dependent, the expenses are treated as paid by the student for purposes of the American Opportunity and Lifetime Learning credits. (However, there could be gift tax consequences for the third party.) If the expenses relate to a dependent, they are in turn considered paid by the taxpayer on whose return the dependent is claimed (usually the parent). [See Regulation Section 1.25A-5(a) and (b).]

Key point: For 2018–2025, the Tax Cuts and Jobs Act (TCJA) suspends dependent exemption deductions. However, for purposes of applying other tax rules that refer to persons for whom dependent exemptions can be claimed, dependent exemption deductions are deemed to still exist for 2018–2025, but the allowable deduction equals zero [IRC Sec. 151(d)(5)]. So, in the context of applying the rules for education tax breaks (as in the following example), the TCJA changed nothing.

Example 7-3

- Monique is a dependent of her parents, Phil and Chelsea.
- Hillary, Monique's wealthy grandmother, offers to pay $20,000 of tuition for Monique's first year at Rice University.
    - Because Hillary is a *third party*, Monique is treated as paying the $20,000 for American Opportunity or Lifetime Learning credit purposes.
    - If Phil and Chelsea claim Monique as a dependent, they are in turn treated as paying the $20,000 for American Opportunity or Lifetime Learning credit purposes.
    - However, if Phil and Chelsea forgo claiming the dependency exemption deduction for Monique, she can claim a credit for herself.

Beating the system

The biggest problems with both the American Opportunity and Lifetime Learning credits are the AGI-based phase-out rules which make many clients ineligible. The planning solution is to arrange for the client's child to take the credit, assuming the child has enough taxable income to benefit from doing so.

Regulation Section 1.25A-1(f) says the child can take the credit for his education expenses as long as the parent does not claim the child as a dependent for IRC Section 151 dependent exemption deduction purposes. It does not matter if the parent pays some or all of the child's education expenses. For 2018–2025, making this choice has no tax cost to the parents because dependent exemption deductions are zero. See the preceding key point.

Deduction for higher education tuition and fees

The American Opportunity and Lifetime Learning tax credits are not always available for family education expenses. For example, the student in question might not meet the eligibility rules (a distinct possibility with the American Opportunity credit) or the client's income might be too high (a distinct possibility with the Lifetime Learning credit; less so with the American Opportunity credit). There was another important break that expired at the end of 2017.

Section 222 of the Internal Revenue Code allowed the client to claim a limited above-the-line deduction for eligible higher education tuition and fees. Depending on the client's income, the maximum write-off was either $4,000 or $2,000.

The IRC Section 222 deduction expired at the end of 2017 and had not been extended by any "extender legislation," but it's possible it could be reinstated by future legislation.

Deduction for student loan interest

IRC Section 221 provides an above-the-line deduction for interest on education loans. However, the deduction is limited to a maximum annual amount of $2,500.

To qualify, the debt must be incurred within a reasonable time before or after eligible higher education expenses are incurred.

Eligible expenses are defined as tuition, fees, room and board, and related expenses such as books and supplies for the taxpayer, spouse, or any dependent of the taxpayer to attend an eligible educational institution. Note that dependent status for a person is determined under the IRC Section 152 rules, without regard to certain restrictions on the taxpayer's ability to claim a dependent exemption deduction for that person. [See IRC Section 221(d).] The deduction is allowed only for expenses attributable to a year during which the student carries, for at least one academic period beginning in that year, at least half of a full-time course load in a program that would ultimately result in an associate's degree, bachelor's degree, or some other recognized credential. [See IRC Section 221(d)(3), IRC Section 25A(b)(3), and Regulation 1.25A-3(d)(1).]

For 2018, the deduction is phased out for unmarried taxpayers between modified AGI (MAGI) of $65,000 and $80,000. For joint filers, the phase-out range is between MAGI of $135,000 and $165,000. For purposes of IRC Section 221, MAGI means *regular* AGI after adding back the deductions under IRC Sections 199 and 222 and the income exclusions under IRC Sections 911, 931, and 933.

Married individuals who file separate returns can forget about this break, regardless of their income level. They are completely ineligible.

Obviously, when the parents won't qualify for the interest deduction because their income is too *high*, the next best thing is to arrange for their child—the student—to get the deduction by taking out the student loan in his or her own name. However, no deduction is allowed to children in years they are dependents on their parents' returns, even when the child is on the hook for the loan and pays the interest. This issue can be finessed by scheduling the start date for loan repayments after graduation. By then the child should be self-supporting and no longer a dependent on his or her parents return.

The bottom line: When the parents' high MAGI level precludes student loan interest write offs, taking the loan out in the student's name and deferring payments until after graduation may salvage the deduction, although the student rather than the parents will be the beneficiary of the deduction.

If an education loan is refinanced, the refinanced loan will also qualify as such [IRC Section 221(d)].

Per IRC Section 221(f)(1), student loan interest is not deductible if it is deductible under another code section.

Knowledge check

1. Married taxpayers who file separately

   a. Are completely ineligible for the student loan interest deduction, regardless of their income level.
   b. Are fully eligible for the student loan interest deduction, regardless of their income level.
   c. Are eligible for the student loan interest deduction, subject to phase-out at higher income levels.
   d. Are exempt from the student loan interest deduction income phase-out rule.

Coverdell Education Savings Accounts

Coverdell Education Savings Accounts (CESAs) can be set up to pay the education expenses of a child (the account beneficiary), pursuant to IRC Section 530.

Contributions—up to $2,000 per year per beneficiary—are non-deductible, but earnings accumulate tax-free. Tax-free withdrawals can then be taken to pay for the beneficiary's postsecondary tuition, fees, books, supplies, and room and board.

The ability to contribute is phased out between MAGI of $95,000 to $110,000 for singles and $190,000 to $220,000 for married filing joint status. For this purpose, MAGI means *regular AGI* increased by amounts excluded under IRC Sections 911, 931, and 933. If the parents' MAGI is too high to allow a contribution, any other person can contribute to the account.

For example, the child's grandparents could contribute the $2,000 annual maximum.

If the taxpayer has several children (or grandchildren), he or she can contribute up to $2,000 annually to separate CESAs set up for each.

Taxpayers can also take tax-free CESA payouts to cover elementary and secondary school (K-12) costs. Under this privilege, eligible expenses include tuition and fees to attend private and religious schools plus room and board, uniform, and transportation costs. Taxpayers can also withdraw CESA money tax-free to pay out-of-pocket costs to attend public K-12 schools. Eligible expenses include books and supplies; academic tutoring; computers, peripheral equipment, and software; and even internet access charges. Starting CESA contributions at an early date is really important if the client wants to benefit from this break.

Taxpayers have until April 15 of the following year (adjusted for weekends and holidays) to make their annual CESA contributions.

A tax-free CESA withdrawal cannot be used to cover the same expenses for which the American Opportunity credit or Lifetime Learning credit is claimed or for the same expenses for which the IRC Section 222 tuition and fees deduction is claimed. [See IRC Section 530(d)(2)(C) and (D) and IRC Section 222(c)(2)(B).]

Tax-free interest from U.S. Savings Bonds

Under IRC Section 135, a taxpayer can exclude all or part of her accrued interest income from Series EE and Series I U.S. Savings Bonds redeemed (cashed in) to pay for certain education expenses of the taxpayer, spouse, and dependents for whom dependent deductions are allowed. However, there are serious restrictions as explained in the following section.

Qualifying savings bonds

The savings bond must be issued after 1989 in the name of an individual, and that person must have attained age 24 before the bond issue date (any person can be named as the beneficiary in the event of the taxpayer's death). In other words, the bonds must be purchased in the name of an older person (typically a parent or grandparent) rather than in the name of the young person who is expected to attend college in the future.

The interest exclusion is unavailable to married taxpayers who file separate returns [IRC Section 135(d)(3)].

Warning

- Savings bonds should not be purchased in the names of the children if the intent is to take advantage of this income exclusion by later cashing in the bonds to pay for college.
- That would violate the age-24 requirement.
- Instead, the bonds should be purchased in the parent's name.
- Old bonds issued in the parent's name when the student was a kid cannot be used to take advantage of the interest exclusion, because that would violate both the age-24 requirement and the issued-after-1989 rule.

Qualifying expenses

Qualified education expenses are limited to tuition and fees net of any assistance from veteran's benefits, tax-free scholarships, employer-provided payments, or any other tax-free educational benefits.

Key point: Qualified expenses do not include any expenses for room and board or books. Also excluded are expenses for courses or programs involving sports, games, or hobbies unless the course or program is part of a degree program.

The educational expenses must be incurred at an eligible educational institution, which includes most colleges, junior colleges, degree nursing schools, and many vocational schools.

Finally, the same tuition expense dollars cannot be used to qualify for the American Opportunity credit or the Lifetime Learning, and also for the tax-free savings bonds interest income break. In other words, expenses used to take advantage of the savings bond break must be reduced by expenses considered in claiming these other breaks. [See IRC Sections 135(d)(2) and 222(c (2)(B).]

Taxpayers can also redeem their qualified savings bonds tax-free (provided the other IRC Section 135 rules are met) if the proceeds are contributed to an IRC Section 529 qualified state tuition program. For purposes of determining the later taxability of education benefits paid for by the qualified state tuition program account, the investment in the tuition program contract will not include the amount of excluded interest income from the redeemed savings bonds. [See IRC Section 135(c)(2)(C).]

Also, qualified savings bonds can be redeemed tax-free (provided all the other IRC Section 135 rules are met) if the proceeds are contributed to a CESA set up for the taxpayer's dependent child [IRC Section 135(c)(2)(C)]. However, the $2,000-per-year CESA contribution limit would still apply.

Computing the amount of excluded interest

If the qualified higher education expenses for the year the qualified savings bond is redeemed equal or exceed the redemption proceeds, all of the accrued interest income is excluded, provided the taxpayer does not run afoul of the AGI-based phase-out rule covered later.

If the proceeds exceed qualifying expenses, only a fraction of the interest income can be excluded. The fraction is calculated by dividing the qualifying expenses for the year by the bond redemption proceeds for that year.

Example 7-4

- Marnie redeems qualified savings bonds for $10,000 ($8,000 original cost plus $2,000 accrued interest). Her daughter's qualifying education expenses for the year are at least $10,000.
    - Marnie can potentially exclude the entire $2,000 of accrued interest (pending the application of the AGI-based phase-out rules).
    - But, if her daughter's qualifying expenses are only $6,000, Marnie can potentially exclude only 60% of the interest, or $1,200 ($6,000 qualifying expenses divided by $10,000 bond redemption proceeds times the $2,000 of interest).

Phase-out rules for higher-income taxpayers

The savings bond interest exclusion is phased out for relatively high-income taxpayers.

For qualified savings bonds redeemed in 2019, the inflation-adjusted phase-out ranges are between the following modified AGI (MAGI) levels:

	Phase-out begins	Phase-out complete
Married filing joint returns	$121,600	$151,600
Single or head of household	81,100	96,100

MAGI means *regular* AGI before any excluded interest from qualified savings bonds under these rules and before income exclusions for employer-provided adoption assistance benefits, foreign income, income from Puerto Rico, and income from U.S. possessions and before the deductions for college loan interest, and qualified tuition and fee expenses (under IRC Sections 137, 911, 931, 933, 221, and 222 respectively).

If the taxpayer's MAGI exceeds the beginning phase-out level but is underneath the complete phase-out level, a fraction is computed to determine how much of the interest exclusion is phased out. The phase-out fraction is the amount of MAGI in excess of the phase-out beginning level divided by $30,000 for joint filers or $15,000 for single and head of household filers.

Example 7-5

- Sean is a married joint filer with 2019 MAGI of $133,500. Remember, the MAGI number includes his interest income from any qualified savings bond redemptions, even if all or part of the interest turns out to be excludable.
    - Sean's phase-out fraction is ($133,500 − 121,600) ÷ $30,000 = .3967.
- Assume Sean had $3,000 of interest income from qualified savings bonds redeemed during 2019. During the year Sean paid $11,000 in qualifying higher education expenses for his son, Bucko. The full $3,000 of interest is potentially excludable because Sean's qualifying education expenses exceeded the qualified savings bond redemption proceeds.
    - However, because Sean's income is too high, he loses 39.67% of the exclusion, or $1,190. In other words, after the AGI-based phase-out rule, Sean can exclude only $1,810 ($3,000 − $1,190) of the interest income.

Example 7-6

- Fred and Wilma are young married parents who anticipate that their income will increase fairly rapidly over the years. The couple is interested in the concept of using tax-free U.S. Savings Bonds to partly finance the college costs for their daughter Bon-Bon. (They like the idea of investing in savings bonds because their investment philosophy is extremely conservative.)
- Although Fred and Wilma's income is currently much less than the AGI-based phase-out start point, they anticipate it will be greater than the cutoff point for tax-free savings bond redemptions by the time Bon-Bon enters college.
    - The couple should consider redeeming qualified savings bonds in a year before they are affected by the phase-out rules and contributing the proceeds to an IRC Section 529 qualified state tuition program account set up for Bon-Bon's benefit. The contribution counts as a qualified education expense and the savings bond interest income exclusion will be available, because Fred and Wilma's income is not yet high enough to be adversely affected by the phase-out rules.

Electing the accrual method for U.S. Savings Bonds

There is another college financing strategy involving U.S. Savings Bonds. This one is for Series EE Savings Bonds issued in the name of the college-bound child, and there are no AGI-based phase-out rules or other tax-law restrictions to worry about. Here is the needed background information:

The 2019 standard deduction amount for a dependent child with only unearned income is $1,100.

If the child is subject to the Kiddie Tax in 2019, it applies only to unearned income greater than $2,200. If the child is age 24 or older as of December 31, 2019, the Kiddie Tax cannot possibly apply for 2019.

The general rule for accrued interest income on U.S. Savings Bonds is that it goes untaxed until the year the bonds are redeemed.

However, an election can be made to report the accrued income on an annual basis [IRC Section 454 and Regulation Section 1.454-1(a)]. This election should be considered if the child has no other unearned income and the annual accrued interest from the savings bonds will always be less than the standard deduction amount (at least $1,100 for 2019 and later years). Making the election in this situation means the interest goes completely untaxed.

Even if the annual accrued interest exceeds the standard deduction amount, the excess will probably be taxed at only 10% or 12% unless the Kiddie Tax applies.

Knowledge check

2. Making the election to report a child's accrued U.S. Savings Bond interest annually
   a. Is always a bad idea, because it accelerates taxation of the accrued interest.
   b. Is a good idea when the child's standard deduction shelters the annual taxable income triggered by making the election.
   c. Has no impact on the child's tax situation.
   d. Is not allowed because individual taxpayers must always use the cash method of accounting for federal income tax purposes.

Example 7-7

- Willie, age 3, owns several U.S. Savings Bonds that mature in future years. Willie has no other income. Assume the annual accrued interest income from the bonds will average $1,000. (Because of compounding, the annual interest income accrual will gradually rise.)
  - If Willie's parents file a return on his behalf and make the election to report the accrued savings bond interest income annually, the annual amounts will be free of any federal income taxes because they will be sheltered by Willie's standard deduction (the standard deduction for dependents with no earned income will be at least $1,100 for 2019 and beyond).

Example 7-7 (continued)

- When Willie eventually redeems the bonds (to pay for college or for any other reason), there will be only the final year's worth of accrued interest to worry about. Again, that amount will be sheltered by Willie's standard deduction in that year.
- A return should be filed in the election year to document the election. Returns need not be filed in later years as long as Willie's income remains less than the filing requirement level.

How to make the election

The following statement should be filed with the return for the election year:

Taxpayer hereby elects pursuant to IRC Section 454 to currently recognize as income the annual increment in the redemption price of U.S. Savings Bonds described in Regulation Section 1.454-1(a)(1). This election applies to such savings bonds owned on January 1 of [*enter year*] and such savings bonds acquired after that date.

Splitting investment income with the kids

Back in the "good old days" it was often possible to save taxes by investing in a college-bound child's name rather than in the parent's name to take advantage of the child's lower federal income tax rates (that is, the rates for a single unmarried person). This strategy is called "splitting income with the child."

The concept of splitting income is simple. The client makes gifts to the college-bound child. Under the $15,000 annual gift tax exclusion (for 2019), a married couple can jointly give up to $30,000 per year to the child without paying any federal gift tax, without diminishing the $11.4m (for 2019) unified federal gift and estate tax exemption allowed to each spouse. [See IRC Section 2503(b).] Investments are then made in the child's name, and the resulting income and gains are split off from the parents' return and hopefully taxed at the child's lower rates. The college fund then compounds that much quicker, because the after-tax rate of return is that much higher.

When parents start a college savings program well ahead of time, they can allocate a relatively large percentage of the college fund to equities (stocks and equity mutual funds) in earlier years. This allows the parents to take advantage of the much higher returns these investments are expected to earn. (Of course, actual returns depend on market conditions.) As the first year of college draws closer, it is best to allocate an increasing percentage of the college fund to fixed-income assets (CDs, treasuries, and high-quality corporate bonds). As the need for funds becomes imminent, risk in the college account's portfolio should be reduced and liquidity increased. However, watch out for the Kiddie Tax rules which are explained in the following section.

Gift away appreciated assets but sell loss assets

The client should not sell appreciated property (like stocks) to free up cash to pay college expenses. Instead, the client should gift appreciated property to the child (up to the $15,000 annual gift tax exclusion limit; $30,000 for a joint gift by both spouses).

The child can then sell the assets, pay tax at a lower rate (probably no more than 10% or 12%; maybe 0%), and use the proceeds for college. With property worth less than its tax basis, use the opposite strategy. The client should sell the property and claim the tax loss. The resulting cash can then be gifted to the child.

The Kiddie Tax rules

Under the Kiddie Tax rules for 2018–2025, part of a dependent child's unearned income (typically from investments) can be taxed at the federal income tax rates that apply to trusts and estates, which can be as high as 37%, or 20% for long-term capital gains and qualified dividends, instead of at the child's lower rates (that is, the rates that would otherwise apply to an unmarried taxpayer with a modest amount of income), which can be as low as 10%, or 0% for long-term gains and dividends. The good news is the Kiddie Tax rules apply only to a dependent child's unearned income greater than the annual threshold, which is $2,200 for 2019. [See IRC Section 1(g).]

2018 Trust and estate rate brackets for ordinary income

10% tax bracket $ 0–2,550

Beginning of 24% bracket 2,551

Beginning of 35% bracket 9,151

Beginning of 37% bracket 12,501

2018 Trust and estate rate brackets for LTCGS and qualified dividends

0% tax bracket $ 0–2,600

Beginning of 15% bracket 2,601

Beginning of 20% bracket 12,701

2019 Trust and estate rate brackets for ordinary income

10% tax bracket $ 0–2,600

Beginning of 24% bracket 2,601

Beginning of 35% bracket 9,301

Beginning of 37% bracket 12,751

2019 Trust and estate rate brackets for LTCGS and qualified dividends

0% tax bracket $ 0–2,650

Beginning of 15% bracket 2,651

Beginning of 20% bracket 12,951

> ### Example 7-8
>
> The client's 10-year-old son owns some investment assets though a custodial account set up in the child's name (managed by the client). The assets produce $5,000 of ordinary investment income in 2019. The first $1,100 is sheltered from any federal income tax by the child's 2019 standard deduction. The next $1,100 is taxed at only 10% (or 0% for long-term gains and dividends). The next $2,800 ($5,000 − $1,100 − $1,100) is taxed at the rates for trusts and estates.

Child's age is the key factor

Until a few years ago, the Kiddie Tax applied only to years when the child was younger than age 14 at year-end. So if the child was age 14 or older at year-end, the Kiddie Tax did not apply to the child for that year or any subsequent year.

Under the current rules, the Kiddie Tax rules can potentially be applied until the year during which the child turns 24. Put another way, the Kiddie Tax will never apply to an individual who is age 24 at year-end or older. For an individual who is age 19–23 at year-end, the Kiddie Tax applies only if he or she is a student for that year. More specifically, the Kiddie Tax is an issue only when all four of the following requirements are met for the year in question:

- **Requirement 1:** One or both of the child's parents are alive at year-end.
- **Requirement 2:** The child does not file a joint return for the year.
- **Requirement 3:** The child's unearned income for the year exceeds the threshold for that year, and the child has positive taxable income after subtracting any applicable deductions, such as the standard deduction. The unearned income threshold for 2019 is $2,200 (in future years, it may be adjusted periodically for inflation). If the unearned income threshold is not exceeded, the Kiddie Tax does not apply for that year. If the threshold is exceeded, only unearned income in excess of the threshold is hit with the Kiddie Tax.
- **Requirement 4:** The child falls under one of the age rules due to his or her age at year-end and other applicable factors. The following three age rules are complicated [IRC Section 1(g)(2)(A)]:
  - **Age Rule 1 (Younger than Age 18).** If the child has not reached 18 at year-end (in other words, he or she is 17 or younger on December 31), the Kiddie Tax will apply if the other three requirements are also met for the year.
  - **Age Rule 2 (Age 18).** If the child is 18 at year-end and does not have earned income [as defined by IRC Section 911(d)(2)] that exceeds half of his or her support (support is generally determined the same as for dependency exemption purposes), the Kiddie Tax will apply if the other three requirements are also met. The child's support does not include amounts received as scholarships.
  - **Age Rule 3 (Age 19–23 and Student).** If the child is age 19–23 at year-end and (1) is a student and (2) does not have earned income that exceeds half of his or her support, the Kiddie Tax will apply if the other three requirements are also met. A child is considered to be a student if he or she attends school full-time for at least five months during the year. The child's support does not include amounts received as scholarships.

Key point: Under the current Kiddie Tax rules, properly determining the amount of a child's support and the amount of a child's earned income are important issues, due to age rules 2 and 3.

Example 7-9

Joseph will be 17 on December 31, 2019. He falls under age rule 1. For 2019, he will be subject to the Kiddie Tax if the other three requirements are also met.

Example 7-10

Susan will be 18 on December 31, 2019. She does not have earned income that exceeds half of her support for the year. She falls under age rule 2. For 2019, she will be subject to the Kiddie Tax if the other three requirements are also met. Susan's support does not include any amounts received as scholarships.

Variation: If Susan has earned income that exceeds half of her support for 2019, she is exempt from the Kiddie Tax for the year because none of the age rules apply to her for the year.

Example 7-11

Baxter will be 19 on December 31, 2019. He does not have earned income that exceeds half of his support for the year, and he is a student for the year. He falls under age rule 3. For 2019, he will be subject to the Kiddie Tax if the other three requirements are also met. Baxter's support does not include any amounts received as scholarships.

Variation: If Baxter is not a student for 2019, he is exempt from the Kiddie Tax because none of the age rules apply to him for the year. However, 2020–2023 could be different stories if he is a student for any of those years.

Example 7-12

Steve will be 21 on December 31, 2019, and he graduates from college in May of 2019. Assume he is subject to the Kiddie Tax for 2019 under age rule 3 (because he is a full-time student for the first five months of the year and has very little earned income for the year). Assuming he is done with school, however, none of the age rules will apply to him for 2020 and beyond, and he will not be subject to the Kiddie Tax in any of those years.

Variation: If Steve gets a job in June of 2019 and, as a result, has earned income in excess of half of his support for the year, age rule 3 does not apply. So Steve is exempt from the Kiddie Tax for 2019.

Example 7-13

Emily will be 24 on December 31, 2019. For 2019 and all subsequent years, she is exempt from the Kiddie Tax because none of the age rules apply to her.

Knowledge check

3. What is the unearned income threshold for the Kiddie Tax in 2019?

    a. $5,000.
    b. $2,100.
    c. Not applicable because the Kiddie Tax was repealed for 2015 and beyond.
    d. $2,200.

4. The Kiddie Tax can potentially apply until the year when an individual turns what age?

    a. It depends.
    b. 27.
    c. 21.
    d. 18.

Kiddie Tax avoidance strategies can save the day

When the Kiddie Tax is applied, it will at least partially defeat the tax-saving purpose behind family income-splitting. That was the intent of the legislation. However, the tax can be minimized or maybe even completely avoided with careful planning.

Key point: The Kiddie Tax applies only to unearned income which basically means investment income and capital gains from stocks, mutual funds, bonds, CDs, and the like. Earned income from jobs or self-employment is always exempt from the Kiddie Tax.

Finesse the age rules

One key thing to remember is that the Kiddie Tax does not apply to any year when the child does not fall within one of the three age rules. For any such year, the child is Kiddie-Tax exempt and is therefore treated like any other unmarried taxpayer (assuming he or she is, in fact, unmarried). To illustrate what this means, consider that a Kiddie Tax-exempt child can have up to $39,475 of taxable income in 2019 (earned or unearned) and never pay more than 10% or 12% (or 0% on long-term capital gains and qualified dividends) to the U.S. Treasury.

Key points

- If the child is not a student for years after reaching age 18, age rule 3 will not apply, and the child will be Kiddie Tax-exempt.
- After the child graduates from college, age rule 3 (for students ages 19-23) will cease to apply (possibly starting with the year of graduation) unless the child goes back to school.
- Age rules 2 and 3 (for ages 18-23) will not apply if the child has earned income that exceeds half of his or her support for the year. So funneling enough earned income to the child can make Kiddie Tax problems vanish. For example, if the child's parent runs a business that can hire the child, the resulting extra earned income could make the child Kiddie-Tax exempt.

Knowledge check

5. What is one way to avoid the Kiddie Tax for a child who will be age 18–23 at year-end?

    a. Arrange for the child to have unearned income in excess of 50% of his or her support for the year.
    b. Arrange for the child to have earned income in excess of 80% of his or her support for the year.
    c. Have the child enlist as an unpaid volunteer in a qualified government-sponsored civic improvement program.
    d. Arrange for the child to have earned income in excess of 50% of his or her support for the year.

Example 7-14

Say the client's 20-year-old child is a college student. The student earns money over the summer doing yard work, cleaning pools, and taking care of pets for taxpayers on vacation. The client also employs the child part-time in the client's sole proprietorship business, because the child is capable of general computer software and hardware maintenance. So the client pays the kid $15 per hour for his or her technical skills. Is any of this child's earned income affected by the Kiddie Tax? No, the Kiddie Tax is not applied to earned income, so it will be taxed at the child's low rates.

The child can also shelter all or part of his or her earned income with the standard deduction. For 2019, the standard deduction equals earned income plus $350 (not to exceed $12,200) if the child is a dependent or $12,200 if the child is not a dependent.

If necessary to gain even more shelter, the child can make a deductible contribution to a traditional IRA based on his or her earned income.

If the child's earned income is enough to exceed half of his or her support, the Kiddie Tax will not apply. That means all the child's unearned income will also be taxed at his or her low rates.

The child may also be entitled to the Hope Scholarship or Lifetime Learning tax credit.

Invest carefully and avoid triggering substantial unearned income in Kiddie Tax years

The truth is, a child can actually have a good deal of money in his or her own name and still avoid the Kiddie Tax with advance planning.

For example, the client's child can invest in growth stocks. There will not be any significant unearned income until shares are sold, because these companies pay little or nothing in dividends. Following a buy and hold strategy with such stocks until a year during which the child is Kiddie Tax-exempt would mean all or a good chunk of the eventual capital gains will probably be taxed at a very low rate; maybe even 0%. Using a buy and hold strategy with tax-efficient mutual funds should also minimize or completely avoid the Kiddie Tax.

Also, a child can have a substantial amount invested in Series EE U.S. Savings Bonds and never pay a dime of Kiddie Tax because the interest is tax-deferred until the bonds are actually cashed in.

If the cash-in date is deferred until a year when the child is Kiddie-Tax exempt, there will not be any Kiddie Tax on the accumulated interest.

Finally, investing for college using an IRC Section 529 plan account or a CESA can avoid Kiddie Tax problems because qualified distributions are federal-income-tax-free and therefore exempt from the Kiddie Tax even when the account is owned by a child.

Key points

- If necessary, a student can attempt to postpone triggering unearned income in excess of the annual threshold until after graduating from college. Until then, the student can try to make ends meet with college loans, work-study income, other sources of financial aid, and loans from the parent. That way, the child can avoid age rule 3 and thereby avoid the Kiddie Tax.
- Similarly, a parent can transfer appreciated assets to a child after he or she graduates from college. Until then, the student can get by with loans and other sources of cash. That way, the child can avoid age rule 3 and thereby avoid the Kiddie Tax when he or she sells the appreciated assets to pay off his or her loans.

Exploit unearned income threshold

Last but not least, please remember that the Kiddie Tax applies only when a child has unearned income for the year in excess of the applicable threshold. For 2019, the threshold is $2,200. In future years, the threshold may be adjusted periodically for inflation.

> #### Example 7-15
>
> In 2019, Zelda is a 20-year-old college student. Her parents provide more than half of her support. For that year, she has no earned income, but she has $2,200 of ordinary unearned income from a custodial account funded with gifts from her parents. Under these facts, the Kiddie Tax does not apply to Zelda in 2019 because her unearned income does not exceed the threshold. Here is how the federal income tax rules will work in this scenario. The first $1,100 of her investment income will be sheltered by her $1,100 standard deduction. The next $1,100 will be taxed at a 10% marginal federal rate. So her federal income tax bill will be only $110 (.10 × $1,100). The effective tax rate is only 5% ($110 ÷ $2,200 = 5%). If Zelda has $2,201 of ordinary investment income, only the last dollar will be taxed at the rates for trusts and estates. The 5% effective rate would still apply to the first $2,200 of ordinary unearned income.

Calculating the Kiddie Tax

The Kiddie Tax is calculated by filling out Form 8615, *Tax for Certain Children Who Have Unearned Income.* The completed Form 8615 is then attached to the child's Form 1040. In effect, the Kiddie Tax

---

calculation taxes the child's unearned income in excess of the $2,200 threshold (for 2019) at the rates that apply to trusts and estates (see the following table). The additional tax that results from the excess unearned income being taxed at the trust and estate tax rates is then reported on the child's Form 1040.

2019 Trust and estate rate brackets for ordinary income

10% tax bracket $ 0–2,600

Beginning of 24% bracket 2,601

Beginning of 35% bracket 9,301

Beginning of 37% bracket 12,751

2019 Trust and estate rate brackets for LTCGs and qualified dividends

0% tax bracket $ 0–2,650

Beginning of 15% bracket 2,651

Beginning of 20% bracket 12,951

Saving for college using parent's taxable account

The client can always choose to save and invest for a child's college expenses by using the client's own taxable brokerage firm account. Under the current rules, the maximum federal income tax rate on long-term capital gains and qualified dividends is 20% for higher-income taxpayers, but most people will pay no more than 15%. If the 3.8% net investment income tax (NIIT) applies, the effective federal rate can rise to 23.8% or 18.8%. If the client still holds appreciated shares in the college account when the child heads off to school, the client should consider giving some to the child. The child can then sell the shares, pay the resulting capital gains tax at a reduced rate, and use the after-tax dollars to pay college costs. If the client's college account holds shares that have declined less than cost, the client can sell them, claim the resulting capital losses on his or her return, and make a cash gift directly to the child's college or to the child (or a combination of both) to cover college costs.

Saving for college using child's Roth IRA

If the client's child has earned income from jobs or self-employment, he or she can make annual non-deductible Roth IRA contributions. For 2019, the maximum contribution is the lesser of (1) $6,000 or (2) earned income. After reaching college age, the child can withdraw up to the cumulative amount of his or her annual Roth contributions without owing any federal income tax or penalties. After that, he or she can withdraw Roth IRA earnings to pay for college costs without being assessed with the 10% premature withdrawal penalty tax. However, withdrawn earnings will be subject to federal income tax at the child's presumably low rates. Of course, it is best to leave as much money as possible in the Roth IRA. That way, the account can continue accumulating tax-free income and gains for the child's retirement years. [See IRC Sections 72(t) and 408A.]

Save for college with parent's taxable account

Here is the story on how IRC Section 529 college savings plan accounts, with their valuable tax benefits and admirable flexibility, can become an important part of the high-income client's overall financial game plan.

Section 529 college savings plans are state-sponsored arrangements named after the section of Tax Code that authorizes very favorable treatment under the federal income and gift tax rules. The parent (or grandparent) of the college-bound child begins by making contributions into a trust fund set up by the state plan that is selected. The money goes into an account designated for the beneficiary specified by the contributor (the client). In most cases, the account beneficiary is the client's child, but it can also be a grandchild or any other young person the client wishes to help.

Contributions can be in the form of a one-time, lump-sum pay-in or in the form of installment pay-ins stretching over several years. The plan then invests the money. Once the account beneficiary reaches college age, withdrawals are taken to pay eligible college expenses (including room and board under most plans). Plans generally cover expenses at any accredited college or university in the country (not just schools within the state sponsoring the plan). Community colleges qualify as well.

In essence, a Section 529 college savings plan account is nothing more than a tax-advantaged way to build up a college fund. The account beneficiary is not guaranteed admittance to any particular college. The cost to attend whichever school that is ultimately chosen is not locked in by the arrangement. Finally, most plans do not guarantee any minimum rate of return. (See the later discussion of the important distinction between IRC Section 529 college savings plans and IRC Section 529 prepaid tuition plans.)

Most college savings plans now permit lump-sum contributions of well over $300,000. So clients can really jump-start the child's (or grandchild's) college fund if they have the money to do so. If not, clients can make installment pay-ins. Of course, the sooner substantial dollars are put into the college savings plan account, the sooner the tax benefits start accruing.

Almost all Section 529 college savings plans now offer several investment alternatives, including equity mutual funds and more conservative options like bond and money market funds. More than a few plans welcome out-of-state investors. There is also a growing trend toward hiring pros to manage the money. For example, the New Hampshire, Delaware, and Massachusetts programs are managed by Fidelity Investments.

Key point: Just a few years ago, critics were complaining that many Section 529 college saving plans did not offer enough really aggressive investment programs, such as strategies emphasizing an unwavering commitment to so-called growth stocks. After several stock market meltdowns, that complaint is not heard much anymore. Relatively conservative investment strategies now seem rather smart, and most Section 529 college savings plans offer at least one of those. That said, many plans now offer relatively aggressive equity-oriented strategies too. Clients can take their choice.

Income tax benefits

Tax-wise, the very best thing about Section 529 college savings plan accounts is they allow earnings to build up federal-income-tax-free. The earnings can be withdrawn federal-income-tax-free to pay college costs.

As for state income taxes, most states provide that there is no liability when both the contributor and the account beneficiary reside in the state sponsoring the plan. However, there are exceptions. For example, California taxes the account beneficiary when he or she withdraws earnings. Until then, earnings are tax-deferred for California state income tax purposes.

When the client invests in an out-of-state plan, the state income tax consequences may be unclear. In fact, this question mark is one of the few potential negatives about Section 529 plans. Presumably, most or all states will eventually offer tax-free treatment just like the federal government, and the state tax questions will die. In any case, the federal tax benefits far outweigh any state tax concerns.

On a brighter note, several states go beyond just allowing state-income-tax-free payouts by offering additional tax incentives to encourage residents to contribute to the in-state plan. New York, for example, allows deductions for contributions to its plan (up to $5,000 annually for singles; $10,000 for married couples).

Estate planning benefits

The most basic estate planning advantage is that contributions to a child's or grandchild's Section 529 plan account reduce the contributor's taxable estate. For federal gift tax purposes, contributions are treated as gifts eligible for the $15,000 (for 2019) annual gift tax exclusion. In addition, the client can elect to spread a large lump-sum contribution over five years and thereby immediately benefit from five years' worth of annual gift tax exclusions. (The election is made on IRS Form 709, Federal Gift Tax Return.)

For example, a single parent or grandparent can make a lump-sum contribution of up to $75,000 (5 × $15,000) on behalf of an account beneficiary without any federal gift tax consequences. A married couple can jointly contribute up to $150,000 ($75,000 × 2). Gifts up to these amounts will not reduce the contributor's $11.4m (for 2019) unified federal gift and estate tax exemption, as long as the five-year spread privilege is elected. However, if the contributor dies during the five-year spread period, a *pro rata* portion of the contribution is added back to his or her estate for federal estate tax purposes. [See Prop. Reg. Sec. 1.529-5 for the gift and estate tax rules.]

Example 7-16

If a client has three young grandchildren, the client and his or her spouse can immediately contribute as much as $450,000 with no federal gift tax consequences ($150,000 to each of three Section 529 plan accounts for each grandchild). As long as the client lives at least five years after making the gifts (the period over which the gifts are deemed to be spread), the taxable estate is reduced by $450,000.

Amounts covered by the annual gift tax exclusion (including under the five-year spread privilege) are also excluded for generation-skipping transfer tax purposes [Prop. Reg. Sec. 1.529-5(b)].

Plus, the client avoids income and estate taxes on future earnings generated by the $450,000 contributed to the Section 529 plan accounts. In contrast, if the client sets up college accounts for the grandchildren in his or her own name, the client could owe up to 37% of the earnings for federal income tax, plus the 3.8% NIIT, plus state income tax, plus estate tax if the client dies before the money gets spent for college costs. Section 529 plans truly are a great tax-saving deal.

Accounts are very flexible

When funding an account for a child's (or grandchild's) college education, the client should always be concerned about what will happen to his or her money if things do not turn out as expected. After all, the child (or grandchild) could decide not to go to college. In this regard, Section 529 college savings plan accounts are pretty wonderful.

First, the IRC gives the client great flexibility to change account beneficiaries without any federal tax consequences. This is allowed as long as the new beneficiary is a member of the original beneficiary's family and in the same generation (or a higher generation). The client's children, stepchildren, and spouses of these individuals are all considered members of the same family and same generation [IRC Section 529(e)(2)]. Therefore, the client can move money from an account set up for any one of these individuals into an account set up for any other of these persons with no federal income tax, gift tax, or generation-skipping transfer tax consequences [IRC Section 529(c)(3)(C) and (c)(5)(B)].

An account beneficiary's first cousin is considered a same-generation family member too [IRC Sec. 529(e)(2)(D)]. For grandparents, that is important. It allows the grandparent to move money from an account set for one grandchild into an account set up for any other grandchild with no federal income tax, gift tax, or generation-skipping transfer tax consequences.

There is also good news when changing plans or investment direction. If, for example, the client decides another state's plan is superior to the current one, he or she can simply switch plans by rolling over the account balance. This can be done as often as once every 12 months without any federal tax consequences [IRC Sec. 529(c)(3)(C)]. In addition, a plan can permit switching investment direction for an account as often as twice in a calendar year [IRC Sec. 529(b)(4)]. So if the existing plan suddenly offers a more attractive investment option, or if the client just changes his or her mind about which existing option seems best, he or she can switch investment direction accordingly. (Of course, the plan's terms must allow such changes for the client to be able to do this, and that should not be taken for granted.)

Finally, what happens if the client wants to or needs to get his or her money back from the Section 529 plan? The federal tax rules allow this too. Of course, the client will be taxed on any withdrawn earnings. Additionally, the IRS is owed a penalty equal to 10% of the withdrawn earnings [IRC Sec. 529(c)(6)]. That is a relatively small price to pay for the privilege of being able to reverse a poor decision and recover one's money.

Key point: The preceding discussion describes what the federal tax law allows. Most Section 529 plans conform to these guidelines, but they are not required to do so. The client should make sure any plan he or she is considering does conform before investing.

Section 529 college savings plans offer big federal income and estate tax advantages, often state income tax benefits as well, and more investment options than ever. Plus, the client has great flexibility to make changes on the fly, including getting his or her money back if worst comes to worst. For college savings fans, especially grandparents with estate tax avoidance goals, this is an almost unbelievably good deal.

Key point: The super-beneficial federal tax rules for Section 529 plans were originally included in 2001 legislation. However, these favorable provisions (which include federal-income-tax-free treatment for qualified Section 529 plan distributions and favorable gift and estate tax rules) were scheduled to "sunset" after 2010. The Pension Protection Act of 2006 made all the existing rules permanent; however, the Pension Protection Act also granted the IRS power to issue "anti-abuse" rules to prevent taxpayers from using Section 529 plans in tax-saving strategies that go beyond what Congress intended. For example, the government does not like the fact that individuals can currently use Section 529 plan accounts as estate tax avoidance vehicles while still retaining lots of control over the how the funds are used.

Computer and internet costs are qualified expenses

Computer and technology costs (including peripheral equipment and software) and internet access charges and related costs count as qualified higher education expenses for purposes of receiving federal income-tax-free distributions from Section 529 plan accounts. However, the cost of software designed for sports, games, and hobbies does not qualify for this break unless the software is mainly educational in nature. [See IRC Sec. 529(e)(3)(A).]

Do not confuse savings plans with prepaid plans

Do not mix up Section 529 college savings plans, which are explained previously, with Section 529 prepaid college tuition plans, which will receive only brief mention here. Both types of plans are properly called Section 529 plans because both are authorized by that section of the Internal Revenue Code. Both receive the same favorable federal tax treatment. That is where the resemblance ends.

The big distinction is that prepaid tuition plans lock in the cost to attend certain colleges. In other words, the rate of return on a prepaid tuition plan account is promised to match the inflation rate for costs to attend the designated schools. Nothing more, nothing less. That is great if that is what the client wants. (The prepaid tuition plan account balance can generally be used to pay eligible costs at any accredited college or university in the nation.)

In contrast, a college savings plan allows the client to benefit if the account earns more than the rate of inflation for costs to attend the college ultimately chosen by the account beneficiary. Earnings greater than the inflation rate mean less money needs to be invested to fully fund the child's (or grandchild's) future college costs.

Of course, there is no guarantee. In fact, the client could actually lose money with a college savings plan. However, that is relatively unlikely if the client makes pay-ins when the account beneficiary is quite young. With enough time on the client's side and the right investment strategy, we can reasonably assume the college savings plan account's rate of return will comfortably exceed the college cost inflation rate. However, if the client is wary of making that assumption, he or she should consider either a prepaid tuition plan or a savings plan that offers suitably conservative investment options.

Key point: When we read about Section 529 plans in the mainstream financial media, we are almost certainly reading about college savings plans and not about prepaid tuition plans. It is important to understand the difference.

Which Section 529 plan is best?

Clients must decide which plan is best. The main consideration should be how closely a particular Section 529 plan's investment options conform to the client's preferences. Of course, a plan that charges low management fees is best, other things being equal. If contributing to the in-state plan would deliver significant state tax benefits to the client, that could be the deciding factor.

Key point: These plans are becoming increasingly competitive. As a result, states are constantly changing and improving their plans by, for example, offering wider arrays of investment options. In evaluating plans, it is very important to work with the most current information. For the latest scoop, visit www.savingforcollege.com. This site also includes details about Section 529 prepaid tuition plans offered by the various states.

TCJA update

The TCJA expands the definition of qualified higher education expenses to cover expenses to attend public, private, and religious elementary and secondary (K-12) schools. Tax-free distributions to cover the account beneficiary's eligible K-12 expenses are limited to $10,000 annually. This permanent change is effective for 529 plan distributions made after December 31, 2017.

Knowledge check

6. Which is correct about Section 529 plan withdrawals?

    a. They are always free of all federal income taxes and penalties.
    b. They are always subject to federal income tax if they include any earnings.
    c. If they include earnings, they must be used for qualified expenses of the Section 529 account beneficiary to be federal-income-tax-free.
    d. They can always be used tax-free to cover qualified expense for the person who set up the account, even if he is not the designated account beneficiary.

How a closely held business can deduct college expenses paid for the owner's adult child

Employer-sponsored educational assistance programs can deliver up to $5,250 in annual tax-free reimbursements to each eligible employee. The employer can deduct the costs whether the business is operated as a sole proprietorship, S or C corporation, LLC, or partnership. The education need not be job-related. Graduate courses are also allowable. This treatment is available under IRC Section 127.

Some people think the IRC Section 127 qualification rules do not apply for employees who happen to be children of small business owners. Not necessarily true. There is a loophole for any child who is

- age 21 or older and a legitimate employee of the parent's business;
- not a more-than-5% owner of the business in his or her own right; and
- not a dependent of the parent (business owner).

Age-21-or-older status is even more likely when the student spends substantial time working in the parent's business.

Finally, working means the student has an income, making it more likely he or she will not be a dependent on the parent's return.

All in all, what starts off looking like a rather narrow loophole ends up being a potentially substantial tax benefit for many small business owners.

Meeting the qualification rules

As mentioned, there are some qualification rules for IRC Section 127 educational assistance programs. Although they are not especially burdensome, they must be scrupulously followed.

- The program must be set up under a written plan of the employer for the exclusive benefit of employees.
- The program must benefit employees who qualify under a classification scheme set up by the employer that does not discriminate in favor of highly compensated employees or their dependents. There is no discrimination problem if all the employees are eligible, even though they all happen to be members of the owner's family. If there are other employees, they may have to be covered as well.
- The program cannot offer employees the choice between tax-free educational assistance and other taxable forms of compensation (like cash). In other words, IRC Section 127 benefits cannot be included as an option in an IRC Section 125 cafeteria benefit program.
- The program need not be prefunded; the employer can pay or reimburse qualifying expenses as they are incurred by the employee (the owner's age-21-or-older child).
- Employees must be given reasonable notification about the availability of the program and its terms.

- The program can't funnel more than 5% of the annual benefits to shareholders or owners, or their spouses or dependents. Only owners with more than 5% of the stock or more than 5% interests in capital or profits of the employer on any day during the year are tainted for purposes of this rule. Here the question is: can ownership be attributed to the owner's child—the student—when the child does not directly own more than 5%?

Dodging the 5% ownership bullet

To avoid having the owner's child become disqualified under the immediately preceding rule, he or she cannot be a more-than-5% owner of the business actual ownership (such as via shares the child directly owns in his or her own right) plus attributed (indirect) ownership under rules explained in the following section.

Stock attribution rules

Stock ownership in the employer corporation is attributed to the owner's child if he or she owns options, is a 5% partner in a partnership that owns stock or is a 5% shareholder in another corporation that owns stock [IRC Sections 127(c)(4) and 1563(e)(1), (2), and (4)]. These rules will rarely cause any attributed stock ownership problems.

Also, an under-age-21 child is considered to own any stock owned directly or indirectly by the parents. However, there is no attribution if the child is age 21 or older [IRC Section 1563(e)(6)(A)]. Actually, there is an attribution rule when an adult child has actual ownership of more than 50% of the stock of the employer corporation, but such actual ownership would probably disqualify the IRC Section 127 program before ever getting to the stock ownership attribution rules [see IRC Section 1563(e)(6)(B)].

In other words, unless the owner's over-age-21 nondependent child has actual direct ownership of more than 5% of the employer company's stock, he or she should pass all the tests. If so, the corporation can set up an IRC Section 127 program and start paying for and deducting college tuition costs right now. The child will owe $0 federal income tax on amounts up to $5,250 per year.

Ownership attribution for unincorporated employers

If the business is unincorporated, there is still concern about ownership being attributed to the owner's child.

The good news is that the rules are analogous to the preceding ones for corporations. So, again, things should work out as long as the child does not have actual direct ownership of a more-than-5% stake in the capital or profits of the business. [Regulation Section 1.127-2(f)(2)(iii) states that the attribution rules under the IRC Section 414(c) regulations apply. Regulation Section 1.414(c)-4(b)(6) includes an ownership attribution rule that is essentially the same as the stock attribution rule explained earlier. See also the example in Regulation Section 1.414(c)-4(b)(6)(iv).]

"Last-minute" suggestions for procrastinators

Sometimes it is simply too late for long-term planning to accumulate college funds and save income taxes along the road. This happens even with high-income taxpayers who earn too much to qualify for juicy benefits like the college tuition tax credits.

All the client wants to do is figure out how to pay college bills right now, snag any tax breaks still available, and avoid *adverse* tax consequences. Here are some thoughts.

Take out home equity loan

Even though TCJA eliminated the itemized interest expense deduction for home equity loans for 2018-2025, these loans can usually be obtained at favorable interest rates. So they can be a good source of money for college.

Tap into IRA funds

To the extent of qualified higher education expenses paid during the same year that early withdrawals (before age 59½) are taken from an account owner's traditional or Roth IRA, the early withdrawals are free of the 10% premature withdrawal penalty tax that might otherwise apply to such early withdrawals. Qualified higher education expenses are defined in the same way as for tax-free withdrawals from Section 529 plans.

The qualified expenses must be for the education of (1) the account owner or the account owner's spouse or (2) a child, stepchild, or adopted child of the account owner or the account owner's spouse. This exception to the 10% penalty tax cannot be used for expenses that are allocable to certain tax-free educational benefits such as scholarships. [See IRC Section 72(t)(2)(E) and (t)(7).]

Key point: To take advantage of the 10% penalty tax exception, the qualified higher education expenses must be paid in the same year during which the early IRA withdrawal is received.
[See *Linda L. Lodder-Beckert,* TC Memo 2005-162 (2005).]

Although early withdrawals from traditional IRAs can qualify for the 10% penalty tax exception previously explained, any earnings included in such withdrawals must still be included in the account owner's gross income. In other words, penalty-free does not equate to income-tax-free.

Make direct gifts to college to cover tuition

An often overlooked fact is that taxpayers can make tax-free gifts of any amount to pay directly for tuition. In other words, these tax-free payments are greater than the $15,000 annual gift tax exclusion limit (for 2019) allowed for regular gifts, and they do not reduce the donor's $11.4m unified federal gift and estate tax exemption (for 2019). [See IRC Section 2503(e).]

The only requirements are that the payment must be made directly to an educational institution described in IRC Section 170(b)(1)(A), and it can be used only for tuition. Payments for room and board, books, supplies, and living expenses do not qualify for the unlimited-gift rule (Regulation Section 25.2503-6). Generous grandparents are the most likely people to want to take advantage of this rule.

Example 7-17

- Henry has secured his own financial future and now wants to help with his grandchildren's college expenses. Henry's granddaughter, Hanna, is entering an expensive private university. Annual tuition and related mandatory fees are $55,000, and Hanna needs at least another $15,000 for room and board, books, and living expenses during the year.
  - Henry can make a tax-free gift of the tuition by cutting a check for $55,000 to the university. He can then make another tax-free gift of $15,000 to Hanna so she can handle the other expenses. The result: Henry gives away $70,000 in a single year without paying any gift tax or reducing his $11.4m unified federal gift and estate tax exemption (for 2019).

Tax Glossary

401(k) plan – A qualified retirement plan to which contributions from salary are made from pre-tax dollars.

Accelerated depreciation – Computation of depreciation to provide greater deductions in earlier years of equipment and other business or investment property.

Accounting method – Rules applied in determining when and how to report income and expenses on tax returns.

Accrual method – Method of accounting that reports income when it is earned, disregarding when it may be received, and expense when incurred, disregarding when it is actually paid.

Acquisition debt – Mortgage taken to buy, hold, or substantially improve main or second home that serves as security.

Active participation – Rental real estate activity involving property management at a level that permits deduction of losses.

Adjusted basis – Basis in property increased by some expenses (for example, by capital improvements) or decreased by some tax benefit (for example, by depreciation).

Adjusted gross income (AGI) – Gross income minus above-the-line deductions (such as deductions other than itemized deductions, the standard deduction, and personal and dependency exemptions).

Alimony – Payments for the support or maintenance of one's spouse pursuant to a judicial decree or written agreement related to divorce or separation.

Alternative minimum tax (AMT) – System comparing the tax results with and without the benefit of tax preference items for the purpose of preventing tax avoidance.

Amortization – Write-off of an intangible asset's cost over a number of years.

Applicable federal rate (AFR) – An interest rate determined by reference to the average market yield on U.S. government obligations. Used in Sec. 7872 to determine the treatment of loans with below-market interest rates.

At-risk rules – Limits on tax losses to business activities in which an individual taxpayer has an economic stake.

Backup withholding – Withholding for federal taxes on certain types of income (such as interest or dividend payments) by a payor that has not received required taxpayer identification number (TIN) information.

Bad debt – Uncollectible debt deductible as an ordinary loss if associated with a business and otherwise deductible as short-term capital loss.

Basis – Amount determined by a taxpayer's investment in property for purposes of determining gain or loss on the sale of property or in computing depreciation.

Cafeteria plan – Written plan allowing employees to choose among two or more benefits (consisting of cash and qualified benefits) and to pay for the benefits with pretax dollars. Must conform to Sec. 125 requirements.

Capital asset – Investments (such as stocks, bonds, and mutual funds) and personal property (such as home).

Capital gain/loss – Profit (net of losses) on the sale or exchange of a capital asset or Sec. 1231 property, subject to favorable tax rates, and loss on such sales or exchanges (net of gains) deductible against $3,000 of ordinary income.

Capitalization – Addition of cost or expense to the basis of property.

Carryovers (carryforwards) and carrybacks – Tax deductions and credits not fully used in one year are chargeable against prior or future tax years to reduce taxable income or taxes payable.

Conservation reserve program (CRP) – A voluntary program for soil, water, and wildlife conservation, wetland establishment and restoration and reforestation, administered by the U.S. Department of Agriculture.

Credit – Amount subtracted from income tax liability.

Deduction – Expense subtracted in computing adjusted gross income.

Defined benefit plan – Qualified retirement plan basing annual contributions on targeted benefit amounts.

Defined contribution plan – Qualified retirement plan with annual contributions based on a percentage of compensation.

Depletion – Deduction for the extent a natural resource is used.

Depreciation – Proportionate deduction based on the cost of business or investment property with a useful life (or recovery period) greater than one year.

Earned income – Wages, bonuses, vacation pay, and other remuneration, including self-employment income, for services rendered.

Earned income credit – Refundable credit available to low-income individuals.

Employee stock ownership plan (ESOP) – Defined contribution plan that is a stock bonus plan or a combined stock bonus and money purchase plan designed to invest primarily in qualifying employer securities.

Estimated tax – Quarterly payments of income tax liability by individuals, corporations, trusts, and estates.

Exemption – A deduction against net income based on taxpayer status (such as single, head of household, married filing jointly or separately, trusts, and estates).

Fair market value – The price that would be agreed upon by a willing seller and willing buyer, established by markets for publicly-traded stocks, or determined by appraisal.

Fiscal year – A 12-month taxable period ending on any date other than December 31.

Foreign tax – Income tax paid to a foreign country and deductible or creditable, at the taxpayer's election, against U.S. income tax.

Gift – Transfer of money or property without expectation of anything in return, and excludable from income by the recipient. A gift may still be affected by the unified estate and gift transfer tax applicable to the gift's maker.

Goodwill – A business asset, intangible in nature, adding a value beyond the business's tangible assets.

Gross income – Income from any and all sources, after any exclusions and before any deductions are taken into consideration.

Half-year convention – A depreciation rule assuming property other than real estate is placed in service in the middle of the tax year.

Head-of-household – An unmarried individual who provides and maintains a household for a qualifying dependent and therefore is subject to distinct tax rates.

Health savings account (HSA) – A trust operated exclusively for purposes of paying qualified medical expenses of the account beneficiary and thus providing for deductible contributions, tax-deferred earnings, and exclusion of tax on any monies withdrawn for medical purposes.

Holding period – The period of time a taxpayer holds onto property, therefore affecting tax treatment on its disposition.

Imputed interest – Income deemed attributable to deferred-payment transfers, such as below-market loans, for which no interest or unrealistically low interest is charged.

Incentive stock option (ISO) – An option to purchase stock in connection with an individual's employment, which defers tax liability until all of the stock acquired by means of the option is sold or exchanged.

Income in respect of a decedent (IRD) – Income earned by a person, but not paid until after his or her death.

Independent contractor – A self-employed individual whose work method or time is not controlled by an employer.

Indexing – Adjustments in deductions, credits, exemptions and exclusions, plan contributions, AGI limits, and so on, to reflect annual inflation figures.

Individual retirement account (IRA) – Tax-exempt trust created or organized in the U.S. for the exclusive benefit of an individual or the individual's beneficiaries.

Information returns– Statements of income and other items recognizable for tax purposes provided to the IRS and the taxpayer. Form W-2 and forms in the 1099 series, as well as Schedules K-1, are the prominent examples.

Installment method– Tax accounting method for reporting gain on a sale over the period of tax years during which payments are made, such as, over the payment period specified in an installment sale agreement.

Intangible property– Items such as patents, copyrights, and goodwill.

Inventory – Goods held for sale to customers, including materials used in the production of those goods.

Involuntary conversion – A forced disposition (for example, casualty, theft, condemnation) for which deferral of gain may be available.

Jeopardy – For tax purposes, a determination that payment of a tax deficiency may be assessed immediately as the most viable means of ensuring its payment.

Keogh plan – A qualified retirement plan available to self-employed persons.

Key employee – Officers, employees, and officers defined by the Internal Revenue Code for purposes of determining whether a plan is "top heavy."

Kiddie tax – Application of parents' maximum tax rate to unearned income of their child under age 19. Full-time students under 24 are also subject to the kiddie tax.

Lien – A charge upon property after a tax assessment has been made and until tax liability is satisfied.

Like-kind exchange – Tax-free exchange of business or investment property for property that is similar or related in service or use.

Listed property – Items subject to special restrictions on depreciation (for example, cars, computers, cell phones).

Lump-sum distribution – Distribution of an individual's entire interest in a qualified retirement plan within one tax year.

Marginal tax rate – The highest tax bracket applicable to an individual's income.

Material participation – The measurement of an individual's involvement in business operations for purposes of the passive activity loss rules.

Mid-month convention – Assumption, for purposes of computing depreciation, that all real property is placed in service in the middle of the month.

Mid-quarter convention – Assumption, for purposes of computing depreciation, that all property other than real property is placed in service in the middle of the quarter, when the basis of property placed in service in the final quarter exceeds a statutory percentage of the basis of all property placed in service during the year.

Minimum distribution – A retirement plan distribution, based on life expectancies, that an individual must take after age 70 ½ in order to avoid tax penalties.

Minimum funding requirements – Associated with defined benefit plans and certain other plans, such as money purchase plans, assuring the plan has enough assets to satisfy its current and anticipated liabilities.

Miscellaneous itemized deduction – Deductions for certain expenses (for example, unreimbursed employee expenses) limited to only the amount by which they exceed 2 percent of adjusted gross income.

Money purchase plan – Defined contribution plan in which the contributions by the employer are mandatory and established other than by reference to the employer's profits.

Net operating loss (NOL) – A business or casualty loss for which amounts exceeding the allowable deduction in the current tax year may be carried back two years to reduce previous tax liability and forward 20 years to cover any remaining unused loss deduction.

Nonresident alien – An individual who is neither a citizen nor a resident of the United States. Nonresidents are taxed on U.S. source income.

Original issue discount (OID) – The excess of face value over issue price set by a purchase agreement.

Passive activity loss (PAL) – Losses allowable only to the extent of income derived each year (such as by means of carryover) from rental property or business activities in which the taxpayer does not materially participate.

Passive foreign investment company (PFIC) – A foreign based corporation subject to strict tax rules which covers the treatment of investments in Sections 1291 through 1297.

Pass-through entities – Partnerships, LLCs, LLPs, S corporations, and trusts and estates whose income or loss is reported by the partner, member, shareholder, or beneficiary.

Personal holding company (PHC) – A corporation, usually closely-held, that exists to hold investments such as stocks, bonds, or personal service contracts and to time distributions of income in a manner that limits the owner(s) tax liability.

Qualified subchapter S trust (QSST) – A trust that qualifies specific requirements for eligibility as an S corporation shareholder.

Real estate investment trust (REIT) – A form of investment in which a trust holds real estate or mortgages and distributes income, in whole or in part, to the beneficiaries (such as investors).

Real estate mortgage investment conduit (REMIC) – Treated as a partnership, investors purchase interests in this entity which holds a fixed pool of mortgages.

Realized gain or loss – The difference between property's basis and the amount received upon its sale or exchange.

Recapture – The amount of a prior deduction or credit recognized as income or affecting its characterization (capital gain vs. ordinary income) when the property giving rise to the deduction or credit is disposed of.

Recognized gain or loss – The amount of realized gain or loss that must be included in taxable income.

Regulated investment company (RIC) – A corporation serving as a mutual fund that acts as investment agents for shareholders and customarily dealing in government and corporate securities.

Reorganization – Restructuring of corporations under specific Internal Revenue Code rules so as to result in nonrecognition of gain.

Resident alien – An individual who is a permanent resident, has substantial presence, or, under specific election rules is taxed as a U.S. citizen.

Roth IRA – Form of individual retirement account that produces, subject to holding period requirements, nontaxable earnings.

S corporation – A corporation that, upon satisfying requirements concerning its ownership, may elect to act as a pass-through entity.

Saver's credit – Term commonly used to describe Sec. 25B credit for qualified contributions to a retirement plan or via elective deferrals.

Sec. 1231 property – Depreciable business property eligible for capital gains treatment.

Sec. 1244 stock – Closely held stock whose sale may produce an ordinary, rather than capital, loss (subject to caps).

Split-dollar life insurance – Arrangement between an employer and employee under which the life insurance policy benefits are contractually split, and the costs (premiums) are also split.

Statutory employee – An insurance agent or other specified worker who is subject to social security taxes on wages but eligible to claim deductions available to the self-employed.

Stock bonus plan – A plan established and maintained to provide benefits similar to those of a profit-sharing plan, except the benefits must be distributable in stock of the employer company.

Tax preference items – Tax benefits deemed includable for purposes of the alternative minimum tax.

Tax shelter – A tax-favored investment, typically in the form of a partnership or joint venture, that is subject to scrutiny as tax-avoidance device.

Tentative tax – Income tax liability before taking into account certain credits, and AMT liability over the regular tax liability.

Transportation expense – The cost of transportation from one point to another.

Travel expense – Transportation, meals, and lodging costs incurred away from home and for trade or business purposes.

Unearned income – Income from investments (such as interest, dividends, and capital gains).

Uniform capitalization rules (UNICAP) – Rules requiring capitalization of property used in a business or income-producing activity (such as items used in producing inventory) and to certain property acquired for resale.

Unrelated business income (UBIT) – Exempt organization income produced by activities beyond the organization's exempt purposes and therefore taxable.

Wash sale – Sale of securities preceded or followed within 30 days by a purchase of substantially identical securities. Recognition of any loss on the sale is disallowed.

Index

CUT YOUR CLIENT'S TAX BILL: INDIVIDUAL PLANNING TIPS AND STRATEGIES

BY WILLIAM BISCHOFF, CPA, MBA

Solutions

The AICPA publishes *CPA Letter Daily*, a free e-newsletter published each weekday. The newsletter, which covers the 10-12 most important stories in business, finance, and accounting, as well as AICPA information, was created to deliver news to CPAs and others who work with the accounting profession. Besides summarizing media articles, commentaries, and research results, the e-newsletter links to television broadcasts and videos and features reader polls. *CPA Letter Daily*'s editors scan hundreds of publications and websites, selecting the most relevant and important news so you don't have to. The newsletter arrives in your inbox early in the morning. To sign up, visit smartbrief.com/CPA.

Do you need high-quality technical assistance? The AICPA Auditing and Accounting Technical Hotline provides non-authoritative guidance on accounting, auditing, attestation, and compilation and review standards. The hotline can be reached at 877.242.7212.

Solutions

Chapter 1

Knowledge check solutions

1.

   a. Incorrect. The 28% maximum rate applies to long-term collectibles gains.

   b. Correct. The 25% maximum rate applies to un-recaptured Section 1250 gains attributable to depreciation deductions; the 20% maximum rate applies to other Section 1231 gains.

   c. Incorrect. The 20% rate is correct, but it is not the full story. The 25% rate applies to un-recaptured Section 1250 gains; the 20% rate applies to other Section 1231 gains.

   d. Incorrect. 28.8% represents the maximum rate on un-recaptured Section 1250 gains, including the 3.8% NIIT.

2.

   a. Correct. Qualified dividends are taxed at a maximum federal rate of 20%.

   b. Incorrect. The 35% rate is currently the second highest rate on ordinary income.

   c. Incorrect. 20% is the maximum rate. The 37% maximum rate is for ordinary income which does not include qualified dividends.

   d. Incorrect. 40.8% represents the maximum rate on ordinary income from investments, including the 3.8% NIIT.

3.

   a. Correct. Un-recaptured Section 1250 gains are in effect a special category of Section 1231 gains that are attributable to depreciation deductions.

   b. Incorrect. The maximum rate on un-recaptured Section 1250 gains is 25%.

   c. Incorrect. The maximum rate on un-recaptured Section 1250 gains is 25%. The 37% rate is the current maximum rate on ordinary income.

   d. Incorrect. 40.8% represents the maximum rate on ordinary income from investments, including the 3.8% NIIT.

4.

   a. Incorrect. The correct answer is 60% LTCG and 40% STCG, not the other way around. This treatment is prescribed because these options are considered Section 1256 contracts.

   b. Incorrect. 60% long-term and 40% short-term treatment is prescribed because these options are considered Section 1256 contracts.

   c. Correct. The 60/40 treatment applies because these options are treated as Section 1256 contracts.

   d. Incorrect. These gains are not taxed as ordinary income. The 60/40 treatment applies.

5.

   a. Incorrect. It is less desirable to offset low-tax long-term gains than high-taxed short-term gains.

   b. Correct. Short-term losses are best used to offset short-term gains that would otherwise be taxed at ordinary income rates of up to 37%.

   c. Incorrect. Net short-term capital losses are subject to the $3,000 annual limitation on deductibility.

   d. Incorrect. There is no such tax credit.

6.

   a. Correct. The realized gain amount includes both the amount of gain taxed currently and the amount of gain that is deferred for tax purposes, while the amount recognized is the currently taxed portion of the gain.

   b. Incorrect. Realized gain includes both gain that is currently taxable and gain that can be deferred for tax purposes, while recognized gain is gain that is taxable in the current year.

   c. Incorrect. They are two different concepts. One refers to taxable gain regardless of when creating a tax liability (realized gain) while the other refers to gain creating a taxable liability in the current year (recognized gain).

   d. Incorrect. Realized gain includes both gain that is currently taxable and gain that can be deferred for tax purposes, but recognized gain is gain that is taxable in the current year. Both terms refer to the profit from a deferred installment sale, not the amount of the sale price for such a sale.

7.

   a. Incorrect. A qualified intermediary is a party who is engaged to facilitate a deferred Section 1031 exchange. The intermediary interacts with both sides to achieve that end.

   b. Incorrect. A qualified intermediary is a party hired to facilitate a deferred Section 1031 exchange. Although achieving this end can have tax advantages for one or both sides, the intermediary is not intended to be a tax expert, but one who works for both parties to meet property holding requirements for a deferred exchange.

   c. Correct. A qualified intermediary is a party hired to facilitate a deferred exchange. Although achieving this end can have tax advantages for one or both sides, the intermediary is not a tax expert, per se. Instead, the intermediary is a facilitator of the transactions that must take place for Section 1031 treatment to be available.

   d. Incorrect. A qualified intermediary is a party hired to facilitate a deferred Section 1031 exchange. A qualified intermediary will not render appraisals.

8.

   a. Incorrect. Under current law, both Starker and reverse-Starker exchanges are allowed. Revenue Procedure 2000-37 provided that properly arranged reverse-Starker exchanges are eligible for Section 1031 treatment.

   b. Correct. Whether replacement property is identified and acquired after relinquished property has been sold (that is, a Starker exchange) or beforehand (that is, a reverse-Starker exchange), like-kind treatment is accorded by Section 1031.

   c. Incorrect. Under judicial precedent and by IRS rulings, deferred exchanges known as Starker and reverse-Starker exchanges are allowed.

   d. Incorrect. Section 1031 exchanges are tax-deferred, except to the extent of boot received.

9.

   a. Incorrect. The NIIT can potentially hit an individual, estate, or trust's income and gains from the investment of business working capital. It does not matter if the business is passive or non-passive with respect to the taxpayer.

   b. Incorrect. The NIIT can potentially hit income and gains passed through by partnerships and S corporations to individuals, estates, and trusts.

   c. Correct. The NIIT cannot be imposed on income and gains accumulated in tax-favored retirement accounts such as 401(k) accounts and IRAs. Distributions from such accounts are also exempt from the NIIT tax.

   d. Incorrect. The NIIT generally hits income from rental activities.

Chapter 2

Knowledge check solutions

1.

    a. Correct. Generally, the two tax-planning objectives are to pay a preferential capital gains tax rate for most if not all of the profit, as well as deferring the tax bill.

    b. Incorrect. The two primary tax-planning objectives are to defer the taxable event and to pay a lower capital gains tax rate when the taxable event occurs. In addition, accelerating the taxable event will often cause profits to be taxed at higher ordinary income rates rather than at lower LTCG rates.

    c. Incorrect. Maximizing the pre-tax profit is always desirable but that is a non-tax objective.

    d. Incorrect. Minimizing risk is desirable but that is a non-tax objective.

2.

    a. Incorrect. There are several scenarios where making a disqualifying disposition is the tax-smart thing to do, including when the shares decline below the exercise price during the year of exercise.

    b. Correct. There are several scenarios where making a disqualifying disposition is the tax-smart alternative if there are benefits to recognizing ordinary income rather than capital gain income.

    c. Incorrect. Disqualifying dispositions are allowed under the tax rules.

    d. Incorrect. SEC rules have nothing to do with disqualifying dispositions.

3.

    a. Incorrect. The bargain element measured as the difference between the exercise price and FMV on the date of exercise is treated as ordinary income from compensation and is subject to all applicable taxes on such income.

    b. Correct. The bargain element is deemed to be ordinary income from compensation and, therefore, subject to all applicable taxes on such income (including federal employment taxes).

    c. Incorrect. The bargain element is taxed as compensation.

    d. Incorrect. The bargain element measured as the difference between the exercise price and FMV on the date of exercise is treated as ordinary income from compensation and is subject to all applicable taxes on such income. However, gains on post-exercise appreciation will be long-term gains if the shares are held for more than one year after the exercise date.

Chapter 3

Knowledge check solutions

1.
    a. Incorrect. There is no requirement that periods of ownership and use as a principal residence overlap. Therefore, it is very important to completely understand the taxpayer's history with a property when determining whether he or she is eligible to claim the home sale gain exclusion privilege for that property.

    b. Correct. The periods of ownership and use as a principal residence are not required to overlap.

    c. Incorrect. The periods of ownership and use as a principal residence are not required to overlap, regardless of the homeowner's filing status.

    d. Incorrect. The periods of ownership and use as a principal residence are not required to overlap, regardless of the homeowner's filing status. However, joint-filing couples are eligible for a larger gain exclusion amount.

2.
    a. Incorrect. It is indeed possible, as long as the new spouse lives in the taxpayer's residence for at least two years during the five-year period ending on the sale date.

    b. Incorrect. It is possible, but there is no special election to be made. Use and ownership tests prevail.

    c. Correct. It is possible, but there are conditions. For a post-marriage sale to qualify for the $500,000 joint return exclusion, both spouses must pass the two-out-of-five-years use test. However, it does not matter which spouse owns the home, as long as at least one spouse also passes the two-out-of-five-years ownership test.

    d. Incorrect. There is no rule requiring five years of marriage.

3.
    a. Incorrect. Each spouse's gain exclusion amount effectively belongs only to that person. There is no ability to use either spouse's exclusion.

    b. Incorrect. One spouse cannot take advantage of any part of the other spouse's "unutilized" gain exclusion.

    c. Incorrect. One spouse cannot take advantage of any part of the other spouse's "unutilized" gain exclusion. This fact may not be understood by clients, which can result in dissatisfaction at tax return time.

    d. Correct. Each spouse's gain exclusion amount effectively belongs only to that person. Therefore, when one spouse does not use her full gain exclusion amount, any "leftover" amount vaporizes.

4.

a. Correct. The fact that there are two separate sales does affect the taxpayer's maximum gain exclusion amount of either $250,000 or $500,000 for the combined gains.

b. Incorrect. The fact that there are separate sales does not increase the taxpayer's maximum gain exclusion amount. Therefore, the maximum exclusion available to shelter the combined gains from the two sales is $250,000 for a single taxpayer or $500,000 for a joint filer.

c. Incorrect. Under the right circumstances, gain from selling land adjacent to a principal residence can be sheltered by the Section 121 home sale gain exclusion.

d. Incorrect. The fact that there are two separate sales does affect the taxpayer's maximum gain exclusion amount of either $250,000 or $500,000 for the combined gains from the two sales. There is no separate $100,000 gain exclusion rule for adjoining land.

5.

a. Incorrect. The timing of the divorce is irrelevant in this context. However, this problem is avoided when the divorce papers explicitly permit the other ex-spouse to continue living in the property.

b. Incorrect. Unless proper language is included in the divorce papers, he will fail the two-out-of-five-years use test after being out of the former marital abode for three years. He will then be completely ineligible to claim the gain exclusion privilege when that property is later sold.

c. Incorrect. Three years (not six years) after he moves out of the former marital abode, he will fail the two-out-of-five-years use test and thus become completely ineligible to claim the gain exclusion privilege when the property is later sold. However, this problem is avoided when the divorce papers explicitly permit the other ex-spouse to continue living in the property.

d. Correct. Three years after he moves out of the former marital abode, he will fail the two-out-of-five-years use test and thus become completely ineligible to claim the gain exclusion privilege when the property is later sold—unless this result is avoided by including the proper language in the divorce papers.

6.

a. Incorrect. Due to the anti-recycling rule, claiming the gain exclusion privilege could make the taxpayer ineligible to claim the exclusion for a later sale that triggers a bigger gain. In such case, the taxpayer should "elect out" of the gain exclusion privilege for the earlier, less-profitable sale.

b. Correct. One would be wise to elect out of the gain exclusion privilege to exclude a bigger gain from a later sale that would otherwise be barred by the anti-recycling rule.

c. Incorrect. The gain exclusion has no impact on whether or not home price appreciation is included in the owner's taxable estate.

d. Incorrect. Divorce-related complications with the gain exclusion rules can usually be avoided by including proper language in the divorce papers.

Chapter 4

Knowledge check solutions

1.

a. Incorrect. Personal residence property taxes are deductible, regardless of how many homes the client owns—subject to the Tax Cuts and Jobs Act limitation on itemized deductions for state and local taxes for 2018-2025.

b. Incorrect. Subject to the rules for qualified residence interest, the client can deduct mortgage interest on up to two (but not three) personal residences.

c. Incorrect. The deductibility of property taxes is not limited to a certain number of personal residences, but for 2018-2025 the Tax Cuts and Jobs Act limitation on deductions for state and local taxes will apply.

d. Correct. Subject to the rules for itemized deductions for qualified residence interest, mortgage interest can be deducted on up to two personal residences.

2.

a. Incorrect. The passive loss rules may limit the client's ability to currently deduct rental losses.

b. Incorrect. The client will be able to deduct expenses, subject to the passive loss rules.

c. Correct. Unfortunately, treatment as a rental property means the passive loss rules may apply.

d. Incorrect. The home will be treated as a rental property for tax purposes. Unfortunately, that means the dreaded passive loss rules may apply. However, the passive loss rules can often be worked around to achieve better tax results.

3.

a. Incorrect. The rental income is tax-free under a special rule.

b. Correct. Under these circumstances the vacation home is treated as a personal residence. Income is not recognized on the few rental days, but correspondingly there is no deduction for operating expenses (such as cleaning costs and utilities) attributable to those days. Interest and taxes attributable to those days are deductible under the normal rules for personal residences.

c. Incorrect. 100% of the rental income is tax-free.

d. Incorrect. The rental income is federal-income-tax-free under a special rule. Therefore, the 3.8% NIIT cannot apply to the rental income.

Chapter 5

Knowledge check solutions

1.
   a. Incorrect. When married individuals file separately, it will not usually result in a lower combined tax bill (although that can happen in limited circumstances).
   b. Incorrect. Filing separately will not usually result in any additional tax breaks. In fact, the more likely outcome is losing some tax breaks, because some are off limits for those who use married filing separate status.
   c. Incorrect. Avoiding the passive loss rules would not usually be facilitated by filing separately.
   d. Correct. By filing a separate return, a married individual avoids joint and several liabilities for tax misdeeds committed by that person's spouse. A spouse who files separately is liable only for tax that is shown or should have been shown on that person's separate return.

2.
   a. Correct. With proper planning, a distribution from a qualified retirement plan will be taxed to the recipient ex-spouse because the retirement plan balance or benefits can be shown to have been transferred to that ex-spouse, pursuant to a divorce or separation agreement.
   b. Incorrect. With proper planning, the ex-spouse who receives the retirement plan balances or benefits will be the one who owes the related taxes when amounts are withdrawn or benefits are received by that ex-spouse. This is only fair. However, this result is not automatic. It requires proper planning.
   c. Incorrect. With proper planning, the ex-spouse who receives the retirement plan balances or benefits will be the one who owes the related taxes when amounts are withdrawn or benefits are received by that ex-spouse. This is only fair.
   d. Incorrect. Without proper planning, the tax results can be unexpected and unfair to the spouse who is the account owner.

3.
   a. Correct. If the transfer is made in this fashion, it is effectively the same as a tax-free rollover between the accounts.
   b. Incorrect. Without a pre-existing divorce or separation agreement calling for the IRA transfer, amounts cannot be transferred tax-free. Instead, the amount withdrawn from the IRA will be treated as a taxable distribution received by the account owner.
   c. Incorrect. If the transfer is made in this fashion, it will be taxable to the recipient ex-spouse.
   d. Incorrect. A transfer done in this fashion will be treated as a taxable distribution to the account owner, and the amount cannot be rolled over into the ex-spouse's IRA.

4.

   a. Incorrect. Generally, transfers of qualified retirement plan assets to anyone other than the plan participant are impermissible. A QDRO establishes a participant's ex-spouse's legal right to plan balances or benefits without violating the plan's rules.

   b. Incorrect. A QDRO establishes that the ex-spouse of a retirement plan participant is entitled to some or all of the participant's retirement plan balance or benefits and that the ex-spouse also owes the related federal income taxes. It is critically important to understand when dealing with divorcing clients that a QDRO is a prerequisite to obtaining equitable results when attempting to split up qualified retirement account funds.

   c. Correct. A QDRO establishes that the ex-spouse of a retirement plan participant is entitled to some or all of the participant's retirement plan balance or benefits and that the ex-spouse also owes the related federal income taxes.

   d. Incorrect. A QDRO has only to do with divorce-related divisions of qualified retirement plan account balances or benefits.

5.

   a. Incorrect. Transfers more than one year (but not more than six years) after the divorce must be pursuant to a divorce or separation instrument to be tax-free. However, tax-free treatment is not automatic unless the transfer occurs within one year of the divorce. Transfers 10 years after the divorce are way too late to be tax-free.

   b. Incorrect. In general, transfers within one year of the divorce are automatically tax-free and transfers within six years can be tax-free if they are called for in the divorce or separation instrument. There is no eight-year rule.

   c. Incorrect. In general, transfers within one year of the divorce are automatically tax-free and transfers within six years can be tax-free if they are called for in the divorce or separation instrument. There is no seven-year rule.

   d. Correct. In general, transfers within one year of the divorce are automatically tax-free.

6.

   a. Incorrect. Such payments are generally treated as either child support or part of the divorce property settlement, either of which are tax-free to the recipient ex-spouse.

   b. Correct. On the payor side, non-qualifying payments are generally considered non-deductible child support or non-deductible divisions of marital property. On the payee side, there is no taxable event for the recipient spouse.

   c. Incorrect. A gift requires donative intent, so court-ordered payments are not gifts.

   d. Incorrect. There is no itemized deduction for spousal support. However, such support can be deducted above the line as alimony if all the requirements for deductible alimony are met.

7.

a. Correct. For federal income tax purposes, payments under pre-2019 divorce agreements that qualify as deductible alimony are deducted by the payor "above the line."

b. Incorrect. Alimony payments under pre-2019 divorce agreements are taxable income to the payee.

c. Incorrect. For federal income tax purposes, payments under pre-2019 divorce agreements that qualify as alimony are deducted by the payor "above the line" and must be reported as taxable income by the payee.

d. Incorrect. Payments under pre-2019 divorce agreements that qualify as alimony are deducted "above the line" rather than "below the line" as an itemized deduction item. This treatment is more beneficial for payors.

8.

a. Correct. For federal income tax purposes, payments that qualify as alimony are deducted by the payor "above the line."

b. Incorrect. Alimony payments are taxable income to the payee.

c. Incorrect. For federal income tax purposes, payments that qualify as alimony are deducted by the payor "above the line" and must be reported as taxable income by the payee.

d. Incorrect. Payments that qualify as alimony are deducted "above the line" rather than "below the line" as an itemized deduction item. This treatment is more beneficial for payors.

Chapter 6

Knowledge check solutions

1.

a. Incorrect. The maximum allowance is $10,000. The $25,500 figure is the maximum Section 179 deduction for a heavy SUV placed in service in tax years beginning in 2019.

b. Incorrect. The maximum allowance for 2019 is $10,000. The $11,160 figure is the maximum 2017 allowance for a new (not used) auto, including first-year bonus depreciation.

c. Correct. The maximum allowance for 2019 is $10,000.

d. Incorrect. The maximum allowance is $10,000. Allowable deductions for "heavy" vehicles used over 50% for business are potentially much higher.

2.

    a. Incorrect. The allowance is not just a proposed rule. It is allowed for 2013 and beyond.

    b. Incorrect. The allowance is allowed for 2013 and beyond and is an alternative to the actual-expense home office deduction method which requires much more recordkeeping.

    c. Correct. The new safe-harbor allowance is allowed for 2013 and beyond. The taxpayer must meet the same eligibility rules that apply to the actual-expense home office deduction method.

    d. Incorrect. Filing status does not affect eligibility.

3.

    a. Incorrect. The rate for the additional Medicare tax is 0.9%. The 2.9% rate is for the "regular" Medicare tax.

    b. Correct. The rate for the additional Medicare tax is 0.9%.

    c. Incorrect. The rate for the additional Medicare tax is 0.9%. The 6.2% rate is the withholding rate for Social Security tax on wages.

    d. Incorrect. The rate for the additional Medicare tax is 0.9%. The 3.8% rate is the *combined* rate for the "regular" 2.9% Medicare tax *plus* the additional 0.9% additional Medicare tax.

4.

    a. Incorrect. The $128,400 figure applied for 2018. For 2019, the Social Security tax cuts out at net SE income above $132,900. That is a big number and explains why cutting a client's SE tax can be a big deal.

    b. Incorrect. The Social Security tax cuts out at net SE income above $132,900.

    c. Incorrect. For 2019, the Social Security tax cuts out at net SE income above $132,900. However, there have been legislative proposals to have the tax cover all net SE income without any upward limit. Thankfully, that has not happened. Yet.

    d. Correct. The Social Security tax cuts out at net SE income above $132,900. However, the "regular" Medicare tax and the additional Medicare tax hit net SE income up to infinity.

5.

    a. Incorrect. It would often have significant SE tax consequences but no federal income tax consequences (assuming the couple files jointly).

    b. Incorrect. It would generally have *no* federal income tax consequences if the couple files jointly. But it could have significant SE tax consequences.

    c. Incorrect. It would not necessitate filing jointly.

    d. Correct. It would often have significant SE tax consequences but no federal income tax consequences (assuming the couple files jointly). In most cases, avoiding partnership status will reduce the couple's SE tax liability.

6.

    a. Incorrect. For calendar-year individuals, contributions can be made as late as April 15 of the following year (adjusted for weekends and holidays). This is the same deadline that applies to IRA contributions.

    b. Correct. Contributions can be made as late as April 15 of the following year (adjusted for weekends and holidays).

    c. Incorrect. For calendar-year individuals, contributions can be made as late as April 15 of the following year (adjusted for weekends and holidays). This is the un-extended due date for the Form 1040 for the previous year.

    d. Incorrect. The federal government's fiscal year-end is irrelevant. So far. Under the current rules, calendar-year individuals can make contributions as late as April 15 of the following year (adjusted for weekends and holidays).

7.

    a. Incorrect. Under an exception to the general month-by-month HSA eligibility rule, an individual's eligibility status as of December 1 (not March 1) can be used to determine the maximum allowable HSA contribution amount for that year. However, a nasty recapture rule applies if an individual takes advantage of the end-of-the-year rule to make a larger HSA contribution and then ceases to be eligible for HSA contributions during the subsequent "testing period."

    b. Incorrect. Under an exception to the general month-by-month HSA eligibility rule, an individual's eligibility status as of December 1 (not July 1) can be used to determine the maximum allowable HSA contribution amount for that year. However, a recapture rule makes taking advantage of the exception a risky venture.

    c. Incorrect. Under an exception to the general month-by-month HSA eligibility rule, an individual's eligibility status as of December 1 (not October 1) can be used to determine the maximum allowable HSA contribution amount for that year. However, a potentially expensive recapture rule makes taking advantage of the exception problematic. Therefore, we doubt too many folks take advantage.

    d. Correct. Under an exception to the general month-by-month HSA eligibility rule, an individual's eligibility status as of December 1 can be used to determine the maximum allowable HSA contribution amount for that year.

Chapter 7

Knowledge check solutions

1.
   a. Correct. The deduction for student loan interest is available only if married taxpayers file joint returns.
   b. Incorrect. This above-the-line deduction is unavailable to married taxpayers filing separately, regardless of their income.
   c. Incorrect. The student loan interest deduction is subject to limitations based upon taxpayer income. However, married taxpayers filing separately are completely ineligible.
   d. Incorrect. That would be nice but the deduction for student loan interest is available only if married taxpayers file joint returns. Those who file separate returns are ineligible regardless of their income level.

2.
   a. Incorrect. Making the election to report a child's accrued U.S. Savings Bond interest annually can be a good idea when the child's standard deduction will shelter most or all of the annual taxable income triggered by making the election.
   b. Correct. Making the election to report a child's accrued U.S. Savings Bond interest annually can be a good idea when the child's standard deduction will shelter most or all of the annual taxable income triggered by making the election. For 2019, the standard deduction for a dependent child with no earned income is $1,100.
   c. Incorrect. Making the election can result in little or no federal income tax on the interest income earned from Savings Bonds. In contrast, not making the election can cause the cumulative amount of interest to be taxed in the year when the Savings Bond matures or is cashed in.
   d. Incorrect. The election is allowed even for cash-method individuals.

3.
   a. Incorrect. For 2019, the unearned income threshold for the Kiddie Tax is $2,200.
   b. Incorrect. For 2019, the unearned income threshold for the Kiddie Tax is $2,200. The $2,100 threshold applied in 2018.
   c. Incorrect. The Kiddie Tax was not repealed for 2015 and beyond. It is still in place.
   d. Correct. For 2019, the unearned income threshold for the Kiddie Tax is $2,200. Unearned income (generally all investment income) over this threshold may be taxed at the rates applicable to estates and trusts.

4.

   a. Correct. Under the current rules, it depends because there are three different age rules that determine whether or not an individual is exposed to the Kiddie Tax.

   b. Incorrect. Under the current rules, there are three different age rules that determine whether an individual is exposed to the Kiddie Tax. One rule applies when a child is age 17 or younger at year-end. Another rule applies when if a child is 18 at year-end. A third rule applies when a child is age 19-23 at year-end. For a child who is 19-23 at year-end, the Kiddie Tax applies only if he or she is a student for that year.

   c. Incorrect. Age 21 has never been the magic age to be free of the Kiddie Tax rules. Under the current rules, it can potentially apply until the year a student turns age 24.

   d. Incorrect. At one time, the Kiddie Tax ceased to apply after a child reached age 18. Under the current rules, the only sure thing is that the Kiddie Tax will not apply after age 24 is attained.

5.

   a. Incorrect. One way to avoid the Kiddie Tax for a student who will be age 19-23 at year-end is to arrange for her to have earned income (not unearned income) in excess of 50% of her support for the year. In such case, the Kiddie Tax will not apply for that year. When the child's parent owns a business, the parent may be able to hire the child, which may result in enough earned income to make the child Kiddie Tax-exempt.

   b. Incorrect. One way to avoid the Kiddie Tax for a student who will be age 19-23 at year-end is to arrange for her to have earned income in excess of 50% (not 80%) of her support for the year.

   c. Incorrect. No, that will have no effect on the child's exposure to the Kiddie Tax rules.

   d. Correct. One way to avoid the Kiddie Tax for a student who will be age 19-23 at year-end is to arrange for her to have earned income in excess of 50% of her support for the year. In some cases, that may be doable without much difficulty.

6.

    a. Incorrect. Earnings can be withdrawn from a Section 529 plan accounts for qualified higher-education expenses to avoid federal income taxes or penalties. Otherwise, the earnings must be included in gross income, and a 10% penalty tax will usually apply to the amount included in gross income.

    b. Incorrect. Earnings can be withdrawn from a Section 529 plan account without any federal income tax or penalty only if the withdrawn earnings are used for qualified higher-education expenses. Otherwise, the earnings must be included in gross income, and a 10% penalty tax will usually apply to the amount included in gross income.

    c. Correct. To be a tax-free qualified withdrawal, the withdrawn amount must be used for the benefit of the account beneficiary (that is, to pay qualified educational expenses for that person). Nonqualified withdrawals of earnings are subject to federal income tax and a 10% penalty tax may apply as well.

    d. Incorrect. To be a tax-free qualified withdrawal, the withdrawn amount must be used for the benefit of the account beneficiary (that is, on qualified educational expenses for that person). However, a person who set up the account with his own money can name his spouse as the new account beneficiary and thereby qualify for tax-free withdrawals to cover the spouse's qualified expenses.

The AICPA publishes *CPA Letter Daily*, a free e-newsletter published each weekday. The newsletter, which covers the 10-12 most important stories in business, finance, and accounting, as well as AICPA information, was created to deliver news to CPAs and others who work with the accounting profession. Besides summarizing media articles, commentaries, and research results, the e-newsletter links to television broadcasts and videos and features reader polls. *CPA Letter Daily*'s editors scan hundreds of publications and websites, selecting the most relevant and important news so you don't have to. The newsletter arrives in your inbox early in the morning. To sign up, visit smartbrief.com/CPA.

Do you need high-quality technical assistance? The AICPA Auditing and Accounting Technical Hotline provides non-authoritative guidance on accounting, auditing, attestation, and compilation and review standards. The hotline can be reached at 877.242.7212.

Learn More

Continuing Professional Education

Thank you for selecting the American Institute of Certified Public Accountants as your continuing professional education provider. We have a diverse offering of CPE courses to help you expand your skillset and develop your competencies. Choose from hundreds of different titles spanning the major subject matter areas relevant to CPAs and CGMAs, including:

- Governmental and not-for-profit accounting, auditing, and updates
- Internal control and fraud
- Audits of employee benefit plans and 401(k) plans
- Individual and corporate tax updates
- A vast array of courses in other areas of accounting and auditing, controllership, management, consulting, taxation, and more!

Get your CPE when and where you want

- Self-study training options that includes on-demand, webcasts, and text formats with superior quality and a broad portfolio of topics, including bundled products like –
  - ➤ CPExpress® online learning for immediate access to hundreds of one- to four-credit hour online courses for just-in-time learning at a price that is right
  - ➤ Annual Webcast Pass offering live Q&A with experts and unlimited access to the scheduled lineup, all at an incredible discount.
- Staff training programs for audit, tax and preparation, compilation, and review
- Certificate programs offering comprehensive curriculums developed by practicing experts to build fundamental core competencies in specialized topics
- National conferences presented by recognized experts
- Affordable courses on-site at your organization – visit **aicpalearning.org/on-site** for more information.
- Seminars sponsored by your state society and led by top instructors. For a complete list, visit **aicpalearning.org/publicseminar**.

Take control of your career development

The AICPA's Competency and Learning website at **https://competency.aicpa.org** brings together a variety of learning resources and a self-assessment tool, enabling tracking and reporting of progress toward learning goals.

Visit www.AICPAStore.com to browse our CPE selections.

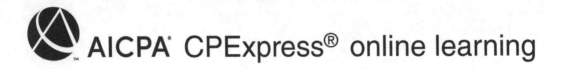
AICPA® CPExpress® online learning

Just-in-time learning at your fingertips 24/7

Where can you get <u>unlimited online access</u> to 600+ credit hours (450+ CPE courses) for one low annual subscription fee?

CPExpress® online learning, the AICPA's comprehensive bundle of online continuing professional education courses for CPAs, offers you immediate access to hundreds of one- to four-credit hour courses. You can choose from a full spectrum of subject areas and knowledge levels to select the specific topic you need when you need it for just-in-time learning.
Access hundreds of courses for one low annual subscription price!

How can CPExpress® online learning help you?

- ✓ Start and finish most CPE courses in as little as 1 to 2 hours with 24/7 access so you can fit CPE into a busy schedule.

- ✓ Quickly brush up or get a brief overview on hundreds of topics when you need it.

- ✓ Create and customize your personal online course catalog for quick access with hot topics at your fingertips.

- ✓ Print CPE certificates on demand to document your training – never miss a CPE reporting deadline.

Quantity Purchases for Firm or Corporate Accounts
If you have 5 or more employees who require training, the firm access option allows you to purchase multiple seats. Plus, you can designate an administrator who will be able to monitor the training progress of each staff member. To learn more about firm access and group pricing, visit aicpalearning.org/cpexpress or call 800.634.6780.

To subscribe, visit www.AICPAStore.com/cpexpress

Your strategic learning partner

Let us help prepare your staff for the future.

What is your current approach to learning? One size does not fit all. Your organization is unique, and your approach to learning and competency should be, too. But where do you start? Choose a strategic partner to help you assess competencies and gaps, design a customized learning plan, and measure and maximize the ROI of your learning and development initiatives.

We offer a wide variety of learning programs for finance professionals at every stage of their career.

AICPA Learning resources can help you:

- Create a learning culture to attract and retain talent
- Enrich staff competency and stay current on changing regulations
- Sharpen your competitive edge
- Capitalize on emerging opportunities
- Meet your goals and positively impact your bottom line
- Address CPE/CPD compliance

Flexible learning options include:

- On-site training
- Conferences
- Webcasts
- Certificate programs
- Online self-study
- Publications

An investment in learning can directly impact your bottom line. Contact an AICPA learning consultant to begin your professional development planning.

Call: 800.634.6780, option 1
Email: AICPALearning@aicpa.org